Modern Finance
and Industrial Economics

Modern Finance and Industrial Economics

Papers in Honor of J. Fred Weston

Edited by
Thomas E. Copeland

Basil Blackwell

First published 1987

Basil Blackwell Inc.
432 Park Avenue South, Suite 1503
New York, NY 10016, USA

Basil Blackwell Ltd
108 Cowley Road, Oxford, OX4 1JF, UK

Library of Congress Cataloging in Publication Data

Modern finance and industrial economics.
Includes index.
1. Finance. 2. Industrial organization (Economic theory) 3. Weston, J. Fred (John Fred), 1916–
I. Weston, J. Fred (John Fred), 1916–
II. Copeland, Thomas E., 1946– .
HG175.M63 1987 332 86-21644
ISBN 0-631-15382-9

British Library Cataloguing in Publication Data

Modern finance and industrial economics:
papers in honour of J. Fred Weston.
1. Economics
I. Weston, J. Fred II. Copeland, Thomas E.
330 HB171
ISBN 0-631-15382-9

Typeset in 10 on 11½ pt Times
by Dobbie Typesetting Service, Plymouth, Devon, England
Printed in the USA

Contents

Contributors

EDWARD I. ALTMAN is professor of finance and chairman of the M.B.A. program at the Graduate School of Business Administration, New York University, and has been a visiting professor in France, Brazil and Australia. Altman has an international reputation as an expert on corporate bankruptcy and credit analysis. Among his books are *Corporate Bankruptcy in America* (1971) and *The Analysis and Prediction of Corporate Bankruptcy* (1982). He was an advisor to the Commission on the Revision of the Bankruptcy Act, and he edits the international publication *Journal of Banking and Finance* and the series *Contemporary Studies in Economics and Finance*. He also serves on the Editorial Board of the *Journal of Business Strategy* and is a member of the Executive Committee of the European Finance Association. His primary areas of research include bankruptcy analysis and prediction, credit and lending policies, and capital markets. The editor of the *Financial Handbook*, he has been a consultant to several government agencies, major financial and accounting institutions, and industrial companies. Altman received the M.B.A. and Ph.D. degrees from the University of California, Los Angeles.

WILLIAM BERANEK is current occupant of the Miles B. Lane chair in banking and finance at the University of Georgia. He received all of his degrees from U.C.L.A.: a B.S. in Accounting, an M.B.A. in Finance, and a Ph.D. in Economics. He is the author of *Analysis for Financial Decisions* (R.D. Irwin, Inc., 1963) and *Working Capital Management* (Wadsworth Publishing Co., 1966). While his research efforts have ranged over a wide variety of issues in both Finance and Economics, he has emphasized the topics of the cost of capital and working capital management. His current research endeavors are focused on attempting to find a role for working capital in a positive theory of Finance.

KWANG S. CHUNG is an Associate Professor of Finance at Chung-Ang University, Seoul, Korea; a Research Fellow at Korea Business Research and Information, Inc. (a credit rating agency); and a Visiting Research

Fellow at Ssangyong Economic Research Institute. Professor Chung was born in 1945 in Korea. He received a B.A. degree from Seoul National University and an M.S. and a Ph.D. from the Graduate School of Management, U.C.L.A. His research and teaching interests include the fields of corporate finance, capital markets, and industrial organization. Among his latest publications is "Mergers in Theory and in Practice" with J.F. Weston, *Journal of the Midwest Finance Association*.

THOMAS E. COPELAND is an Associate Professor of Finance at the Graduate School of Management, U.C.L.A., and has been a visiting professor in Holland. He is co-author with J. Fred Weston of *Financial Theory and Corporate Policy*, 2nd edition, and *Managerial Finance*, 8th edition. He has published articles on a theory of sequential information arrival, liquidity effects following stock splits, a theory of the bid-ask spread, account receivables management, cancellable operating leases, and portfolio performance measurement. He is currently working in the field of experimental economics. Active in executive education, he has twice won awards as best teacher at the Graduate School of Management and has been twice nominated for the U.C.L.A. campus-wide teaching award. He has been Finance Area Chairman and Department Vice Chairman at the Graduate School of Management. He is on the editorial board of the *Financial Review* and the *Midland Corporate Finance Review*. The editor of this *Festschrift*, he is also an expert on the valuation of privately held corporations, and has served as expert witness on many occasions. He received his B.A. from Johns Hopkins University, his M.B.A. from the Wharton School, and his Ph.D. in Applied Economics from the University of Pennsylvania.

HARRY DeANGELO is Associate Professor of Finance at the University of Rochester, with primary research interests in corporate finance and corporate control. Professor DeAngelo's research has appeared in the *American Economic Review*, and *Journal of Financial Economics*, the *Journal of Finance*, and the *Journal of Law and Economics*. He is an Associate Editor of the *Journal of Financial Economics* and the recipient of M.B.A. teaching awards at the University of Washington and the University of Rochester. Professor DeAngelo received his Ph.D. from U.C.L.A. in 1977, and was also the 1977 recipient of the U.C.L.A. Alumni Association Award for Academic Achievement. He served as research assistant to J. Fred Weston during his entire doctoral program at U.C.L.A.

LINDA DeANGELO is Associate Professor of Accounting at the University of Rochester, with primary research interest in the role of financial accounting in corporation contracting. Her research has been published in the *Journal of Financial Economics*, the *Journal of Accounting and Economics*, the *Journal of Law and Economics*, the *Journal of Accounting*

Research, and *The Accounting Review*. She is currently an Associate Editor of the *Journal of Accounting and Economics* and has also served on the Editorial Board of *The Accounting Review*. Professor DeAngelo received her Ph.D. in Accounting from the University of Washington in 1980.

MANAK GUPTA is a former student of Dr. J. Fred Weston and completed his Ph.D. dissertation under his able guidance and supervision. He has published widely in the *Journal of Finance, Journal of Financial and Quantitative Analysis, Journal of Accounting Research*, etc. Also he has chaired sessions, presented papers, and acted as a discussant in various annual meetings of AFA, FMA, EFA, Econometric Society, Operations Research Society of America, etc. Currently, he is working on analyzing the determinants of foreign investments, especially in the developing countries.

CHI-CHENG HSIA received his B.A. in Economics from Taiwan University and his Ph.D. in Management (finance) from University of California at Los Angeles (U.C.L.A.). He has taught at the Graduate School of Business Administration, Taiwan University, for three years, at the Graduate School of Management, U.C.L.A. as visiting faculty for one year, and at Washington State University. He has written articles published in the *Financial Review*, the *Financial Analysts Journal*, and the *Journal of Financial Research*. He has co-authored with Dr. J. Fred Weston the article: "Price Behavior of Deep Discount Bonds," which was published in the *Journal of Banking and Finance* (1981). He is currently Associate Professor of Finance at the College of Business and Economics, Washington State University.

JEFFREY F. JAFFE is Associate Professor of Finance at the Wharton School. He has been active in the areas of research and consulting, with particular interest in the effect of inflation on the returns to stock and bonds, valuation of the firm, and the effect of regulation on trading of corporate insiders. Dr. Jaffe has been a financial consultant to corporate, governmental, and individual clients. His articles have appeared in such leading professional journals as the *Quarterly Journal of Economics*, the *Bell Journal of Economics and Management Science*, the *Journal of Business*, the *Journal of Finance*, the *Journal of Financial and Quantitative Analysis*, and the *Journal of Portfolio Management*. Dr. Jaffe is a member of the American Finance Association, the American Economic Association, and the Financial Management Association. He received his Ph.D. in Finance from the University of Chicago.

CLEMENT G. KROUSE is Professor of Economics at the University of California, Santa Barbara. He has published a variety of studies in both industrial organization and financial economics. His most recent publications include "Competition and Unanimity Revisited, Again" (*American Economic Review*, December 1985) and *Capital Markets and Prices: Valuing Uncertain Income Streams* (North-Holland Publishing Co., 1986).

EDUARDO LEMGRUBER received his Ph.D. from the Graduate School of Management, U.C.L.A. From 1971 to 1977 he was the general manager of the Rio de Janeiro branch of Serasa S/A. In 1978 he started teaching at the Federal University of Rio de Janeiro, Brazil, where he is an Associate Professor of Finance at the COPPEAD Institute (M.B.A. program). He received the B.E. (Civil Engineering) and the M.B.A. degrees from the Federal University of Rio de Janeiro. He has published an article about the implications of short term revolving credit agreements on the firm's cash flow, *Revista de Administracão* U.S.P., University of São Paulo, Brazil. His research and teaching interests include the fields of corporate finance and capital markets. His thesis work is in the area of managerial compensation and insider trading.

DAVID MAYERS is Professor of Finance at the Graduate School of Management, University of California at Los Angeles. He is an Associate Editor of the *Journal of Financial Economics*. His research interests have included asset pricing, portfolio performance measurement and various topics on insurance markets.

SCOTT A. NAMMACHER currently works for the Treasury Department at PepsiCo, in the mergers and acquisition area. Prior to joining PepsiCo, he was a research consultant for the investment banking firm of Morgan Stanley & Company. During that time he and Edward Altman co-authored and published three studies on the high yield bond marketplace. These studies will be published in book form by John Wiley & Sons. Their study on default rates also appeared in the *Financial Analysts Journal*. Prior to receiving his M.B.A. in finance from New York University, Nammacher was involved in the publishing industry where he cofounded the trade magazine *Recreation, Sports and Leisure*.

STANLEY I. ORNSTEIN received a Ph.D. in Economics from the University of California, Los Angeles. He is currently an Associate Research Economist and Associate Director of the Research Program in Competition and Business Policy at the graduate School of Management, U.C.L.A. Previously he was an economic analyst at Planning Research Corporation. At U.C.L.A. he has engaged in research in the fields of Industrial Organization and Antitrust. He has served as an economic consultant to firms on a number of antitrust cases. He was a member of the research staff at the U.C.L.A. Alcohol Research Center, conducting studies on the beer, wine, and distilled spirits industries. His books include co-editor of *The Impact of Large Firms on the U.S. Economy* and author of *Industrial Concentration and Advertising Intensity*. He has written a number of papers which have appeared in *The Journal of Business, Journal of Industrial Economics, Southern Economic Journal, Antitrust Bulletin, Journal of Consumer Research, Journal of Studies on Alcohol*, and *The International Journal of Advertising*, as well as chapters in various books.

EDWARD M. RICE is an Associate Professor of Finance and Business Economics at the University of Washington. He received his Ph.D. degree in Economics from the University of California at Los Angeles in 1978, and worked there as a research assistant for the Research Program in Competition and Business Policy directed by J. Fred Weston. His earlier degrees, Bachelor of Arts degrees (in Applied Economics and Finance), are both from the University of Rochester. Professor Rice has published important papers in leading journals in economics and finance, such as the *Journal of Financial Economics, Journal of Finance*, and *Journal of Law and Economics*. He previously was an Assistant Professor of Economics at the University of Illinois at Champaign-Urbana. He is currently a Visiting Associate Professor of Finance at the University of Chicago.

RICHARD ROLL holds the Allstate chair in Finance and Insurance at the Graduate School of Management, U.C.L.A. Currently on leave, he is Vice President for new product development in the mortgage finance department at Goldman, Sachs & Company and co-director of Mortgage Securities Research. He has published two books and over 50 papers in technical journals. He is an associate editor of the *Journal of Finance*, the *Journal of Financial Economics*, and the *Journal of Portfolio Management*. He is currently president of the American Finance Association.

MARK RUBINSTEIN is Professor of Finance at the University of California at Berkeley. He has recently published a book, written with John Cox of M.I.T. titled *Options Markets* (Prentice-Hall, 1985). He has been awarded the C.B.O.E. Pomeranze Prize for excellence in options research, has twice received prizes for papers related to options from the Institute for Quantitative Research in Finance, and in 1985 received the Graham and Dodd Plaque Award from the Financial Analysts Federation for excellence in financial writing. For the last decade he has been an associate editor of the two leading academic finance journals – *Journal of Finance* and the *Journal of Financial Economics*. Recently, he was appointed to the editorial advisory board of the *Journal of Portfolio Management*. Between 1983 and 1986 he was chairman of the Finance Group at Berkeley and prior to that served for three years as Director of the Berkeley Program in Finance. In addition, he has had a varied business background including acting as a market-maker in options on the floor of the Pacific Stock Exchange. In 1981, he, together with Hayne Leland (also from Berkeley) and John O'Brien, formed the firm Leland O'Brien Rubinstein Associates, which specializes in institutional portfolio risk management using Dynamic Asset Allocation™ (or more simply known as portfolio insurance). The firm now manages over $13 billion in assets.

RICHARD L. SMITH II is Associate Professor and Chairman of the Department of Finance at Arizona State Univeristy. He is also Senior Vice President of Economic Analysis Corporation, a Los Angeles based consulting firm specializing in antitrust, merger and securities valuation matters. Professor Smith's recent research is concentrated in the area of informational asymmetry on security issuance practices. He received his Ph.D. in Management from U.C.L.A. in 1979 and also holds a B.B.A. from Southern Methodist University, an M.B.A. from Washington University and an M.A. in Economics from U.C.L.A.

RANDOLPH WESTERFIELD is a Professor of Finance at the Wharton School, Chairman of the Finance Department, and a Research Associate of Wharton's Rodney L. White Center for Financial Research. He has been visiting professor at Stanford University, University of California at Los Angeles, and the University of Lisbon, Portugal. He is a member of the Pension Research Council and is on the Trust Committee of Continental Bank. He has published many articles in areas of corporate finance and investments. Dr.Westerfield has served as a consultant to the U.S. Department of Labor, the United Nations, and many private firms. He received his Ph.D. from the University of California at Los Angeles in 1968.

Introduction

Literally translated, a *Festschrift* is a writing in celebration of an important event, in this instance the retirement of J. Fred Weston, Cordner Professor of Money and Financial Markets at the Graduate School of Management, U.C.L.A. Spanning over 40 years, his career has been devoted to scholarship in two major fields of intellectual endeavor, industrial organization and financial economics. Both have seen rapid advances to which he has contributed significantly. What makes this collection of research papers special is that they have been written primarily by Weston's former doctoral students and colleagues. Each paper is preceded by a preface which describes the special relationship which the contributor has had with Fred. There is little that I can add to these sincere personal statements. My objective here is dual – to describe the accomplishments of J. Fred Weston as a scholar and teacher, and to provide continuity among the papers contained in this book.

J. Fred Weston got his start at the University of Chicago. Born in Fort Wayne, Indiana, he arrived in the Windy City to begin his studies at the age of sixteen. Political Science occupied his interest as an undergraduate, after which he worked for General Electric for a few years before returning to Chicago for his Masters degree in Business Administration. The Second World War intervened before he returned once more to the University, this time to receive his Ph.D. in finance in 1948. He joined the faculty at the University of California at Los Angeles in 1949 and has been there ever since.

At U.C.L.A. Fred distinguished himself as a teacher, researcher, and architect of one of the leading finance faculties in North America. Certainly his greatest achievement there has been his on-going commitment to doctoral studies. In 1978 he was honored with the U.C.L.A. campus-wide teaching award in recognition of his guidance of doctoral students. He has chaired over 30 doctoral committees, and been a member of at least 24 others. The majority of the authors who have contributed to this Festschrift are Fred's former students – each now a major scholar in his own right. I once asked Fred his prescription for motivating doctoral students. "You have to engage them intellectually and work with them on a weekly basis,'' he commented. ''And you have to work hard. One of my pleasures in life has been learning from my students.'' Without exception, Fred's students have commented that his door is never closed. He always has time for a new idea.

Along with Fred's work with students has gone his commitment to establishing the pre-eminence of U.C.L.A.'s Graduate School of Management. In this effort he has served in numerous roles including those of Associate Dean and Department Chairman. In addition to his administrative work at the university, he has made his mark in the government and industry as a consultant to the Council of Reserve Bank Presidents, the Committee for Economic Development, the National Bureau of Economic Research, the Commission on Money and Credit, the Ford Foundation, the Sloan Foundation, the U.S. Department of Energy, the National Science Foundation, and to many corporations, including, among others, General Motors, General Electric, and American Telephone and Telegraph.

While Fred Weston's teaching and administrative work have contributed directly to the lives of individuals and institutions, his writing has reached and enriched a far broader audience, that of financial economists and students around the world. Weston has published 19 books, chapters in 28 other books, 5 monographs, 71 articles, and 21 book reviews. His textbook, *Managerial Finance*, was first published in 1962 and has dominated graduate business education for 25 years. Now in its eighth edition, it has been translated into eleven foreign languages. Weston has served on the boards of editors of the *Journal of Finance, Financial Analysts Journal, Journal of Business Economics, Western Economic Journal, Journal of Business Research, Journal of Corporate Accounting and Finance*, and *Journal of Accounting, Auditing and Finance*. He has served as president, member of the Board of Directors, and member of the Advisory Board of the American Finance Association. He has also been president of the Western Economics Association, and the Financial Management Association.

Weston's research has spanned two major fields of academic endeavor – industrial organization and financial economics. Both have developed rapidly since the early 1950s and both now bear his mark.

Weston is renowned for his studies on mergers, beginning with his seminal 1953 book, *The Role of Mergers in the Growth of Large Firms*. His research has shown that conglomerate mergers are efficient and are the result of strong competitive behaviour. His later articles included work on alternative theories of mergers, a synthesis and analysis of market event studies on the efficiency of mergers, and numerous conference papers on antitrust policy. Weston is often asked to testify before Congressional Committees on merger policy, and has been an expert witness in merger litigations for over 25 years. Three particularly significant cases come to mind: the F.T.C.'s shared monopoly case against four ready-to-eat cereal firms, where he testified for Quaker Oats; the Justice Department suit against A.T.&T.; and the F.T.C. investigation and subsequent Chrysler Corporation suit against the General Motors–Toyota joint venture.

In 1968 Weston, along with Neil Jacoby, founded the Research Program in Competition and Business Policy, following many years of research in industrial organization. Fred was dissatisfied with the direction of Federal antitrust policy, and with its reliance on the prevailing structure–performance model of industrial organization. He became a leader in the "New Learning" on industrial concentration in the early 1970s, which established the intellectual foundation for the transformation of antitrust policy in the late 1970s and early 1980s. His studies include the first simultaneous equation structure–performance model, tests of the determinants of market structure, the effects of international competition on measures of industrial concentration, changes in aggregate concentration, and tests of the relationship of industry concentration to industry price changes.

Weston has also done ground-breaking work in the area of pricing policy. His first contribution in this area was a theory of large firm pricing. Subsequently, in a series of detailed studies, he examined pricing policies in such industries as pharmaceuticals, steel, automobiles, and petroleum refining. He also contributed studies on the administered price hypothesis, finding strong evidence to reject it.

Weston's commitment to public policy extends well beyond antitrust and pricing policy. He has testified before Congressional Committees on consumer product safety, and energy policy as well. In each case, he is always a strong advocate of policies to improve consumer welfare.

The inception of modern finance can be dated from roughly 1958 when Markowitz published his work on portfolio theory and Modigliani and Miller published their famous proposition that the financial structure of the firm would have no effect on the value of the firm. It is in the area of cost of capital and capital structure that Weston had an early significant impact on the field of finance, although he has certainly published on many other topics in the field, such as pension plans, leasing, forecasting financial requirements, tax incidence, planning and control, and credit policy. Early on, Fred had the idea that it is impossible to assess corporate performance without taking into account the fact that industries with different risk should have different profitability. When Modigliani and Miller (1958) supported their proposition that the cost of capital was unrelated to capital structure with cross-sectional data from the oil and electric utilities industries, Weston responded (1963) with his own analysis. He criticized their work on two counts: (1) The oil industry is not even approximately homogeneous in terms of business risk, and (2) the valuation model from which they derived the cost of capital assumed that cash flows are perpetuities which do not grow.

In an empirical study of his own, Weston documented a significant negative relationship between the cost of capital and financial leverage. The obvious and important implication was that the financial structure of the firm did affect its value. Subsequently, Modigliani and Miller revised their work (1966) and also found results consistent with a gain from higher financial leverage. The stimulating intellectual interchange among these early pioneers in the field has helped to delineate and clarify the thinking of those of us who have followed. Even today, the question of optimal capital structure remains at the very heart of corporate finance. The paper by Jaffe and Westerfield in this book represents new thinking based on the earlier work of giants in the field such as Modigliani, Miller, and Weston.

This volume is divided into two parts. The first four papers are topics in the field of industrial organization, while the remaining nine are subjects in financial economics. All are related to Weston's work.

Chapter 1, the first of the four papers on industrial organization, by Clement Krouse, examines the issue of factor supply: Is it better to have share contracting (contracts which stipulate delivery of a given fraction of a supplier firm's output regardless of who is the buyer and regardless of which state of nature occurs) or is vertical integration preferable? As the title of the chapter suggests, share contracting is a possible alternative to vertical integration, but it isn't likely.

Ed Rice discusses the classical question of barriers to entry in chapter 2. He points out conflicts and inconsistencies among definitions proposed by other scholars and comes up with a new approach.

Manak Gupta, in chapter 3, develops a model of an optimal long-run pricing policy for a profit-maximizing monopolist confronted with stochastic entry which is a function of the firm's existing pricing policy.

Chapter 4, by Stanley Ornstein, is an empirical study and critique of simultaneous equation methods of structure–performance relationships such as profitability, concentration, and advertising intensity. He argues that simultaneous equation bias is unlikely to be a problem in many hypothesized structure–performance relationships, and that many common estimation techniques, such as two or three stage least squares often introduce far more econometric problems than they theoretically resolve.

Weston, in his work on industrial organization, has touched on each of the aforementioned topics. His approach has always been to try to understand why the existing structure of industrial organization has come to be what it is, rather than to begin by assuming monopolistic practices. For example, high profits and high concentration ratios may occur because the most efficient firms are the most likely to succeed, not because they are unfair competitors. The efficiency of vertical integration, the definition of barriers to entry, the determination of pricing policy in the face of stochastic entry, and the econometric estimation of industry structure–performance relationships are all important parts of the story.

Part 2 is a collection of nine articles in finance. The first three, however, represent a bridge between industrial organization and finance, because they deal with corporate restructuring – mergers and acquisitions, leveraged buyouts, and spinoffs.

Richard Roll (chapter 5) reviews the empirical evidence on the effect of merger activity on shareholder wealth. It isn't surprising that Fred Weston (with Ansoff (1962), with Mansinghka (1971), with Smith and Shrieves (1972), and with Chung (1982)) did important early work in the area. The empirical evidence supports the conclusion that target firm shareholders are materially benefited by merger, but the evidence for shareholders of bidding firms is less conclusive. There is no support, however, for the theory that monopoly is a takeover motive.

Harry and Linda DeAngelo study a particular form of takeover in chapter 6, buyouts by management. Their sample includes 64 buyout proposals in the 1973–1982 period. All but four were completed, all of those which were completed went private, and the majority were leveraged buyouts. The paper describes the financial arrangements in detail, the role of the buyout specialist, and the costs and benefits of going private.

Copeland, Lemgruber and Mayers (chapter 7) study spinoffs, the opposite of mergers. They document statistically significant increases in shareholders' wealth at the first announcement date, at successive announcement dates, and at the spinoff ex-date. They estimate that the increase in shareholders' wealth averages 7.3 percent for completed spinoffs.

Chapter 8, by Jaffe and Westerfield, is concerned with the optimal capital structure debate where Weston was, again, an early contributor. They demonstrate that financial leverage may be an increasing function of the firm's variability, not a decreasing function as is suggested in most textbooks. The intuitive explanation for this surprising result is that the firm trades off two deadweight costs – the cost of bankruptcy if the firm's value falls too low, and the cost of taxes, if the firm's value is high. The costs are not symmetric, however. The cost of bankruptcy is not a function of the shortfall of cash flow, while the corporate tax paid is a positive function of the firm's pre-tax cash flow. With higher variance, the marginal cost of bankruptcy from a debt increase is greater than the marginal tax benefit, hence debt rises.

Chung and Smith also study the optimal financial structure question in chapter 9. They show that when product quality is costly to determine prior to purchase, a firm may use nonsalvageable capital to signal its commitment not to depreciate quality for opportunistic gain. The nonseparability between capital structure and the incentive to provide a high level of product quality is shown to give rise to a cost of using financial leverage which militates against extreme levels of financing.

Chapters 10, 11, and 12 are related, from different perspectives, to the problem of assessing risk and return. Ed Altman and Scott Nammacher explore the anatomy of the high yield debt (junk bond) market. They report the default experience of high yield debt securities, and compare the risk and return of active and passive investment strategies over the period 1978–1984. Chi-Cheng Hsia ranks eight widely-used market indices using two mean-variance efficiency scores developed from Roll's geometric representation of Shanken's C.R.S. T^2 test statistic and the likelihood ratio test statistic of Kandel. Over the period 1973–1982 the C.R.S.P. equally-weighted, C.R.S.P. value-weighted, and the S and P 500 indices emerge consistently as the three most efficient indices under all market conditions. William Beranek studies the risk induced by parent and subsidiary debt financing. Parents may support the debt of some or all of their subsidiaries, and consolidated financial statements may overstate the total obligation of the parent. The value and risk of a parent's shares depend on the extent to which it has assumed liability for subsidiary debt.

The final chapter, chapter 13 by Jeffrey Jaffe and Mark Rubinstein, models the value of information in personal and impersonal markets. They find that, in general, there is less incentive than one might expect for trading based on private information. In impersonal markets, if the market for information can be efficiently organized, it is better to sell information than to trade on it. And in personal markets, there may be no benefit to trading on information.

As a concluding thought, I am sure that I speak on behalf of all of the contributors to this book, when I express my gratitude to J. Fred Weston, mentor, scholar, and friend.

Thomas E. Copeland
Los Angeles, California, 1986

Part 1
Topics in Industrial Organization

1

Share Contracting to Assure Factor Supply? Possible, But Not Likely

CLEMENT G. KROUSE

PREFACE

It is usually argued that vertical integration in moderate scale is the preferred method for assuring factor supply under conditions of uncertainty. Markets in share contracts, which simply stipulate delivery of a given fraction of a supplier firm's output regardless of who is buyer and regardless of which future state of nature occurs, are considered as an alternative. What is "lost" by this sort of a negotiable contract is not an exhaustive specification of factor supply conditions, but rather the patterns of supply that buyers might achieve across state contingencies. The effect of this limitation is shown to depend on the form of the production technology of the factor using firms. Finally, vertical integration is shown to be a special case of share contracting, which means that the ability to insure against factor supply risk by vertical integration is never better than by share contracting. That we generally see vertical integration, and not share contracts, depends on other considerations as noted.

While the general problem dealt with in this paper is one frequently addressed in industrial organization economics, the specific questions, relating to the efficiency of risk allocation, are ones more usually addressed in financial economics. Fred Weston has been a research pioneer in merging these two fields of economics. And, as in this paper, many of his students have followed his leadership.

The author would like to thank H. E. Frech and J. Fred Weston for helpful comments.

INTRODUCTION

The list of motives for vertical integration is quite long. For example, such integration can (1) extend monopoly profits when production is subject to variable proportions (see Schmalensee, 1973; Warren-Boulton, 1974); (2) achieve technological advantages through increasing returns, information discovery, or decreased transactions costs owing to a minimization of opportunistic bargaining (see Williamson, 1975; Klein *et al.*, 1978; Hess, 1983); (3) provide advantages in dealing with regulation and tax law (see Kessler and Stern, 1958; Weston, 1981); and, (4) assure factor supply under conditions of uncertainty.[1] While our interest finally lies in "share" contracts to resolve the uncertainty associated with factor supply, it is instructive to make the usual vertical merger solution a starting point.

To begin in this way, let the production of some specific intermediate good by upstream (or supplier) firms be subject to uncertainty. Represent the uncertainty by states of nature and hold fixed the aggregate supply of the good in every such state. Three market arrangements are typically considered to allocate this aggregate among downstream (or user) firms: competitive spot markets, competitive markets in state-contingent forward contracts, and vertical integration. The obvious limitations of risk diversification offered by spot markets, which occur conditional on the realization of the uncertain state and thus allow no state-to-state exchanges among the firms, usually lead to their dismissal. The second alternative, exchange by state-contingent forward contracts, generally implies extraordinary transaction costs either in negotiating comprehensive contract specifications or in *ex post* haggling over an incomplete specification of states.

Williamson (1975, esp. pp. 67–70) has argued cogently that vertical integration in moderate scale is preferred from among the three alternatives. Because of bounded rationality, he maintains it is prohibitively costly to write contracts in which contingent supply conditions are exhaustively specified. And, contracts with only a partial specification of exchange conditions pose trading risks since there are real incentives for each party to bargain "opportunistically" when contractual ambiguities develop. Haggling is likely to ensue, and when the potential gains are large the haggling process can become costly. The resulting allocation by contracts is thus ineffective, for vertical integration provides equivalent factor supply patterns at lower cost.[2]

It is the last part of this analysis that provides the starting point here. As Williamson notes, it is the specification of a comprehensive state-contingent contract that becomes inordinately expensive; a full list of "if this then this" contract provisions governing factor supply surely involves prohibitive costs in complex lines of business. While Williamson is correct in this, what of a second possibility: a market in fully comprehensive contracts which define an allocation rule for each supplier's output under all contingencies. We here consider such contracts in their most tractable form, as linear sharing rules which stipulate delivery of a given fraction of a supplier's output regardless of which state of nature obtains. What is "lost" by this sort of a negotiable contract is not an exhaustive specification of factor supply conditions, but rather the patterns of supply downstream firms might achieve across state contingencies. What is gained is a significant reduction in the kinds of negotiation and enforcement costs which concern Williamson.

A detailed description of such a share contract market is set out in the next section. Two questions are then considered: (1) are there reasonable conditions such that a competitive market in these contracts provides an allocation of the supplier's outputs which is preferred by downstream firms; and, when these (and possibly less restrictive) conditions are met, (2) what can be said about the relative preference of the downstream firms for such share contracting compared to vertical integration?

INTERMEDIATE GOOD SUPPLY:
CONTRACT COMPLEXITY AND VERTICAL INTEGRATION

Consider a two-period model economy with two kinds of firms. Supplier firms offer an intermediate factor. Owing to technological uncertainty in their production processes, and incentives to invest in production as noted below, the exact amount they offer is, however, dependent on the realization of a state of nature. Users in turn employ the intermediate good as a factor in their production of final goods. To avoid confusing motives for alternative supply arrangements between these vertical stages, suppose there is no uncertainty in this latter production process and further assume there to be competition in the final goods market. Finally, to focus here on the contract arrangement between suppliers and users, it is assumed that planned levels of investment are fixed for the supplier firms at the time they offer their output. This does not mean that their investment level is exactly known by the user firm. Rather, some combination of this investment uncertainty plus the technological uncertainty inherent in the supplier's production process means that the outputs of these firms are viewed as random variables by the users.

How can users best arrange for factor supply under these conditions? Holding aside the possibility of vertical integration for the moment, and as a reaction to the costs of state contingent forward contracts, consider exchanges by *share* contracts.[3] As noted earlier, such a share contract would promise delivery, regardless of the state of nature to obtain, of a pro rata, constant portion of the upstream firm's output. As a result, for any (and all) possible states of nature the amount of intermediate good to be supplied by such contracts is unambiguous. This comprehensiveness notwithstanding, the contracts can be expected to economize on exchange costs for several reasons: they have an uncomplicated specification; they are based on market observable variables; and, they are (not individually tailored but) common to all user firms. Moreover, the costs of verifying output do not appear prohibitive as the monitoring problem is not different from that frequently faced in licensing arrangements where the owner of the scarce resource, including patented inventions, generally specifies royalty fees on a per unit output basis and closely monitors that output.[4]

While the exact costs of negotiating and enforcing such contracts finally involve questions of fact specific to the given intermediate good, it none the less seems reasonable to suppose that such costs are relatively small. As a consequence, it is an arrangement for upstream to downstream supply which is of *a priori* interest. It is therefore somewhat of a surprise that only very few examples of the use of share contracts are known.[5] The question then arises as to *why* it is that share contracting is ineffective?

This shifts attention to the specific patterns (across states) of supply that are available using share contracts and to the conditions under which such restrictions in achievable patterns adversely affect downstream firms. If the conditions for no adverse effects are fairly general, then share contracts should stand as an alternative to other arrangements, and particularly to the moderate scale vertical integration generally proposed. As the next sections show, these conditions are somewhat restrictive and the inability to properly insure risks therefore contributes to the infrequent use of share contracts for allocating the supply of factors. The exact manner in which share contracts fail is of special interest, for the analysis also explains why vertical integration is likely to be an even less effective solution to factor supply uncertainty. That vertical integration prevails, and share contracts do not, must then owe generally to the first three advantages of integration noted in the initial paragraph of this chapter and not its ability to insure risk.

BASIC MODEL AND NOTATION

We consider $j = 1,2, \ldots, J$ upstream suppliers, $k = 1,2 \ldots, K$ downstream users, and uncertain states of nature designated by $s = 1,2, \ldots, S$. (J, K, and S are assumed to be finite.) The following notation is employed throughout:[6] $Q_j(s)$ the intermediate good output of upstream firm j if state s obtains; v_j the market value of firm j's share contracts; α_{kj} the fraction of firm j's share contracts held by downstream firm k (note that $\Sigma_k \alpha_{kj} = 1$ is required for market clearing); $q_k(s)$ the total amount of the intermediate good received from suppliers by user firm k if state s obtains;

and, $h_k(q_k(s))$ the amount of *final* good produced by firm k, with h_k its production function.

From these definitions it follows directly that firm k's total of intermediate good acquired by share contract can be written as (for each state s)

$$q_k(s) = \sum_j [\alpha_{kj} Q_j(s)] \tag{1.1a}$$

and, associated with the combination of contracts held, firm k's total factor cost is[7]

$$C_k = \sum_j [\alpha_{kj} v_j] \tag{1.1b}$$

In turn, state contingent net income for each downstream firm, $\pi_k(s)$, can be written

$$\pi_k(s) = p(s) h_k(q_k(s)) - \sum_j [\alpha_{kj} v_j] \tag{1.1c}$$

where $p(s)$ is the price prevailing in the final good spot market. While this price generally depends on the state, each user firm is assumed small relative to the total market in any state and thus a price-taker (of the random price).

Given its choice of production plan, each supplying firm sells share contracts as claims to its output. Downstream firms bid competitively for the uncertain supply of the intermediate good and in the process establish market prices and holdings for the various contracts. To avoid side issues associated with the financing of corporations, assume that the actual payment for contracts is deferred until the end of the period *then*, even though the contracts are formally exchanged and their prices are established at the beginning of a period *now*. To further confine attention to a two-period model without carrying discount parameters, allow the production of downstream firms to be instantaneous and occur at the moment the (uncertain) upstream output is realized. These simple time relationships are set out in Table 1.1.

Radner (1974) has shown that necessary and sufficient conditions for unanimous stockholder support for a production rule are that the capital

Table 1.1   Two-period events

Now (s uncertain)	Then (s realized)
1 Share contracts exchanged, and 2 $[v_j]$ share prices established.	1 $Q_j(s)$ known, 2 intermediate goods delivered according to share contracts, 3 downstream firms complete production of final good, selling at price $p(s)$, and 4 upstream firms make deferred share contracts payments.

market be (perceived) competitive *and* that it be possible to replicate any firm's capital market returns at the margin as a linear combination of the returns of all firms. (This second condition is, of course, less restrictive than presuming the *capital* markets to be complete.) As one suspects, the unanimously supported rule is (perceived) capital market value maximization. When these conditions hold, there exist positive, state claim prices $[\Phi(s)]_s$, fixed under the output decisions of any firm, such that the market value of any firm can be written as a weighted sum of its distribution of returns across states, i.e.[8]

$$v_k = \sum_s \Phi(s)\pi_k(s) \quad \text{for all } k \tag{1.2}$$

Importantly, the $[\Phi(s)]_s$ provides weights for valuing the return distribution of any firm.

Given that the capital market has those conditions which yield value maximization as the optimal investment rule for firms, each downstream firm acts in its selection of share contracts to solve the problem

$$\max_{\alpha_k} \sum_s \Phi(s)\pi_k(s) \tag{1.3}$$

where $\pi_k(s)$ depends on the *J*-vector of contract fractions $\alpha_k = [\alpha_{k1} \; \alpha_{k2} \ldots \alpha_{kJ}]$ given in equation (1.1c). If these user firms are takers of the contract prices $[v_j]_j$, then *contract* demand functions are derived from the necessary conditions of equation (1.3)

$$v_j = \sum_s \Phi(s)[p(s)h_k'(q_k(s))Q_j(s)] / \sum_s \Phi(s) \tag{1.4}$$

for all *j* and *k*, where $h_k'(q_k(s))$ is the marginal physical product of the factor in state *s* and $\sum_s \Phi(s)$ is (one plus) the riskless rate of return.[9]

As a final bit of bookkeeping, we note that the *KJ* equations (1.4) and *J* market clearing equations $\sum_k \alpha_{kj} = 1$ for all *j* form $(K+1)J$ relations. The *J* equilibrium contract prices $[v_j]_j$ and the *KJ* equilibrium holdings $[\alpha_{kj}]_{kj}$ are associated with the solution of the equations.

EFFECTIVENESS OF INTERMEDIATE GOODS ALLOCATION BY SIMPLE CONTRACTS

Consider some original allocation of intermediate goods by markets in share contracts and, with the supplier firms' output fixed, consider all feasible reallocations. If any such reallocation fails to increase the market value of the (typical) *k*th user firm, then the original exchange by share contracts is said to be *effective* from that firm's viewpoint. There is then no incentive for it to seek an alternative allocative mechanism, either by markets in a more complex form of contract or by an internal organization of dealing (among divisions). If share contract markets economize on transmission costs, then the conclusions hold *a fortiori*.

The conditions under which markets in share contracts are effective for *each* downstream firm k are stated as a proposition below. Two foundations of that proposition are of special interest in themselves and first set forth as lemmas.

Lemma 1 Effective Allocations. An allocation is effective from the standpoint of every downstream firm if and only if

$$\frac{\partial \pi_k(s)}{\partial q_k(s)} = \gamma_k \frac{\partial \pi_1(s)}{\partial q_1(s)} \tag{1.5}$$

for all s and k, where γ_k is a positive constant.

Proof. Hold constant the amount of intermediate good produced in each state and consider an allocation (by market or internal directive) of this output to user firms. A reallocation of the intermediate good will be desired and possible for some specific firm k only if that reallocation increases its market value while not adversely affecting the value of any other downstream firm. We first prove sufficiency by considering some reallocation from $q_k(s)$ to $[q_k(s) + dq_k(s)]$ for an arbitrary firm k. If conditions (1.5) hold in this case then

$$d\pi_k(s) = \sum_s \frac{\partial \pi_k(s)}{\partial q_k(s)} \, dq_k(s)$$

$$= \gamma_k \sum_s \frac{\partial \pi_1(s)}{\partial q_1(s)} \, dq_k(s) \tag{1.6}$$

If the reallocation is to be feasible it is required that $\sum_k dq_k(s) = 0$ for all s. Summing (1.6) over all downstream firms then gives

$$\sum_k d\pi_k(s) = \sum_k \gamma_k \sum_s \frac{\partial \pi_1(s)}{\partial q_1(s)} dq_k(s)$$

$$= \sum_s \frac{\partial \pi_1(s)}{\partial q_1(s)} \sum_k \gamma_k dq_k(s) = 0 \tag{1.7a}$$

With each $\gamma_k > 0$, then the differential profits $d\pi_k(s)$ for all k cannot all be of the same sign (unles they are all zero). As a result there can be no reallocation of the intermediate factor which will be uniformly agreed to and, therefore, condition (1.5) is sufficient for an effective allocation.

To demonstrate necessity, consider the case of only two firms (k and m) and two states (s and θ). We then must have $dq_k(s) = - dq_m(s)$ and $dq_k(\theta) = - dq_m(\theta)$. The changes in profitability associated with the proposed reallocation are

$$d\pi_k(s) = \pi_k'(s)dq_k(s) + \pi_k'(\theta)dq_k(\theta) \tag{1.7b}$$

$$d\pi_m(s) = - \pi_m'(s)dq_k(s) - \pi_m'(\theta)dq_k(\theta) \tag{1.7c}$$

where we use the notation $\pi_k'(s) = \partial \pi_k / \partial q_k(s)$. When one of the firms incurs negative profits the reallocation will not be agreed upon; thus $(d\pi_k)(d\pi_m) \le 0$, for all possible $dq_k(s)$ and $\partial q_k(\theta)$, stands as a condition for the original allocation to be effective. Using equations (1.7b) and (1.7c) this inequality is rewritten as

$$\pi_k'(s)\pi_m'(s)[dq_k(s)]^2 + [\pi_k'(s)\pi_k'(\theta) + \pi_k'(\theta)\pi_m'(s)]dq_k(s)dq_k(\theta) \\ + \pi_k'(\theta)\pi_m'(\theta)[dq_k(\theta)]^2 \ge 0 \tag{1.7d}$$

It is clear that (1.7d) can be satisfied only when

$$[\pi_k'(\theta)\pi_m'(s) - \pi_k'(s)\pi_m'(\theta)]^2 \le 0$$

This weak inequality immediately, and finally, implies

$$\frac{\pi_k'(s)}{\pi_k'(\theta)} = \frac{\pi_m'(s)}{\pi_m'(\theta)} \tag{1.7e}$$

which occurs only when condition (1.5) is satisfied.

Lemma 2 Effective Allocations and Aggregate Output. Let $q_k(\cdot)$ be the general rule specifying the allocation of each supplier to user k, i.e.

$$q_k(s) = q_k(Q_1(s), Q_2(s), \ldots, Q_j(s))$$

where $Q_j(s)$ is upstream firm j's state s output. An allocation is effective only if this rule is of special form, for all s,

$$q_k(s) = q_k(Q(s)) \tag{1.8}$$

where $Q(s) = \Sigma_j Q_j(s)$ is the aggregate supply of the intermediate good.

Proof. Differentiate the definition $Q(s) = \Sigma_k q_k(s)$ and equations (1.5) with respect to $Q_j(s)$ to obtain, respectively,

$$\frac{\Sigma_k \partial q_k(s)}{\partial Q_j(s)} = 1 \tag{1.9}$$

and

$$\frac{\partial^2 \pi_k}{\partial q_k(s)^2} \frac{\partial q_k(s)}{\partial Q_j(s)} = \gamma_k \frac{\partial^2 \pi_1}{\partial q_1(s)^2} \frac{\partial q_1(s)}{\partial Q_j(s)} \tag{1.10}$$

Solving equation 1.10 yields

$$\frac{\partial q_k(s)}{\partial Q_j(s)} = \gamma_k \frac{\partial^2 \pi_1}{\partial q_1(s)^2} \frac{\partial q_1(s)}{\partial Q_j(s)} \bigg/ \frac{\partial^2 \pi_k}{\partial q_k(s)^2}$$

which when summed over all k and (1.9) is employed gives

$$\frac{\partial q_1(s)}{\partial Q_j(s)} = \frac{1/[\partial^2 \pi_1/\partial q_1(s)^2]}{\Sigma_k\{\gamma_k/[\partial^2 \pi_k/\partial q_k(s)^2]\}} \tag{1.11}$$

Note that the right-hand side of this expression does not depend on any specific supplier firm's output $Q_j(s)$, and therefore the rule for determining an effective allocation of intermediate good depends only on the aggregate factor supply in each state.

Lemma 2 requires that downstream firms optimally choose factor supply arrangements which shed all risks except those associated with the total industry output of the intermediate good; any other plan of factor acquisition is ineffective. *All* effective allocations plans for intermediate goods must therefore be constructed by pooling the suppliers' outputs into one aggregate and then specifying a rule for sharing that total among user firms. As a consequence, what any downstream firm needs to know generally is not the output pattern across states of a single supplier firm, or a subset of them, but the total industry output pattern. One would therefore turn to, say, a supplier industry trade association or sales bureau in formulating purchase plans.[10] Implications of this result for vertical integration are noted in a moment.

Lemma 2 is an optimal "diversification" rule. If the aggregate (state contingent) supply in some two states is the same, the lemma tells us it is non-optimal for user firms to create additional risk by varying their demand across factor suppliers. More generally, if the aggregate supply of the factor differs across states it is not optimal for the user firms to create a balance of risk bearing where one user's reduced variation comes at the expense of another's increased variation.

One must not, however, read more into the lemma than is really there. For example, Lemma 2 does not simply mean that share contracts written on aggregate supply represent an effective allocation. Consider, as an illustration of this, an industry with two downstream firms with profit functions, for all s,

$$\Pi_1(q_1(s)) = \xi_1(q_1(s))^{3/4}$$
$$\Pi_2(q_2(s)) = \xi_2(q_2(s))^{1/2}$$

where ξ_1 and ξ_2 are parameters representing the excess of average revenue product over factor price. An effective allocation requires (see equation (1.5)),

$$\frac{\xi_2}{2}(q_2(s))^{-1/2} = \lambda_2 \frac{3\xi_1}{4}(q_1(s))^{-1/4}$$

$$q_2(s) = \xi(q_1(s))^{1/2}$$

where $\xi = [3(\xi_1/\xi_2)\lambda_2]^{-2}$. Let $Q(s) = [q_1(s) + q_2(s)]$ be aggregate supply in state s, solve this for $q_2(s)$, and substitute in the above equation to give

$$q_1(s) = a + [b + cQ(s)]^{1/2}$$

where a, b, and c are appropriate constants. A similar expression obtains for $q_2(s)$. Of special note is the fact that here the optimal demands for factors by the two users are non-linear functions of the (state contingent) aggregate supply. Share contracts, which provide only for *linear* sharing of the factor, could not generally assure the effective allocation in this case.

We now see that all effective rules for allocating the upstream output by share contracts must be written in the general form

$$\mathbf{q}_k = \lambda_{0k}\mathbf{1}_S + \lambda_{1k}\mathbf{Q} \tag{1.12}$$

where $\mathbf{q}_k$ and $\mathbf{Q}$ are state contingent *vectors* of inputs and outputs, $\mathbf{1}_S$ is an S-vector of 1s, and the scalar constants λ_{0k}, $\lambda_{1k} \geq 0$ are generally different for each firm. If s and θ are arbitrary pairs of states, then equation (1.12) requires the rate of input usage to be constant for all pairs of states, i.e.

$$\frac{dq_k(s)}{dq_k(\theta)} = \beta(s, \theta) \tag{1.13}$$

for all k regardless of specific input (and thus output) levels. That is, an effective allocation of the intermediate good requires the "input expansion path" for each downstream firm to be linear, each expansion path relating demands for *state contingent* amounts of intermediate goods as expected output varies. What restrictions does this place on the production technology of these firms?

Proposition. Production Technologies for Effective Share Contract Allocations. Share contracts provide an effective allocation of the intermediate good only if the profit function of each downstream firm is of the form, for all s,

$$-\frac{\partial\Pi_k(s)/\partial q_k(s)}{\partial^2\Pi_k(s)/\partial q_k^2(s)} = \delta_k + \delta q_k(s), \tag{1.14}$$

where $\delta_k > 0$ is a firm k specific parameter and $\delta > 0$ is a parameter common to all downstream firms. In turn, this requires production functions of the form

$$h_k(q_k(s)) = \ell n[q_k(s) + 1] \tag{1.15a}$$

for $\delta = 1$, and

$$h_k(q_k(s)) = \alpha\{[\delta_k + (\frac{\alpha+1}{\alpha})q_k(s)]^{1/\alpha} - \delta_k^{1/\alpha}\} \tag{1.15b}$$

for $\delta \neq 1$, where $\alpha = 1/(\delta - 1)$.

Proof. Differentiate (1.5) first with respect to $Q(s)$ and then γ_k. Substitute from the second equation into the first, use the linearity requirement (1.12) and rearrange to derive condition (1.14) of the proposition:

$$-\frac{\partial \Pi_k / \partial q_k(s)}{\partial^2 \Pi_k / \partial q_k^2(s)} = \delta_k + \delta_k q_k(s)$$

where the δ are generally functions of γ_k. Solving this differential equation gives two solutions: case one,

$$\partial \Pi_k / \partial q_k(s) = \exp[-q_k(s)/\delta_k] + i_k \tag{1.16}$$

for $\delta_k = 0$; and case two

$$\frac{\partial \Pi_k}{\partial q_k(s)} = [\delta_k + \hat{\delta}_k q_k(s)]^{-1/\hat{\delta}_k} + i_k \tag{1.17}$$

when $\hat{\delta}_k \neq 0$. In both cases i_k indicates the constant of integration. As (1.16) requires that profits be a uniformly decreasing function of output we dismiss this case. When case two satisfies (1.5) then

$$[\delta_k + \hat{\delta}_k q_k(s)]^{-1/\delta_k} + i_k = \gamma_k \{ [\delta_1 + \hat{\delta}_1 q_1(s)]^{-1/\delta_k} = i_1 \}$$

This gives linear sharing rules (that is, outputs can be allocated by share contracts) if and only if $i_k = 0$ and $\hat{\delta}_k = \delta$ for all k. Finally, integrating (1.17), solving for $h_k(q_k(s))$ from $\Pi_k(s)$ and imposing the condition $h_k(0) = 0$ gives equations (1.15). Q.E.D.

An example is helpful in understanding the proposition. Consider two downstream firms with production techniques given by (1.15b) and parameters $\alpha = 0.5$, $\delta_1 = 1$, $\delta_2 = 2$: namely,

$$h_1(s) = 0.5[1 + 3q_k(s)]^2 - 5 \tag{1.18a}$$
$$h_2(s) = 0.5[2 + 3q_k(s)]^2 - 2 \tag{1.18b}$$

The optimality condition (1.5) then requires

$$\frac{p(s)h_2'(s) - c(s)}{p(s)h_2''(s)} = \gamma_2 \frac{p(s)h_1'(s) - c(s)}{p(s)h_1''(s)} \tag{1.19}$$

where primes indicate the usual derivatives. Forming the appropriate derivatives from (1.18) and substituting these in (1.19) gives the equilibrium condition

$$\frac{2[1 + 3q_2(s)]}{9} = \frac{2\gamma_2[2 + 3q_1(s)]}{9}$$

Finally, using the identity $q_1(s) + q_2(s) = Q(s)$ and solving gives

$$q_2(s) = a_2 + b_2 Q(s) \tag{1.20}$$

Where a_2 and b_2 are parameters dependent upon α, δ_1, δ_2, and γ_2.

Equation (1.20) is more useful if written in vector form (and for some kth firm generally):

$$\mathbf{q}_k = a_k \mathbf{1}_S + b_k \mathbf{Q}$$
$$= (a_k + b_k) \mathbf{1}_S + b_k \mathbf{Q}^* \qquad (1.21)$$

where $\mathbf{q}_k$ and $\mathbf{Q}$ are the S-vectors of state-contingent amounts of the firm k factor usage and the aggregate factor supply respectively, $\mathbf{1}_S$ is an S-vector of ones, and $\mathbf{Q}^* = (\mathbf{Q} - \mathbf{1}_S)$. $\mathbf{1}_S$ may be thought of as representing a riskless factor plan (vector), making $\mathbf{Q}^*$ the residual, risky plan. Equation (1.21) informs us that an effective plan of factor usage for every downstream firm is a linear combination of these riskless and risky plans. Thus, if the conditions on user production technologies given by the proposition hold, suppliers can optimally issue two types of shares contracts to their output: those which provide riskless claims and then those which provide the residual (state contingent) amounts. In turn, users purchase both riskless contracts and a combination of the residual, risky contracts. (Each user's portfolio of risky contracts will optimally be a scalar multiple of $\mathbf{Q}^*$ the aggregate, residual risk.) The proportions of the $\mathbf{1}_S$ and $\mathbf{Q}^*$ used to form $\mathbf{q}_k$ will reflect the relative risk adverseness of the user firm.

MARKET EXCHANGE OR VERTICAL INTEGRATION

By specific choice of the parameters in equation (1.15), the downstream production functions can be made to possess constant, increasing, or decreasing return of any degree. In this respect the functions are of flexible form and the linearity requirement of share contracts does not appear to be unduly restrictive. On the other hand, the requirement that the parameter δ (or α) be common means that the downstream firms can differ only to the extent allowed by the parameter δ_k. A degree of equal access to production technology which provides for this extent of commonality is necessary. Given the economist's general inclination to think that representative firm analysis provides an accurate description of actual industries, then the restriction to a common δ, but differing δ_k, should not be viewed too skeptically. (The special case of equation (1.15a) does, of course, require identical production technologies.)

With respect to vertical integration, for any such merger plan to be effective it is necessary that the downstream firm merge backwards to acquire a sufficient number of supplier firms such that they have an output distribution that is, except for scale, equal to a linear combination of (is "spanned" by) a riskless plan and the original producers' aggregate output. If this spanning condition is not satisfied, then vertical integration of an amount which economizes on transaction costs cannot be effective. This is equivalent to the observation that vertical integration is a means of specializing in share contracts, with the downstream firm buying 100 percent of the output shares of *one* supplier firm. As an effective allocation requires full diversification in the purchase of shares, this polar case can be effective only if the selected supplier's output is spanned by the riskless and residual risky plans.

This view of vertical integration, as specialization in share contracts, is of further importance. In the specialization by integration one generally loses valued diversity. This means that vertical integration cannot yield patterns of supply significantly more valued than those achievable by trading in share contracts. If, in contrast to our reasoning above, there are significant costs associated with writing share contracts (or with enforcing them) and if intermediate outputs are highly (but not perfectly) correlated across firms, then integration could dominate market exchanges by share contracting.[11] This, however, leads to consideration of specific industry facts which are beyond the present study.

NOTES

1 See, generally, Adelman (1955), Mueller (1969), Williamson (1975), and Scherer (1980, pp. 89–91). DeChazeau and Kahn (1959, p. 415) claim this to be the principal reason for the vertical integration of production, refining and distribution stages in petroleum:

> The essence of integration, it seems to us, is the protection it offers or seems to offer against the uncertainties and instabilities of reliance on often highly imperfect intermediate markets. It is a means by which oil companies have attempted, in a industry that is potentially highly unstable, to stake out and insulate market positions by securing dependable sources of supply.

McLean and Haig (1954, pp. 101–2, 224–6, 420–3) offer a similar explanation for vertical integration in the petroleum industry and Teece (1976) provides a list of specific cases based on this explanation.

2 Moreover, Williamson finds that these hazards of contractual incompleteness generally cannot be circumscribed by the construction of a multi-firm sharing rule with joint profit maximizing behavior.

3 Spot market transactions for the intermediate good are generally omitted on an a priori basis from the subsequent analyses, for the immediate concern is with problems of supply assurance and spot markets, occurring state conditionally as they do, which simply do not provide for exchanges across states.

4 A sequence of well-known cases where there has been close monitoring of license output (and prices) is especially relevant evidence here. See *U.S.* v. *General Electric Co.*, 272 U.S. 476 (1926), then *U.S.*v. *Line Material Co., et al.*, 382 U.S. 197 (1965). Cartel arrangements provide another example where output

plans are generally required to be verified by agents outside the producing firm. Industry sales bureaus, trade associations, and agricultural co-operative agencies are generally established in these cases with power not only to collect detailed output information, but also to perform routine audits of company records. Such verification activities, legal and illegal, have been repeatedly found to function with great precision and efficiency. (See *Appalachian Coals, Inc.* v. *U.S.*, 288 U.S. 344 (1933) as a premier example of an efficiently operated sales bureau. Also, Stocking (1954) summarizes a wide range of case studies of successful output monitoring by industry trade associations.)

5   White (1972, ch. 18) notes some share contracting for crude petroleum was used in California at the turn of the century. Jones (1914) describes similar contracts by railroads for the output of hard coal in the Appalachian region. And, of course, agricultural sellers' co-operatives serve this same purpose. I cannot find cases other than these.

6   Throughout, j will be used to index upstream firms and indicate a representative one of them. The letter k will be used similarly for downstream firms.

7   Without loss of generality the intermediate good is considered to be homogeneous and firm k's only factor of production.

8   The $[\Phi(s)]_s$ are implicit prices for consumption in states, being marginal rates of substitution (M.R.S.) between investor consumption in the state and income. When the *capital* market is complete (there are as many linearly independent securities as states) or when conditions for universal portfolio separation obtain, see Cass and Stiglitz (1970), these M.R.S.s will be common across all individuals. In the case that the M.R.S.s are not common, then the prices $[\Phi(s)]_s$ can be selected as any convex combination of the individual M.R.S.s.

9   In passing, it is seen that equation (1.4) implies a proportional valuation rule: when one firm's output is a constant multiple of another's in all states, then the total market value of its share contracts differs by that same constant.

10   This result is analogous to the Brainard and Dolbear (1971) finding that private risk can never be "less" than the social (aggregate) risk.

11   Klein *et al.* (1978) provide a systematic analysis of one specific kind of contracting cost which provides incentives for vertical integration. No other clear analysis of such costs exists in the literature.

BIBLIOGRAPHY

Adelman, M. 1955: Concept and statistical measurement of vertical integration. *Business Concentration and Public Policy*. Princeton: Princeton University Press.

Arrow, K. 1975: Vertical control with variable proportions. *Journal of Political Economy*, July/August, 783–802.

Brainard, W. and Dolbear, F. T. 1971: Social risk and financial markets. *American Economic Review*, May, 360–70.

Cass, D. and Stiglitz, J. 1970: The structure of investor preferences and asset returns, and separability in portfolio allocation: a contribution to the pure theory of mutual funds. *Journal of Economic Theory*, 122–60.

DeChazeau, M. and Kahn, A. E. 1959: *Integration and Competition in the Petroleum Industry*. New Haven: Yale University Press.

Diamond, P. 1967: The role of a stock market in a general equilibrium model with technological uncertainty. *American Economic Review*, September, 759–76.

Hess, J. 1983: *The Economics of Organization*. Amsterdam: North-Holland.

Jones, E. 1914: *The Anthracite Coal Combination in the United States*.

Kessler, F. and Stern, R. 1959: Competition, contract, and vertical integration. *Yale Law Journal*, November, 1–129.

Klein, B., Crawford, R. C. and Alchian, A. A. 1978: Vertical integration, appropriable rents, and the competitive contracting process. *Journal of Law and Economics*, October, 297–326.

McLean, J. and Haig, R. 1954: *The Growth of Integrated Oil Companies*. Cambridge: Harvard University Press.

Mueller, W. F. 1969: In J. Fred Weston and S. Peltzman (eds). *Public Policy Towards Mergers*. Pacific Palisades: Goodyear Publishing.

Radner, R. 1974: A note on unanimity of stockholders' preferences among alternative production plans. *Bell Journal of Economics*, Spring, 181–4.

Scherer, R. 1980: *Industrial Market Structure and Economic Performance*. Chicago: Rand McNally.

Schmalensee, R. 1973: A note on the theory of vertical integration. *Journal of Political Economy*, March/April, 442–9.

Stocking, G. W. 1954: The rule of reason, workable competition, and the legality of trade association activities. *University of Chicago Law Review*, Summer, 527–619.

Teece, D. T. 1976: *Vertical Integration and Vertical Divestitures in the U.S. Oil Industry*. Stanford University.

Warren-Boulton, F. 1974: Vertical control with variable proportions. *Journal of Political Economy*, July/August, 783–803.

Weston, J. Fred 1981: Industrial concentration, mergers, and growth. In *Mergers and Economic Efficiency*, vol. 2. U.S. Department of Commerce (June).

White, G. T. 1972: *Formative Years in the Far West*. New York: Appleton-Century-Crofts Press.

Williamson, O. 1975: *Markets and Hierarchies: Analysis and Anti-Trust Implications*. New York: Free Press.

2

A New Look at Disagreements About Barriers to Entry

EDWARD M. RICE

PREFACE

This chapter is a discussion of the role played by barriers to entry in economic analysis. It represents part of my continuing interest in the relationships between industrial structure, pricing, and economic efficiency. This interest first began with my contact with J. Fred Weston.

Much of Dr. Weston's career has focused on these issues in industrial organization. The first academic literature I read on the subject was his book with Stanley Ornstein, The Impact of Large Firms on the U.S. Economy. *He taught me much about this area when I worked under him at U.C.L.A. – especially that one should be very careful about the link between the theoretical concepts addressed by research and the data proxies used for empirical measurements. This concern about measurement problems shows clearly in the present piece as well as most of my other work in the industrial organization area.*

Corporate finance is my other principal general area of research interest, and Dr. Weston has had a powerful influence on my thinking there as well. My first exposure to corporate finance was through his Managerial Finance *textbook with Eugene Brigham. His many papers which link industrial organization theory and corporate finance theory, provide the basis for much of my corporate finance work.*

This chapter represents an extension of a paper presented to the Western Economic Association Meetings several years ago while I was at the University of Illinois. Financial support along the way was received from the Bureau of Economic and Business Research at the University of Illinois and from the University of Washington. This work has benefited from suggestions by many people, especially H. DeAngelo, L. DeAngelo, S. Ornstein, and J. Simon. The economics workshops at the Universities of Illinois and Washington also assisted the paper's development substantially. Of course all errors are mine.

It is hard to imagine how anyone's influence on my academic career could have been larger than J. Fred Weston's.

INTRODUCTION

Fundamental disagreement among economists arises over whether or not barriers to entry exist in various industries. The confusion is not only about where barriers to entry (B.T.E.) are, but about what they are. Studies which classify industries according to the height of their barriers to entry use nebulous criteria and reach conflicting conclusions.

This chapter will attempt to reconcile disagreements about barriers to entry to the extent possible. It will first mention the most important definitions of barriers that have been offered in the literature, and apply the definitions in several situations. It will then discuss the uses that economists have made of the B.T.E. notion; that is, it will analyze the implications barriers to entry are said to have for prices and market structure. It will demonstrate the essential points, that the definitions must be matched to the implications–a different definition is relevant for each implication drawn – and that none of the existing definitions relate directly to social inefficiency. For these reasons, a redirection of the policy debate over barriers to entry is necessary, away from definitional issues toward more fundamental issues. The next section will discuss the problems in both the theoretical and empirical literature involving barriers to entry. The concluding section will summarize.

DEFINITIONS

Several different definitions of barriers to entry have been offered in the literature. This section will review some prominent ones offered to date.

Six definitions will be considered. A B.T.E. is defined as:

Definition 1. (Stigler, 1968)[1] Anything giving cost advantages in the long run to existing firms relative to potential entrants. A transaction cost or other imperfection in any input market may give rise to these cost advantages. Since existing firms have already acquired the relevant inputs, these imperfections reduce the opportunity cost of inputs for existing firms relative to the prospective outlays for potential entrants.

Definition 2. (Bain, 1956; 1968) Anything allowing existing firms to raise price over minimum long-run average cost. The height of B.T.E. is defined by Bain as the difference between minimum average cost for the most efficient existing firm and the maximum price it could charge without inducing entry. This is essentially 1, with the addition of economies of scale (limit pricing) and strategic behavior as possible B.T.E.

Definition 3. (Caves and Porter, 1976) A durable asset specific to a particular firm. This formulation has actually been used by Caves and Porter as a definition of "barriers to exit."[2] Specifically, it implies that the value of the asset in alternative use is small; thus its cost is sunk. This leads to a lower opportunity cost of the asset for existing firms relative to potential entrants, as in 1.

Definition 4. (Bork, 1978; Needham, 1969)[3] Anything that acts as an obstacle to entry. This definition encompasses most of the others, but is extremely vague.

Definition 5. (Brozen, 1974; 1975) Contrived or artificial impediments to entry. While not clearly stating how "contrived" and "artificial" are to be defined, Brozen supplies examples that suggest that such barriers are imposed by government for no "good" reason.

Definition 6. (Weizsacker, 1980) A cost of producing borne by entrants but not by incumbents, and which implies a distortion away from the socially optimal allocation of resources. This is exactly the Stigler definition, but with the additional requirement of social misallocation.

While the foregoing definitions sound reasonable and quite similar, closer investigation reveals serious problems with them and differences between them. These problems and differences can most clearly be seen by applying the definitions directly to various potential sources of B.T.E. and seeing how these potential sources are classified. The direct application of these definitions often classifies things to be B.T.E. that neither the "authors" of the definition, nor anyone else, would intend to classify this way.

Low Demand.[4] This would seem to be a B.T.E. under Definition 4, since clearly demand encourages entry. It would seem to be unrelated to other measures (except perhaps to 2 very indirectly, in increasing the importance of economies of scale).

Taxicab Medallions. In New York City one needs to buy a medallion (very expensive) to be allowed to operate a taxi. The supply of these medallions is severely constrained tending to create the high price. Stigler uses this as a classic example of what a barrier to entry is. Unfortunately, it does not fall under his B.T.E. Definition 1. Since the medallions are bought and sold in a fairly well-organized market, they are equally costly to current cab owners (as an opportunity cost) and potential entrants (as a prospective outlay).[5] For similar reasons, Definitions 2, 3, and 6 would not classify this as a B.T.E. For obvious reasons, 4 and 5 would.

Bain and Stigler would probably argue that the medallions really are a B.T.E. under their definitions on the grounds that buying a medallion does not constitute "true" entry. They would say that, since such a purchase does not expand output, it merely amounts to a renaming of existing firms. A slight change in the situation to allow government to sell new medallions, while still permitting resale of existing medallions, would circumvent their exception. That is, suppose government prices the medallions at the price currently prevailing in the resale market for medallions (and government will continue to price them at whatever level this latter price would take in the future). Such pricing ensures that the amount of medallions in circulation is exactly the amount currently existing. This pricing will also ensure that the price of cab services, the quantity sold, and the market structure will be the same as under the current medallion policy. Here, there will be no cost advantage or B.T.E. in Definitions 1 and 2, "true" entry will be possible, yet the economic effects of this policy will be the same as under the current restriction.

High Price. A firm, or many of the firms in an industry, may elect to follow a policy of charging a high price, so as to earn returns earlier than otherwise. Such a policy encourages entry by the more efficient potential entrants. However, when the more efficient potential entrants have entered the industry, the price can be raised to an even higher level without inducing further entry. Thus, according to Definition 2, this policy will result in a *higher* B.T.E.! B.T.E. may also be higher according to Definitions 1 and 6, since potential entrants will now have higher costs, although 6 would also require a judgement on the social misallocations from the policy. Under Definition 4, this high price will definitely lower barriers to entry. It seems irrelevant to 3 and 5 which concern only structural and cost conditions within an industry.

Advertising and Product Differentiation. Such advertising has all the essential features of an asset and is specific to the firm. It would thus be a B.T.E. according to Definition 3 and also 4 (as any asset would be). Whether it is a B.T.E. according to Definitions 1, 2 and 6 would depend on whether it is more costly for an entrant to differentiate his product (build up reputation) than it is for the first firms. Whether advertising is a B.T.E. would also depend, in 2, on whether there are economies of scale in advertising and, in 6, on whether the advertising results in social waste. Brozen, 1974, makes clear that he does not consider advertising a barrier according to 5.

Bain claims that, according to his Definition 2, product differentiation is a barrier to entry because it enables existing firms to charge higher prices than entrants. This argument is extremely misleading, ignoring the expenditure on building the differentiation asset (reputation) that has already been incurred by existing firms. It is equivalent to an argument that a production plant is a barrier to entry, since an entrant must incur the expense of building one if he is to produce any output.[6]

Superior Efficiency. Some firms seem to have lower costs than other firms because of superior team production techniques. This cost advantage will be a B.T.E. in Definitions 1 and 2. This efficiency can be considered a durable, specific asset and thus will be a B.T.E. according to 3. A very efficient firm will also be an "obstacle" to a potential entrant – thus a B.T.E. in Definition 4. This obstacle, however, will neither be "artificial" nor socially wasteful; thus, it will not be a B.T.E. in Definitions 5 and 6.

USES OF BARRIERS

While the preceding applications of the definitions often appear odd, one cannot judge the appropriateness of a B.T.E. definition without knowing the purposes for which B.T.E. are used. The B.T.E. concept has been used for the following positive and normative purposes:

(1) Explaining different rates of entry across industries – for this purpose, Definition 4 is probably most appropriate. Low demand, or any other "obstacle", should reduce the amount of entry we find in an industry.

(2) Determining the number of firms in an industry – here, all definitions are somewhat appropriate. Stigler's classification of things affecting industry structure to include B.T.E. (in Definition 1), economies of scale, and the extent of demand seems useful. This classification might also include legal impediments to entry, although these could be included in the demand function or the cost function (where they show up as economies of scale).

(3) Determining how dangerous and powerful collusion would be in an industry – for this purpose, probably the best definition is 2, although all definitions are again somewhat appropriate. While it might seem at first glance that Definition 2 is perfect for this purpose, a deeper look shows problems. That is, the implicit assumptions necessary to apply 2 directly here are that:

(a) all firms currently producing in an industry can costlessly be brought into collusion;
(b) no potential entrant can ever be included in the collusion.

Without (a), rivalry among existing firms might make collusion no problem at all, even with B.T.E. high in Definition 2. Without (b), collusion might

be a very large problem, even with low cost potential entrants and thus
low B.T.E. in Definition 2.

Many who have worked in the B.T.E. area have corrected for
assumption (a) to some degree by noting that B.T.E. create collusion
problems only in more concentrated industries, where collusion among
existing firms is easier. As Posner (1976) notes, however, there are many
factors other than concentration which affect the costs of collusion.
Assumption (b) has been ignored in work to date.[7]

(4) Determining where there are inefficiently too few firms and/or
inefficiently high pricing – for this purpose, none of the definitions are
satisfactory. Definition 1 is designed to explain industry structure and has
little relation to efficiency. Definition 2, however, attempts to deal directly
with efficiency questions. Bain argues that his measure of B.T.E. is an
index of potential inefficiency, since it enables firms to raise price above
minimum average cost. But the reference to cost results in an avoidance
of the central issue. That is, what is to be included in cost? Is the price
of a taxicab medallion to be included in the cost calculation? How are
rents to specific assets, with little alternative use, to be accounted for?
Such specific assets cannot be valued without reference to demand and
price. The indeterminacy of the Bain definition eliminates its usefulness
for this purpose.[8]

It is difficult to relate Definitions 3 and 4 to efficiency. Surely *some*
durable, specific assets (3) are necessary and efficient for production in
any industry. Similarly some obstacles to entry (4), e.g. low prices, are
efficient. There can be entry that is too "fast" as well as too "slow",
as far as efficiency is concerned.

One can see a further crippling problem with all definitions other than
5 and 6 in dealing with efficiency questions. Under Definitions 1–4,
superior firm efficiency will be designated a barrier to entry. Such efficiency
is the antithesis of social waste.

The most direct attempts to deal with inefficiency are in 5 by Brozen
and 6 by von Weizsacker. Yet Brozen's definition is too vague to provide
clear guidance in this matter. What impediments are artificial? Are
government impediments the only artificial ones? Is everything done by
government artificial? Government actions are neither necessary nor
sufficient for inefficiency, thus government should not be the criterion
to determine B.T.E. If other agents can create barriers, the Brozen
definition does not give us much guidance on how to determine where
these barriers are.

Definition 6 is plagued by its stress on costs borne by entrants and
not incumbents. Taxicab medallions create serious social waste and a
structure with fewer firms, as do other restrictions imposed on industries
as a whole. It seems useful to classify medallions and these other
restrictions as B.T.E. Yet Definition 6 does not so classify such overall
restrictions.

ANOTHER DEFINITION

The use of barriers to entry as an index of inefficiency is probably their most important use. The interest in B.T.E. to predict different rates of entry across industries as well as to predict market structure differences (purposes 1 and 2), in the final analysis, is usually motivated by efficiency considerations. Thus, the failure of any B.T.E. definition to relate directly to efficiency is an egregious state of affairs.

A definition of B.T.E. that directly confronts the efficiency issue would be the following:

A pure *barrier to entry* is an asset possessed by incumbents which yields private returns by enabling price to rise above the socially optimal price without inducing entry, but has zero or negative social value. To the extent that any asset has a private value in excess of its social value, even if the social value is not zero, the asset would constitute a barrier to entry.[9]

This definition and inefficiency are linked as follows. A firm's expected returns can be tautologically defined as normal returns to assets the firm owns.[10] (If, for example, a firm earns monopoly rents, its excess return can be regarded as normal returns to its "monopoly asset.") If these returns are to assets where private and social values are equal, as in the competitive situation, there is no inefficiency. Only if these returns are to assets where private and social values are unequal will there be social waste. Such inefficiency takes the form of pricing above marginal and average social cost, thus generating the returns that give B.T.E. their private value.

Crucial to determining what constitutes a B.T.E. under this definition is how social value is to be determined. In one sense this is not a problem for the definition; it is a problem for normative economics in general. Whatever definition of social value one prefers can be employed in the B.T.E. definition.

Economics does, however, provide a useful definition of social value. The social value of an asset is the net amount of surplus created by its existence. In principle one measures this value by summing the amounts (in dollars) by which people who benefit from the asset are made better off, and then subtracting the amounts (in dollars) by which people who suffer from the asset's existence are made worse off. This net quantity equals the social value of the asset.

To understand this alternative definition of B.T.E., it may be helpful to investigate how the suggested barriers mentioned earlier would be classified here. Low demand would involve no asset yielding any return, hence would not be a B.T.E. under the definition here. Taxicab medallions, on the other hand, would be an obvious B.T.E. example. The social value of this asset is nonexistent – in fact, consumers would benefit *more* from eliminating these medallions than producers would benefit from retaining them – yet the medallions are definitely valuable to the owner. A high price would not in itself be a B.T.E.; however, if such pricing were socially wasteful, what led to the charging of such a high price might be a barrier. Product differentiation, which involves the building of a reputation asset, would be a barrier if the reputation had no social value. If the social value of the reputation equalled the private value, it would not be a B.T.E. Finally, superior firm efficiency would in no way be a B.T.E.

One might note that this definition of B.T.E. does not focus on differences between incumbents and potential entrants. This is because social waste has little to do with such differences. Perhaps the concept here defined should be given a name different from B.T.E., but it is the correct concept to apply in social waste determination.

CONFUSION IN THE THEORETICAL LITERATURE

As previously stated, barriers to entry are primarily important as indicators of inefficiency. Also, the extant B.T.E. definitions are not appropriate for this use. It is not surprising, therefore, that there is confusion in both the theoretical and empirical literature on B.T.E.

The theoretical confusion is most obvious in the debate about whether advertising is a B.T.E. Comanor and Wilson (1967), for example, say it is a B.T.E., while Brozen says it is not. The reason for their differences is primarily due to their use of different definitions of B.T.E. Comanor and Wilson say advertising creates a B.T.E. because it involves scale economies and aids in product differentiation, thereby following Bain's B.T.E. Definition 2. Brozen is using his Definition 5, and does not consider advertising contrived or artificial.

The disagreement lurking below the surface, however, is about social waste. Comanor and Wilson (1967), for example, conclude by saying:

Current policies which tend to emphasize the role played by concentration may need to be supplemented by those concerned directly with the nature and extent of product differentiation. Policies dealing with these matters would be an important component in a general policy designed to promote competition.

Comanor and Wilson would certainly not put forth this policy prescription if they felt that advertising was socially productive information dissemination. Would they criticize capital intensive production processes, which seem to have all the characteristics they ascribe to advertising, as a barrier to entry? Brozen is direct in his defense of advertising as a socially beneficial tool of competition.

The discussion of the social costs and benefits of advertising has here been obfuscated by the term "barriers to entry." The term serves no useful purpose in this debate. A potentially substantive discussion has been reduced to semantic bickering. The discussion must be redirected to focus on the social value of advertising.

THEORETICAL ASIDES

At this point, it may be useful to address the issue of whether advertising is socially wasteful in general. Much of the belief in wastefulness is based on either or both of two questionable premises – that information should be free or that economists are smarter than consumers. The first premise shows through in the forementioned Bain argument that product differentiation is a B.T.E. He allows no cost of building reputation, an information asset, to be imputed into firm cost functions.[11] The second premise is implicit in the inadmissability, in the advertising–social waste logic, of consumers' willingness to pay as a measure of social value. It must be that consumers are duped by advertising (while economists are not), for otherwise socially wasteful advertising would not persist. When consumers are not duped, Demsetz (1972) has argued that a cheaper, unadvertised product can penetrate the market and reap high profits.[12]

As an additional aside, the question of whether private firms can ever create barriers to entry (in the inefficiency sense) should be faced. Taxicab medallions, referred to above, are a B.T.E., but are government created. Many other examples of barriers are cited by Brozen, but all involve government. If advertising is not socially wasteful, as has just been argued, then what B.T.E. can private firms create?

A simple case of a privately created B.T.E. arises in a Mafia-run market. Here firms that dare compete with the Mafia must do so at the risk of grave physical injury to their workers. The threat of Mafia retaliation will dissuade some firms from entering the industry. The threat will enable the Mafia to charge high prices, and thus has substantial value to the Mafia. However, this threat has no social value – i.e. the benefits derived from eliminating the threat in total would at least be as great as the Mafia's loss.

This simple case corresponds to a more general class of privately created barriers. Any credible predatory (or other) threat a firm can create will be valuable in deterring potential entry. These threats may be created where firms would have no cause to carry out such a threat, were it not for the value in entry deterrence. In such cases, the threat will cause social waste, and thus be a B.T.E. in the inefficiency sense.[13] Whether such predatory threats are important in practice is unclear, as the existing evidence suggests their importance may have been overestimated (see Koller, 1975, for example).

CONFUSION IN THE EMPIRICAL LITERATURE

There are two types of problems with empirical studies that involve barriers to entry. The first lies in the necessarily somewhat arbitrary nature of B.T.E. classifications. The second has to do with the misuses of profit rates or similar industry variables to infer effects and causes of B.T.E.

The first problem is that classifying industries as having very high, substantial, or moderate to low B.T.E. is a highly suspect procedure. Economists who engage in such classifications must of necessity exercise substantial personal judgement in murky areas. Since the judgement is so subjective, there exists substantial danger of unintentionally choosing classifications that are biased toward the chooser's predispositions.

Evidence that different authors arrive at very different classifications increases one's skepticism of empirical B.T.E. studies. Comparing Bain's (1956) classifications with Shepherd's (1970) clearly provides evidence of differences. Shepherd uses the same criteria as Bain and even makes explicit reference to Bain's classifications as the starting point of his own. Yet the classifications made by these two authors differ on more than a third of the identical industries they investigate. Although when comparing other authors' B.T.E. classifications there is often strong agreement, this agreement is usually caused by the authors' acceptance of previous classifications (usually Bain's) without exercising much independent judgement.[14]

The second problem with B.T.E. empirical studies involves misconceptions about the relation of profit rates or similar variables to B.T.E. and social waste. As previously alluded to, the profit rate (profit divided by equity or profit plus interest paid divided by assets) should be approximately[15] normal for *all* firms if *all* assets are properly capitalized (as they are in the capital market) into the asset base of the profit calculation. Examination of differences in accounting profit rates, therefore, primarily identifies differences in the values of assets in the capital markets as compared to the values on the balance sheet. That is, high profit rates generally reflect the existence of assets uncapitalized by accountants.[16] These assets are likely to be uncapitalized only because of difficulties that accountants have in assessing their values.

B.T.E. studies use profit rates for one of two purposes: either to show that social inefficiency is higher where B.T.E. are higher or to argue that some industry variable is a B.T.E. since it is associated with high profits. Studies using profit rates for the first purpose are implicitly assuming that there is a one-to-one relationship between uncapitalized assets and socially wasteful or monopoly assets. No such relationship can be justified by existing accounting procedures. Many socially productive assets (such as efficient team production techniques) go uncapitalized because of the difficulty of measuring their value, while potentially monopoly type assets (such as entry licenses) are capitalized because their values are easier to determine. These studies implicitly let accountants determine what is socially productive, yet accountants have neither the expertise nor the inclination to make judgements about social efficiency.[17]

Studies arguing that various industry variables cause B.T.E. because of a profit association have similar problems. That is, these studies implicitly define B.T.E. as assets uncapitalized by accountants. This definition has little to do with industrial organization economics or social efficiency questions. Again, an unwillingness to directly address questions of social efficiency has caused misunderstanding and confusion.

CONCLUSIONS AND REMAINING PROBLEMS

This paper argues that economists should clearly specify what they mean when they refer to "barriers to entry." It is senseless to discuss whether something is a B.T.E. when different B.T.E. definitions are used by different people.

The paper goes on to show serious problems in most of the empirical literature involving B.T.E. These problems stem from the subjectivity of B.T.E. classifications as well as the misunderstanding of accounting profit and related measures.

Policy prescriptions about barriers also are misguided, since no definition of B.T.E. to date directly addresses the social waste question. An alternative definition is offered in the paper to remedy this deficiency. But perhaps the term "barriers to entry" should be avoided altogether in policy discussions, since it seems to cloud the issues at least as often as it clarifies them.

This argument should not be taken to mean that B.T.E. definitions have been valueless. In particular, the extent of durable specific assets in an industry, or sunk costs, may be useful in predicting varieties of market behavior. Such definitions have, unfortunately, often been used inappropriately.

NOTES

1 The names after the definitions refer to the authors in whose work the definitions "arose" – it does not necessarily follow that these writers consistently employ these definitions in the use of the B.T.E. term.

2 The difference between B.T.E. and exit barriers is unclear to me, although the distinction is made by Caves and Porter (1976).

3 Needham (1969) actually adheres to the Bain definition after suggesting this one – Bork (1978) suggests this definition as the current, but not very desirable, usage of the term.

4 This example is suggested by Stigler (1968, ch. 6) as something that should not be classified as a B.T.E.

5 This point is also recognized in Demsetz (1982).

6 Similar points are made by many authors, including Demsetz (1982) and Fisher *et al.* (1983).

7 Assumption (b) is probably of major importance only in industries with only one or two relatively efficient potential entrants.

8 Those questions of how costs are calculated also arise with respect to discussions of B.T.E. that stress the existence of economic profits (see, for example, Fisher *et al.*, 1983).

9 Such social inefficiency would necessarily arise from some transaction cost which prevents all costs from being internalized by the owner.

10 Note that the capital market returns of all firms are expected to be normal because the capital market capitalizes the value of *all* assets of the firm, whether socially valuable or not.

11 Such ignoring of information costs is also evident in the argument that imperfect capital markets are a B.T.E. It seems that the reputation asset of existing borrowers is ignored.

12 Recent literature on information problems, stemming from Akerlof (1970), has pointed out the social value of brand names in insuring product quality and economizing on information costs. Reasons for consumers' willingness to pay premiums for brand named goods seem much more sensible than economists have sometimes admitted.

13 Much recent theoretical work has focused on the positive and normative implications of strategic behavior by firms (see, for example, Spence, 1979).

14 For one example among many of this type of acceptance, see Qualls (1975).

15 This point abstracts from timing and depreciation problems in accounting returns. See Fisher *et al.* (1983) for a discussion of these problems.

16 Notice that uncapitalized assets will not always increase profit rates (see Demsetz, 1979).

17 Using Tobin's q (see Lindenberg and Ross, 1981) instead of profit rates does not solve this problem either. That is, someone must decide *which assets are to be included* in calculating replacement cost, and accounting procedures are not designed for this purpose.

BIBLIOGRAPHY

Akerlof, G. 1970: The market for 'Lemons'. *Quarterly Journal of Economics*, August.

Bain, J. 1956: *Barriers to New Competition*. Cambridge, Mass: Harvard University Press.

Bain, J. 1968: *Industrial Organization*, 2nd edn. New York: Wiley and Sons.

Bork, R. 1978: *The Antitrust Paradox: A Policy at War with Itself*. New York: Basic Books.

Brozen, Y. 1974: Entry barriers: advertising and product differentiation. In H. Goldschmid, H. M. Mann, and J. F. Weston (eds) *Industrial Concentration: The New Learning*. Boston, Mass: Little Brown and Co.

Brozen, Y. 1975: Competition, efficiency, and antitrust. In Y. Brozen (ed.) *The Competitive Economy*. Morristown, New Jersey: General Learning Press.

Caves, R. and Porter, M. 1976: Barriers to exit. In R. Masson and P. D. Qualls (eds) *Essays in Industrial Organization in Honor of Joe S. Bain.* Cambridge, Mass: Ballinger.

Comanor, W. and Wilson, T. 1967: Advertising, market structure and performance. *Review of Economics and Statistics,* November.

Demsetz, H. 1972: The inconsistencies in monopolistic competition: a reply. *Journal of Political Economy,* May.

Demsetz, H. 1979: Accounting for advertising as a barrier to entry. *Journal of Business,* July.

Demsetz, H. 1982: Barriers to entry. *American Economic Review,* March.

Fisher, F., McGowan, J. and Greenwood, J. 1983: *Folded, Spindled, and Mutilated: Economic Analysis and U.S. vs. IBM.* Cambridge, Mass: MIT Press.

Koller, R. 1975: The myth of predatory pricing: an empirical study. In Y. Brozen (ed.) *The Competitive Economy.* Morristown, New Jersey: General Learning Press.

Lindenberg, E. and Ross, S. 1981: Tobin's q ratio and industrial organization, *Journal of Business,* January.

Needham, D. 1969: *Economic Analysis and Industrial Structure.* New York: Holt, Rinehart and Winston.

Posner, R. 1976: *Antitrust Law: An Economic Perspective.* Chicago and London: University of Chicago Press.

Qualls, D. 1975: Price stability in concentrated industries. *Southern Economic Journal,* October.

Shepherd, W. 1970: *Market Power and Economic Welfare.* New York: Random House.

Spence, A. M. 1979: Investment strategy and growth in a new market. *Bell Journal of Economics,* Spring.

Stigler, G. 1968: *The Organization of Industry,* Chs. 6 and 10. Homewood, Illinois: Richard D. Irwin, Inc.

Weizsacker, C. C. von 1980: A welfare analysis of barriers to entry. *Bell Journal of Economics,* Autumn.

3
Monopoly Pricing With Stochastic Demand and Rate of Entry

MANAK C. GUPTA

PREFACE

The contributions of Dr. J. Fred Weston to the academic world are phenomenal. Fred has done high quality work in a wide spectrum of fields. The present paper relates to Fred's earlier paper in the A.E.R. *where he tests the administered price thesis, and also his 1973 monograph,* The Impact of Large Firms on the U.S. Economy, *where he discusses varied aspects of monopolies in the United States. The present paper outlines the monopoly pricing with certain constraints such as threat of entry.*

The author acknowledges with gratitude the immense support with which Fred has provided him, while he was a student and also thereafter. Fred was always there when he was needed. Talking to other students of Fred's, I know that this feeling is shared by us all. Surprisingly, every one of his students feels that he has a unique bond with Fred; I certainly do.

INTRODUCTION

The departure of pricing from the classical behavior over cycles in industries with a high degree of concentration has been studied at length by Weston *et al.* (1974), Philips (1971), and Stigler and Kindahl (1971). Weston *et al.* examine both the truncated and the full versions of the administered price thesis using data from a recent business cycle. This paper develops a model to examine pricing in industries that exhibit a high degree

Temple University Research Committee provided financial support for this project.
To Fred Weston who readily shared the knowledge and learning with me, I shall ever be grateful.

of concentration but still face potential entrants. Leland (1972), Gaskins (1971), and Kamien and Schwartz (1971) have done much to enhance our understanding of the monopoly pricing and this paper takes a step further in that direction by introducing both the dynamic and stochastic properties in the model. Also, the model incorporates the effects of the following on the optimal price trajectory: price elasticity of demand, stochasticity of rate of entry, risk aversion of the dominant firm, variations in the capitalization rate, and uncertainty of the demand function. As a result, some interesting insights into the price behavior of the monopolist emerge. Some of the implications should be helpful in developing a dynamic model of the firm, especially monopolies and oligopolies. Most current financial models, such as the capital asset pricing model (C.A.P.M.), are equilibrium restricted, ie. they do not allow for changing market and environmental conditions. The model presented in this paper, however, incorporates both dynamic and stochastic conditions, thus providing a vehicle with which to study transitional phenomena.

The procedure followed in this paper will be first to develop certain essential concepts for our model. The solution to the model is then obtained and final optimality conditions are established. In the next section, the economic implications of the results obtained in the earlier section are explored.

THE MODEL

Let the following be defined: $p(t)$ is the price per unit, $\tilde{q}(p(t), t)$ is the industry demand, a normal random variable (r.v.), with mean μ_q and variance σ_q^2, R is the present value of all future profits, r is the capitalization rate, and $z(t)$ is the quantity sold by the competitors, a random variable with mean μ_z and variance σ_z^2.

Thus, the time-adjusted profits for the firm, $\pi(t)$, is also a random variable and is given by equation (3.1).

$$\tilde{\pi}(t) = \{[p(t) - c][\tilde{q}(p(t)) - \tilde{z}(t)]\} \exp^{-rt} \qquad (3.1)$$

where $[q(p(t)) - z(t)]$ denotes the quantity sold by the dominant firm and c is the cost per unit. Also, the rate at which the rivals enter into the market can be described by the stochastic differential equation

$$\tilde{z} = \tilde{k}[p(t) - p\ell] \qquad (3.2)$$

where $p\ell$ is the limit price, and the rivals' response coefficient, a random variable, is denoted by $\tilde{k}$. Equation (3.2) states that the rate of entry by rivals into the market has a linear but uncertain relationship to the dominant firm's price $p(t)$.

The model thus recognizes that uncertainties are associated with the industry demand, the competitors' response coefficient and competitors' rate of entry into the market. The uncertainty in $q(p(t))$ is caused by the fact that the industry demand is not simply a function of $p(t)$. It is a more complex process and may be dependent upon factors such as the state of the economy and disposable personal income. By assuming $q(p(t), t)$ to be a stochastic process, it is possible to derive a relatively simple model and still account for these other factors. Also, the rivals' response coefficient $\tilde{k}$ is a random variable, as is their rate of entry into the market, $\tilde{z}(t)$. The rate of market entry again could be a function of a host of other factors besides $p(t)$. The random variable $\tilde{k}$ takes into account all these extraneous factors and ensures that $\tilde{z}(t)$ is actually a stochastic process. Thus, we let the random variable $\tilde{k}$ have the following properties:

$$E[k] = \mu_k \quad and \quad V(k) = \sigma_k^2 \tag{3.3}$$

Equation (3.3) defines the expectation and the variance of $\tilde{k}$. Also, from equation (3.1) we have

$$E[\tilde{\pi}(t)] = [p(t) - c][\mu_q - \mu_z]$$
$$V[\tilde{\pi}(t)] = [p(t) - c]^2[\sigma_q^2 - \sigma_z^2] \tag{3.4}$$

assuming $\sigma_{q,z}$ to be zero. Let us postulate a Von Neumann–Morgenstern utility function of the form

$$U[\tilde{\pi}] = -\exp^{(-a\tilde{\pi})} \tag{3.5}$$

Equation (3.5) has the desirable properties that

$$U'[\tilde{\pi}] = a\exp^{(-a\tilde{\pi})} > 0$$
$$U''[\tilde{\pi}] = -a^2\exp^{(-a\tilde{\pi})} < 0 \tag{3.6}$$

implying an increasing total utility but decreasing marginal utility. Taking the expected value of the utility function, we obtain

$$E[U(\tilde{\pi})] = -\exp^{[-aE(\tilde{\pi}) + (a^2/2)V(\tilde{\pi})]} \tag{3.7}$$

The certainty equivalent of $\tilde{\pi}$, denoted by π, should have the property

$$U[\hat{\pi}] = E[U(\tilde{\pi})] \tag{3.8}$$

Therefore, substituting from equation (3.1) we obtain the following expression for the time adjusted certainty equivalent of profits:

$$\hat{\pi} = \{[p(t) - c]\hat{q} - [p(t) - c]\hat{z}\}\exp^{(-rt)} \tag{3.9}$$

and from equation (3.4)

$$\hat{\pi} = \{[p(t) - c]\mu_q - \alpha[p(t) - c]^2\sigma_q^2 - [p(t) - c]\hat{z}\}\exp^{(-rt)} \tag{3.10}$$

where $\hat{z}$ is the certainty equivalent of uncertain entry by competitors and $\alpha = a/2$.

Also, from equation (3.3) we can obtain the expression for the certainty equivalent of the entry response coefficient

$$\hat{k} = \mu_k + \alpha \sigma_k^2 \tag{3.11}$$

Combining equations (3.2) and (3.11), the certainty equivalent of the uncertain rate of entry by potential competitors is given by

$$\hat{z} = \mu_k [p(t) - p_\ell] + \alpha \sigma_k^2 [p(t) - p_\ell] \tag{3.12}$$

where $[p(t) - p_\ell]$ is the excess of price charged over the entry preventing price, p_ℓ.

Thus, the objective of the firm can be expressed as the maximization of the certainty equivalent of the profit stream, that is

$$\max_{p(t)} R = \int_0^T \{[p(t) - c] \mu_q - \alpha [p(t) - c]^2 \sigma_q^2 - [p(t) - c] \hat{z}\} \exp^{(-rt)} dt \tag{3.13}$$

for $T \to \infty$, and

$$\hat{z} = \mu_k [p(t) - p_\ell] + \alpha \sigma_k^2 [p(t) - p_\ell] \tag{3.14}$$

SOLUTION TO THE MODEL

Equations (3.13) and (3.14) present a typical control problem with $p(t)$ as the control variable and $\hat{z}(t)$ as the state variable. To obtain optimal price policy for the firm, let us form the Hamiltonian, H, that is

$$H = \{[p(t) - c] \mu_q - \alpha [p(t) - c]^2 \sigma_q^2 - [p(t) - c] \hat{z}\} \exp^{(-rt)}$$
$$+ \lambda(t) \{\mu_k [p(t) - p_\ell] + \alpha \sigma_k^2 [p(t) - p_\ell]\} \tag{3.15}$$

For simplifying the notation, let index (t) be dropped from price and also denote

$$V_q = \sigma_q^2 \tag{3.16}$$
$$V_k = \sigma_k^2 \tag{3.17}$$
$$V_z = \sigma_z^2 \tag{3.18}$$

The optimal price p will be such that $\dfrac{\partial H}{\partial p} = 0$. Therefore,

$$0 = \frac{\partial H}{\partial p} = [\mu_q + (p - c) \frac{\partial \mu_q}{\partial p} - 2\alpha(p - c) V_q - \alpha(p - c)^2 \frac{\partial V_q}{\partial p} - \hat{z}]$$
$$\exp^{(-rt)} + \lambda(t) [\mu_k - \alpha V_k] \tag{3.19}$$

Differentiating equation (3.19) again with respect to price, we obtain

$$
\frac{\partial^2 H}{\partial p^2} = \left[\frac{\partial \mu_q}{p} + (p-c) \frac{\partial^2 \mu_q}{\partial p^2} + \frac{\partial \mu_q}{\partial p} - 2\alpha V_q - 2\alpha(p-c) \frac{\partial V_q}{\partial p} \right.
$$

$$
\left. - 2\alpha(p-c) \frac{\partial V_q}{\partial p} - (p-c)^2\alpha \frac{\partial^2 V_q}{\partial p^2} \right] \exp^{(-rt)} \tag{3.20}
$$

For H to have a maximum, $(\partial^2 H/\partial p^2) < 0$. In equation (3.20), $\exp^{(-rt)}$ is always positive, and therefore,

$$
2\frac{\partial \mu_q}{\partial p} + (p-c)\frac{\partial^2 \mu_q}{\partial p^2} - 4\alpha(p-c) \frac{\partial V_q}{\partial p} - 2\alpha V_q - \alpha(p-c)^2 \frac{\partial^2 V_q}{\partial p^2}
$$

must be negative. This will always be true if profit is a smooth concave function of price.

Equation (3.19) may be rewritten as

$$
-\lambda(t)[\mu_k - \alpha V_k] = \exp^{(-rt)} [\mu_q + (p-c) \frac{\partial \mu_q}{\partial p}
$$

$$
- 2\alpha(p-c)V_q - (p-c)^2\alpha \frac{\partial V_q}{\partial p} - \hat{z}]
$$

Differentiating both sides with respect to time, we have

$$
-\dot{\lambda}[\mu_k - \alpha V_k] = e^{(-rt)} \left[\frac{\partial \mu_q}{\partial p}\dot{p} + \dot{p}\frac{\partial \mu_q}{\partial p} + (p-c)\frac{\partial^2 \mu_q}{\partial p^2} - 2\alpha \dot{p}V_q \right.
$$

$$
\left. - 2(p-c)\alpha \frac{\partial V_q}{\partial p}\dot{p} - 2(p-c)\dot{p}\alpha \frac{\partial V_q}{\partial p} - (p-c)^2\alpha \frac{\partial^2 V_q}{\partial p^2}\dot{p} - \dot{\hat{z}} \right] \exp^{(-rt)}
$$

$$
r\exp^{-rt} \ [\mu_q + (p-c)\frac{\partial \mu_q}{\partial p} - 2\alpha(p-c)V_q - \alpha(p-c)^2\frac{\partial V_q}{\partial p} - \hat{z}] \tag{3.21}
$$

The adjoint equation is obtained by differentiating the Hamiltonian with respect to the state variable, that is,

$$
-\dot{\lambda} = \frac{\partial H}{\partial \hat{z}} = -(p-c)\exp^{(-rt)} \tag{3.22}
$$

Substituting the value of $-\dot{\lambda}$ from equation (3.22) and the value of $\dot{\hat{z}}$ from equation (3.14) into equation (3.21), we have

$$-(p-c)[\mu_k-\alpha V_k]=\dot{p}[2\frac{\partial\mu_q}{\partial p}-4\alpha(p-c)\frac{\partial V_q}{\partial p}+(p-c)\frac{\partial^2\mu_q}{\partial p^2}$$

$$-2\alpha V_q-(p-c)^2\alpha\frac{\partial^2 V_q}{\partial p^2}]-(\mu_k-\alpha V_k)(p-p_\ell)-r[\mu_q+(p-c)\frac{\partial\mu_q}{\partial p}$$

$$-2\alpha(p-c)V_q-(p-c)^2\alpha\frac{\partial V_q}{\partial p}-\hat{z}]$$

or

$$\dot{p}=$$

$$\frac{(\mu_k-\alpha V_k)(p_\ell-c)+r[\hat{z}-\mu_q-(p-c)\frac{\partial\mu_q}{\partial p}+2\alpha(p-c)V_q+(p-c)^2\alpha\frac{\partial V_q}{\partial p}]}{-2\frac{\partial\mu_q}{\partial p}-(p-c)\frac{\partial^2\mu_q}{\partial p^2}+4\alpha(p-c)\frac{\partial V_q}{\partial p}+(p-c)^2\alpha\frac{\partial^2 V_q}{\partial p^2}-2\alpha V_q}$$

and $\qquad\qquad$ (3.23)

$$\dot{z}=(\mu_k-\alpha V_k)(p-p_\ell) \qquad\qquad (3.14)$$

If we assume V_q to be constant and independent of p, equation (3.23) reduces to

$$\dot{p}=\frac{(\mu_k-\alpha V_k)(p_\ell-c)+r[\hat{z}-\mu_q-(p-c)\frac{\partial\mu_q}{\partial p}+2\alpha(p-c)V_q]}{-2\frac{\partial\mu_q}{\partial p}-(p-c)\frac{\partial^2\mu_q}{\partial p^2}-2\alpha V_q} \qquad (3.24)$$

Setting $\dot{p}=0$, equation (3.24) yields

$$(\mu_k-\alpha V_k)(p_\ell-c)+r[\hat{z}-\mu_q-(p-c)\frac{\partial\mu_q}{\partial p}+\alpha^2(p-c)V_q]=0 \quad (3.25)$$

or

$$p=\left(\frac{\partial\mu_q}{\partial p}-2\alpha V_q\right)^{-1}\hat{z}+\left(\frac{\partial\mu_q}{\partial p}-2\alpha V_q\right)^{-1}$$

$$[-\mu_q+c\frac{\partial\mu_q}{\partial p}-2c\alpha V_q+\frac{(\mu_k-\alpha V_k)(p_\ell-c)}{r}] \qquad (3.26)$$

In equation (3.14), set $\hat{z}=0$; since the certainty equivalent value of k, that is $(\mu_k+\alpha V_k)$, is nonzero, therefore $p=p_\ell$. Also, consider the phase plane $p-\hat{z}$. From (3.26), since $(\partial\mu_q/\partial p)$ is negative, the curve $\dot{p}=0$ on the $p-\hat{z}$ plane will have a negative slope as shown in figure 3.1.

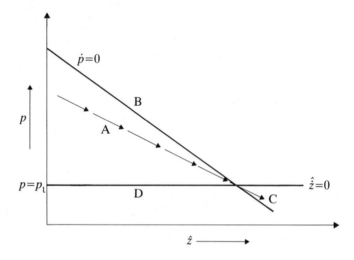

Figure 3.1

Thus, the loci of $\dot{p}=0=\hat{z}$ divide the phase plane in figure 3.1 into four distinct regions, A, B, C, and D. The equilibrium point where $\hat{z}=0$ and $\dot{p}=0$ intersect is obviously a saddle point. Now, any trajectory originating in regions B or D will always remain in that region. Also notice that if a trajectory originates in B, $\hat{z}$ and p will increase without bounds; if a trajectory originates in D, $\hat{z}$ and p will decrease without bounds. An inspection of the objective function R in equation (3.13) convinces us that no trajectory in regions B or D could represent an optimal path. We further observe that because $\hat{z}(p)$ and $p(\hat{z})$ are continuous and continuously differentiable in the $\hat{z}$–p plane, and because $\tilde{\pi}$ is a strictly concave function of p, there is only one optimal price trajectory in the region of interest A from $\hat{z}=0$ to the equilibrium point $p=p_\ell$ and $\hat{z}=0$.[1]

IMPLICATIONS

In this section we wish to explore the implications of the following for the optimal price path and the final share of the dominant firm: (1) price elasticity of demand; (2) uncertainty about the market entry of potential competitors; (3) risk aversion characteristics of the dominant firm, (4) variations in the capitalization rate; and (5) uncertainty about the demand function. Analysis of the effects of these factors is undertaken in the order presented above.

Price Elasticity

We shall first examine the effects of variations in the elasticity of demand for $p(0)$ and the final market share of the dominant firm. An evaluation of these effects for the entire price trajectory will be presented later, with an analysis of variations in the potential competitors' market rate of entry and uncertainty about it.

Rearranging equation (3.26), for $V_q = 0$, we obtain

$$p = \left[\frac{\partial \mu_q}{\partial p} \right]^{-1} \hat{z} + \left[\frac{\partial \mu_q}{\partial p} \right]^{-1} [-\mu_q + c \frac{\partial \mu_q}{\partial p} + \frac{\mu_k + \alpha V_k}{r}(p_\ell - c)]$$

(3.27)

At the initial time $t = t_0$, let $\hat{z} = 0$. Thus, equation (3.27) reduces to

$$p(0) = \left[\frac{\partial \mu_q}{\partial p} \right]^{-1} [-\mu_q + \frac{\mu_k + \alpha V_k}{r}(p_\ell - c)] + c$$

(3.28)

Differentiating (3.28) with respect to the elasticity of demand, $(\partial \mu_q / \partial p)$,

$$\frac{\partial p(0)}{\partial (\mu_q / \partial p)} = - \left[\frac{\partial \mu_q}{\partial p} \right]^{-2} [-\mu_q + \frac{\mu_k + \alpha V_k}{r}(p_\ell - c)] + c$$

(3.29)

From (3.28), since $p(0)$ must be greater than c, we observe that

$$[-\mu_q + \frac{\mu_k - \alpha V_k}{r}(p_\ell - c)] < 0$$

(3.30)

Therefore,

$$\frac{\partial p(0)}{\partial [\frac{\partial \mu_q}{\partial p}]} > 0$$

(3.31)

that is, with an increase in $(\partial \mu_q / \partial p)$, $p(0)$ increases. This implies that as the elasticity of demand decreases, that is as $(\partial \mu_q / \partial p)$ becomes less negative, the initial price charged by the monopolist optimally increases.

To examine the effect of variations in price elasticity on the final market share of the dominant firm, equation (3.27) may be solved for $\hat{z}$ to get

$$\hat{z} = \left[\frac{\partial \mu_q}{\partial p}(p - c) + \mu_q - \frac{\mu_k + \alpha V_k}{r}(p_\ell - c) \right]$$

(3.32)

As $t \to \infty$, $p \to p_\ell$. Therefore, from (3.32),

$$\hat{z}(\infty) = \left[\left(\frac{\partial \mu_q}{\partial p} \right) (p_\ell - c) + \mu_q - \frac{\mu_k + \alpha V_k}{r}(p_\ell - c) \right]$$

(3.33)

Differentiating (3.33) with respect to the price elasticity, $(\partial \mu_q / \partial p)$, we obtain (3.34)

$$\frac{\partial [\hat{z}(\infty)]}{\partial (\partial \mu_q / \partial p)} = (p_\ell - c) \tag{3.34}$$

and since $(p_\ell - c) > 0$, then

$$\frac{\partial [\hat{z}(\infty)]}{\partial (\partial \mu_q / \partial_p)} > 0 \tag{3.35}$$

Equation (3.35) implies that as $(\partial \mu_q / \partial_p)$ becomes less negative, that is as price elasticity increases, $\hat{z}$ decreases and, therefore, the final market share of the dominant firm increases. Also, (3.31) and (3.35) imply that the $\dot{p} = 0$ curve for the higher price elasticity lies below the original $\dot{p} = 0$ curve throughout the $\hat{z}-p$ plane, although the dislocation of the curve is not necessarily lateral. However, for fixed values of r, μ_q, and $(\mu_k - \alpha V_k)$, there can be determined a unique value of $(\partial \mu_q / \partial p)$ where the slopes in equations (3.31) and (3.35) become equal, and the new $\dot{p}$ curve runs parallel to the original curve. We now proceed to explore the implications of price elasticity together with those of variations in V_k and μ_k for the entire price trajectory.

Uncertainty About Entry

To examine the implications of uncertainty about the competitors' rate of entry into the market for the monopolist firm's optimal price trajectory, equation (3.28) may be differentiated with respect to V_k to obtain

$$\frac{\partial p(0)}{\partial V_k} = \frac{\alpha(p_\ell - c)}{r} \left(\frac{\partial \mu_q}{\partial p} \right)^{-1} \tag{3.36}$$

The R.H.S. of (3.36) is negative, since $p_\ell > c$, and $(\partial \mu_q / \partial p)$ is negative. This implies that the higher the uncertainty about competitors' entry into the market, the higher the initial price, $p(0)$, charged by the monopolist firm.

Also, differentiating (3.33) with respect to V_k we obtain

$$\frac{\partial [\hat{z}(\infty)]}{\partial V_k} = \frac{(p_\ell - c)\alpha}{r} \tag{3.37}$$

By definition, $p_\ell > c$, and therefore (3.37) is positive. This implies that the higher the V_k, the higher the competitors' final share of the market, and lower the dominant firm's final share of the market.

Furthermore, comparison of (3.36) and (3.37) reveals that $|\partial p(0)/\partial V_k|$ is larger or smaller than $|\partial [\hat{z}(\infty)]/\partial V_k|$ depending upon whether the price elasticity of demand $|\partial \mu / \partial p|$ is less than or greater than unity. For the unitary price elasticity of demand, (3.36) equals (3.37).

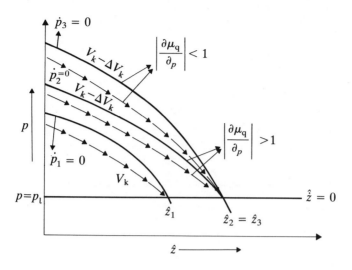

Figure 3.2

As mentioned earlier because $\hat{z}(p)$ and $p(\hat{z})$ are continuous and continuously differentiable in the $\hat{z}$–p plane, and π is a strictly concave function of p, there is only one optimal price trajectory in the region of interest, A, from $\hat{z}=0$ to the equilibrium point $\hat{z}=0=\dot{p}$.

The shape and position of optimal price trajectories, the $\dot{p}=0$ curves, $\hat{z}$ for various values of V_k, and price elasticity following the results established in equations (3.36) and (3.37) are shown in figure 3.2.

Examination of figure 3.2 and equations (3.36) and (3.37) brings out several points. (1) For a given decrease in V_k, the price trajectory moves above the original price trajectory; also, the new price trajectory becomes flatter should the demand be highly elastic, that is, $|\partial\mu_q/\partial p|$ is greater than unity. This implies that the price charged by the firm all along the time path is higher, but the final share of the market of the dominant firm is lower since $\hat{z}_2$ lies to the right of $\hat{z}_1$. (2) If the demand is relatively inelastic and $|\partial\mu_q/\partial p|$ is less than unity, the new price trajectory for lower V_k, though still above the original price trajectory, is now steeper. This implies that the monopolist firm charges still higher prices all along the time path. However, notice that the dominant firm's final share of the market is independent of the price elasticity and $\hat{z}_2=\hat{z}_3$ as shown in figure 3.2. (3) In the case where price elasticity equals unity, the optimal price trajectory is laterally displaced and all price trajectories run parallel to one another for different values of V_k on the $\hat{z}$–p plane. The lower the uncertainty about the competitors' entry, that is the lower the V_k, the farther to the right the optimal price trajectory shifts, and vice versa.

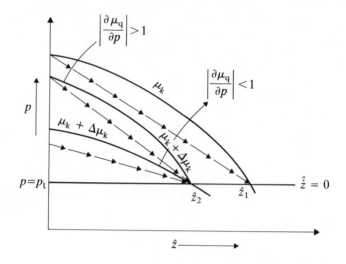

Figure 3.3

To see the effect of variations in the mean rate of competitors' market entry on the optimal price trajectory and the final market share of the dominant firm, differentiate (3.28) and (3.33) with respect to μ_k to get (3.38) and (3.39) respectively,

$$\frac{\partial p(0)}{\partial \mu_k} = \frac{p - c}{r} \left(\frac{\partial \mu_q}{\partial p} \right)^{-1} \tag{3.38}$$

$$\frac{\partial z(\infty)}{\partial \mu_k} = - \frac{(p_\ell - c)}{r} \tag{3.39}$$

Notice that since $p_\ell > c$ and $(\partial \mu_q / \partial p)$ is negative, equations (3.38) and (3.39) are both negative. However, it may further be noted that while (3.38) is dependent upon the price elasticity, (3.39) is not. The $\dot{p} = 0$ curves, the optimal price trajectories, and the final market shares, $\hat{z}$, for various values of price elasticity and μ_k are shown in figure 3.3.

It is obvious from equations (3.38), (3.39), and figure 3.3 that for higher values of μ_k the optimal price trajectory lies below the original price trajectory and the dominant firm's final share of the market is larger, since $\hat{z}_2$ is less than $\hat{z}_1$. Furthermore, though $\hat{z}$ is not affected by the price elasticity of demand, following equations (3.38) and (3.39), the optimal price trajectory is flatter for $|\partial \mu_q / \partial p| < 1$ and steeper for $|\partial \mu_q / \partial p| > 1$. Also, the initial price $p(0)$ charged by the monopolist firm is higher for $|\partial \mu_q / \partial p| < 1$ than for $|\partial \mu_q / \partial p| > 1$.

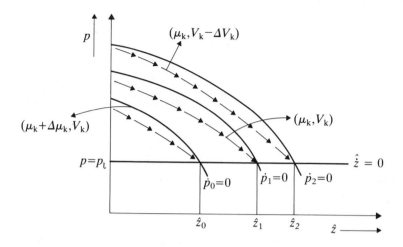

Figure 3.4 Effect of changes in μ_k and V_k on the optimal price trajectories

Figure 3.4 presents the analysis of variations in μ_k, V_k and their effect on the optimal price policy of the dominant firm and its final market share for a simple case where the price elasticity is unitary.

It is evident from figure 3.4 that a lower value of V_k results in the optimal price path that lies above the original price path and a higher value of μ_k results in a price path that lies below it. That is, for a given market share, the firm charges a higher price with a decrease in V_k and a lower price with an increase in μ_k. It may further be noticed that the final optimal price at the equilibrium point is p_ℓ and is the same for all values of μ_k and V_k. But, the firm's share of the market at the equilibrium point goes up with, *ceteris paribus*, an increase in V_k or a decline in μ_k.

The α and r Effects

At this point a word about the effect of the firm's risk aversion characteristics denoted by α on its optimal price policy would be appropriate. From equation (3.28) it is apparent that an increase in α results in a lower $p(0)$. That is, *ceteris paribus*, a more risk averse firm would initially charge a lower price. Also, from equation (3.33) it can be seen that the higher the value of α, the lower the value of $z(\infty)$. That is, with an increase in risk aversion, the final market share increases. Thus, it may be stated that for a given market share, the more risk averse a firm is, the lower the price it would charge. Also, the more risk averse a firm is, the larger its final share of the market will be. This is also evident upon examination of equations (3.36) and (3.37), which indicate a further downward shift in the optimal price trajectory with higher values of the risk aversion coefficient.

Variations in Capitalization Rate

To examine the effects of variations in the capitalization rate on the optimal price trajectory, differentiate (3.28) and (3.33) with respect to r to obtain equations (3.40) and (3.41) respectively:

$$\frac{\partial p(0)}{\partial r} = \left(\frac{\partial \mu_q}{\partial p}\right)^{-1} [-(\mu_k - \alpha V_k)(p_\ell - c)\frac{1}{r^2}] \qquad (3.40)$$

$$\frac{\partial \hat{z}(\infty)}{\partial r} = (\mu_k - \alpha V_k)(p_\ell - c)\frac{1}{r^2} \qquad (3.41)$$

Notice that $(\mu_k - \alpha V_k) > 0$ and $p_\ell > c$, and, therefore, equations (3.40) and (3.41) are both positive. Following the arguments advanced previously about the uniqueness of the price trajectory, it is evident from (3.40) and (3.41) that with an increase in the capitalization rate the entire price trajectory shifts upward. This implies that, *ceteris paribus*, the firm charges a higher price and finally settles for a lower share of the market since $\hat{z}$ is larger. The conclusion is intuitively reasonable since with an increase in capitalization rate, the firm values immediate profits more than future profits.

However, it may be that a change in r would not cause lateral dislocation in the optimal price trajectory if the price elasticity of demand is non-unitary. It can be seen from equations (3.40) and (3.41) that the new price trajectory would have a steeper or flatter slope depending upon whether $|\partial \mu_q / \partial p|$ is less than or greater than unity respectively.

Demand Uncertainty

To examine the effect of uncertainty on the optimal price policy of the monopolist confronting potential entry, consider the line $\dot{p} = 0$ on the $\hat{z}-p$ plane as given by equation (3.26). We reproduce equation (3.26) for convenience:

$$p = \left(\frac{\partial \mu_q}{\partial p} - 2\alpha V_q\right)^{-1}\hat{z} + \left(\frac{\partial \mu_q}{\partial p} - 2\alpha V_q\right)^{-1}$$

$$[-\mu_q + c\frac{\partial \mu_q}{\partial p} - 2c\alpha V_q + \frac{(\mu_k - \alpha V_k)(p_\ell - c)}{r}] \qquad (3.26)$$

At the initial time $t = t_0$, let $\hat{z} = 0$. Therefore, equation (3.26) reduces to

$$p(0) = \frac{-\mu_q + \frac{\mu_k - \alpha V_k}{r}(p_\ell - c)}{\frac{\partial \mu_q}{\partial p} - 2\alpha V_q} + c \tag{3.42}$$

Differentiating (3.42) with respect to V_q we obtain

$$\frac{\partial p(0)}{\partial V_q} = \frac{2\alpha[-\mu_q + \frac{(\mu_k - \alpha V_k)}{r}(p_\ell - c)]}{\left(\frac{\partial \mu_q}{\partial p} - 2\alpha V_q\right)^2} \tag{3.43}$$

From equation (3.30) we know that

$$-\mu_q + \frac{\mu_k - \alpha V_k}{r}(p_\ell - c) < 0$$

This implies that,

$$\frac{\partial p(0)}{\partial V_q} < 0 \tag{3.44}$$

Thus, $p(0)$ increases with decreases in V_q. That is, the firm initially sets the price at a higher level as the uncertainty about the demand function declines.

At the equilibrium point, $p = p_\ell$; also let $\hat{z}_e = z(\infty)$. From equation (3.26), on rearranging, we get

$$z(\infty) = \frac{\partial \mu_q}{\partial p}\bigg|_{p=p_\ell}(p_\ell - c) - 2\alpha V_q(p_\ell - c) - \mu_q|_{p=p_\ell}$$

$$+ \left(\frac{\mu_k - \alpha V_k}{r}\right)(p_\ell - c) \tag{3.45}$$

Differentiating (3.45) with respect to V_q, we get

$$\frac{\partial z(\infty)}{\partial V_q} = -2\alpha(p_\ell - c) \tag{3.46}$$

Since $(p_\ell - c)$ is positive, therefore, $(\partial z(\infty)/\partial V_q)$ is negative. This implies that $z(\infty) = z_e$ decreases with an increase in V_q.

Thus, examination of the effect of variations in V_q on the $\dot{p} = 0$ curve shows that with an increase in uncertainty about demand function both $p(0)$ and $z(\infty)$ decrease. The expressions for $(\partial z(\infty)/\partial V_q)$ and $(\partial p(0)/\partial V_q)$ are not directly comparable, but for fixed values of r, μ_q,

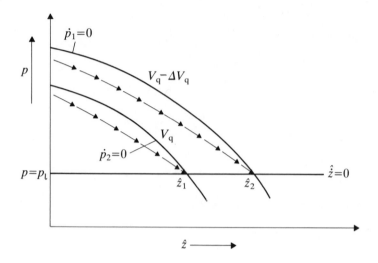

Figure 3.5

α, $\mu_k - \alpha V_k$, and $\partial \mu_q / \partial p$, there exists a unique value of V_q where the slopes given in equations (3.43) and (3.46) are equal, and the optimal trajectory runs parallel to the original trajectory. However, examination of $(\partial p(0)/\partial V_q)$ in (3.43) further reveals that as V_q decreases, $p(0)$ increases but at a diminishing rate. Thus, $z(\infty)$ and $p(0)$ are both higher for $(V_q - \Delta V_q)$ than for V_q, but as further declines in V_q take place, the $\dot{p} = 0$ curve and also the optimal price trajectory become flatter as shown in figure 3.5.

The shifts in the optimal price trajectory for the monopolist confronting potential entry with variations in the uncertainty about the demand functions are shown in figure 3.5. Notice that the optimal price trajectory for $V_q - \Delta V_q$ lies above the one for V_q. Note also that $\hat{z}_2$ is to the right of $\hat{z}_1$. This implies that with a decline in V_q, the monopolist charges a higher price but his final market share at the equilibrium point is lower.

CONCLUSION

We have considered the problem of optimal pricing for a long-run profit maximizing monopolist firm confronting market entry by potential competitors. The rate of rivals' entry into the market, as a function of the existing firm's pricing policy, is recognized as a stochastic process. It was recognized that the quantity of product demanded, as a function of the monopolist firm's pricing policy, is a stochastic process. We explored the impact of these stochastic processes and variations in the price elasticity of demand on the optimal trajectory and the final share of the market of the dominant firm. The implications of variations in the risk aversion characteristics of the firm and its capitalization rate for the managerial decision making were explored as well.

In detail it has been shown that the optimal price trajectory shifts downward and the firm charges a lower price all along the time path with an increase in uncertainty about the competitors' rate of entry into the market. As the mean rate of entry declines, the optimal price trajectory shifts outward and to the right. The shift in the price trajectory is lateral in the case where the elasticity of demand is unitary. In the case where the demand is highly elastic, the price trajectory becomes flatter, and in the case where demand is relatively inelastic, the price trajectory becomes steeper. However, the elasticity of demand does not influence variations in the final market share of the dominant firm arising from changes in the mean rate of entry or uncertainty about it. Also the final equilibrium price remains at the same level regardless of variations in price elasticity, mean rate of entry, and uncertainty about entry. The effect of an increase in the risk aversion of the firm is that the firm charges a lower price all along the time path but its final market share increases. The effect of an increase in the firm's capitalization rate is that the optimal price trajectory shifts upward and the final market share of the firm decreases. However, the shape of the altered price trajectory depends upon the price elasticity of demand. The effect of *ceteris paribus* variations in the price elasticity itself is to shift the price trajectory outward, if the price elasticity decreases, and downward, if it increases, though the displacement is not necessarily lateral. Finally, the final market share of the dominant firm is shown to be larger if the price elasticity is lower, and vice versa.

NOTES

1 There will be another unique trajectory in region C for $z(0) > z(\infty)$. In this case, however, $p > 0$ and $\hat{z} < 0$ and the trajectory starting from $z(0)$ goes to $z(\infty)$ from the right to the left in region C. This would imply exit from the industry rather than entry and will not be explored here.

BIBLIOGRAPHY

Aoki, M. 1967: *Optimization of Stochastic Systems*. New York: Academy Press.

Gaskins, D. W. 1971: Dynamic limit pricing: optimal pricing under threat of entry. *Journal of Economic Theory*, September.

Kamien, M. I. and Schwartz, N. L. 1971: Limit pricing and uncertain entry. *Econometrica*, May.

Leland, H. E. 1972: Theory of the firm facing uncertain demand. *American Economic Review*, June.

Philips, L. 1971: *Effects of Industrial Concentration: A Cross-section Analysis for the Common Market*. Amsterdam: North-Holland.

Stigler, G. and Kindahl, J. K. 1971: Industrial prices, as administered by Dr. Means. *American Economic Review*, September.

Weston, J. F., Lustgarten, S. and Grottke, N. 1974: The administered price thesis denied: note. *American Economic Review*, March.

4
An Analysis of Advertising, Concentration, Profit Studies

STANLEY I. ORNSTEIN

PREFACE

The industry structure–performance model dominated analysis in the field of industrial organization in the 1950s and 1960s and provided the intellectual basis for much of antitrust policy during that era, particularly with respect to mergers. Fred Weston believed the structural model lacked a sound theoretical base and that its empirical results served the nation poorly by misdirecting antitrust enforcement and blocking the efficient utilization of resources by firms. In Fred's view, competition is a dynamic, multidimensional process which is best understood by examining the fundamental determinants of supply and demand in an industry. The single-equation, concentration–profit models of the time, with their view that competition can be measured by concentration ratios and proxies for barriers to entry, failed completely in capturing the essence of competition and gave repeated false signals of a lack of competition in high concentration industries. Fred started the Research Program in Competition and Business Policy in 1968 to address these weaknesses and to advance knowledge generally in industrial organization and antitrust.

Fred held that at a minimum a multi-equation model capturing the feedforward and feedback effects between demand, supply, industry structure, and industry performance measures needed to be tested. Such a model, he hypothesized, would show that profits were a function of firm efficiencies and not, as held at the time, of collusion and artificial barriers to entry. Working with Michael Intriligator, Ronald Shrieves, and myself,

This study was supported by the Research Program in Competition and Business Policy, U.C.L.A. I am indebted to Larry Kimbell, Dominique Hanssens, and Gregory Carpenter for discussions on the estimation of simultaneous equation systems. Computer assistance was provided by Allen Krug and Ken Heyer.

Fred developed a multi-equation, block recursive model which was grandly called an econometric model of industrial organization. The framework of the model was first sketched out in our jointly edited book, The Impact of Large Firms on the U.S. Economy. *Testing of the model supported our view that industry profit rates were explained by the fundamental determinants of supply and demand and by competitive superiority in an industry. Although not subsequently published, Fred's model provided the foundation for the simultaneous equation models of structure and performance that followed. Unfortunately, these models simply extended the original structural orthodoxy without considering more fundamental economic determinants of structure and performance.*

The present chapter is in the spirit of Fred's original work and had its intellectual origins in that early period. It shows that simultaneous equation estimations of structure–performance models have often erred both theoretically and econometrically and that such models have likely not advanced understanding of industrial competition. The results support Fred's long held view that the traditional industrial organization approach was incorrect.

Fred's earlier minority views have been adopted by a wider audience and are now the majority position. The structural model of industrial organization has lost its dominance in the field. Antitrust policy has undergone a major transformation due to the research of Fred and many other scholars and is now oriented toward supporting economic efficiency and consumer welfare, instead of protecting competitors and preventing firms from consummating efficient distribution relationships.

I have been fortunate to have had the opportunity to work with Fred for many years in his research program and to have participated in this transformation of industrial organization. Fred has provided me with an ideal environment to do research and to grow as an economist. My initial post-graduate training was under his tutelage. He has provided ongoing encouragement for my work and generous intellectual and emotional support. Our applied work on antitrust cases has been exciting and has provided me with an invaluable learning experience by being able to study firms and industries from the inside. Without Fred's assistance I would not have had this opportunity. My debt to him is deep in many ways, as is my gratitude.

Fred Weston is a scholars' scholar, one of the premier figures in his fields. I am honored to be able to contribute to this volume.

INTRODUCTION

Empirical tests of structure–performance models in industrial organization have progressed through distinct stages of statistical methodology. The first tests were across simple group means, such as whether the mean profit rate in high concentration industries was significantly different from the mean profit rate in low concentration industries (Bain, 1951; Brozen, 1970; Mann, 1966). The next step was multiple regression analysis in order to hold constant all relevant variables related to the performance variable under examination (Weiss, 1974). In recent years, in order to capture the hypothesized interactions between performance and structure variables, such as profitability, concentration, and advertising intensity, simultaneous equation models have been tested (Caves *et al.*, 1980; Martin, 1979; Pagoulatos and Sorensen, 1981; Strickland and Weiss, 1976). The rationale for going to simultaneous equation models was: on first approximation certain structure–performance relationships appear to be simultaneous, so in theory single equation models would suffer from simultaneous equation bias, and, second, single equation models often produced weak (low R^2) and inconsistent results across studies, which some claimed was due to simultaneous equation bias. In point of fact, many simultaneous equation studies have found that their results simply confirm single equation results, with such findings as positive relationships between profit and concentration, profit and advertising intensity, concentration and advertising intensity, and a negative relationship between profit and import to sales ratios.

The primary purpose of this chapter is to call into question the increasing use of simultaneous equation models and estimation by two-stage and three-stage least squares in industrial organization, with specific application to models of advertising, concentration, and profitability. The paper argues that simultaneous equation bias is unlikely to be a problem in many hypothesized structure–performance relationships, and that common estimation techniques, such as 2SLS or 3SLS, often introduce far more econometric problems than they theoretically resolve. A second area investigated is the logical consistency of, and direct empirical support for, the commonly tested relationships between advertising, concentration, and profitability.

The chapter first presents and criticizes a stereotypical advertising, concentration, and profit model, pointing out problems in such eclectic models (i.e. lumping together separately developed theories) due to inconsistent theories and weak empirical support for individual linkages in the model. The next section discusses the potential misuse of simultaneous equation estimation in this area and the econometric problems introduced by 2SLS. The final section presents and tests a representative simultaneous equation model, providing evidence of serious problems in the use of 2SLS and 3SLS.

SOME PROBLEMS IN ECLECTIC MODEL BUILDING

Figure 4.1 depicts a schematic diagram of the commonly hypothesized interrelationships between advertising, concentration, and profitability.

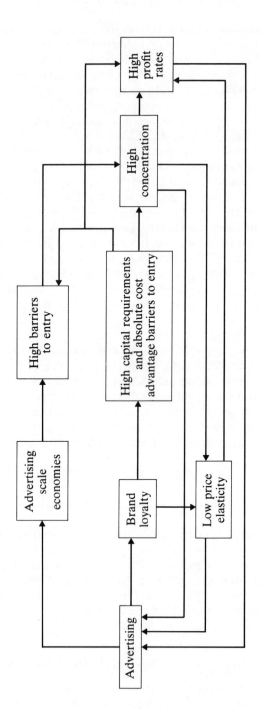

Figure 4.1

The detailed theory underlying individual relationships is discussed elsewhere and need not be repeated (Martin, 1979; Pagoulatos and Sorensen, 1981; Strickland and Weiss, 1976). In broad terms the conventional argument goes as follows. Large-scale advertising of individual brands leads to strong consumer brand loyalty. This results in lower price elasticity, leading to higher price–cost margins and still higher advertising expenditures. Firms attracted by high margins are blocked from entry owing to a variety of advertising created barriers to entry, including large advertising economies of scale, high capital requirements needed to overcome existing brand loyalty, and cost advantages of existing firms in establishing brand loyalty via advertising. These alleged barriers to entry, in turn, are said to increase concentration, leading to collusion and still higher price–cost margins. Finally, there are feedback effects; high concentration and high profit rates leading to higher levels of advertising intensity.

This type of eclectic model building attempts to bring a logical order to a disparate set of hypotheses. As a consequence, it is vulnerable to inconsistencies and ambiguities in hypothesized relationships. As an example, take the various hypotheses offered for expecting a relationship between concentration and advertising intensity. Four principal arguments are made: two that concentration increases advertising, one that advertising increases concentration, and one that concentration reduces advertising. First, advertising intensity is claimed to increase with concentration due to the greater ability of top firms in highly concentrated industries to internalize advertising induced increases in industry demand. Second, it can be shown using a dominant firm model that, under certain assumptions, concentration is inversely related to firm demand elasticity (Geroski, 1982; Saving, 1970), and, by Dorfman and Steiner's (1954) result, that advertising intensity for a monopolist is inversely related to firm price elasticity. It follows that the higher concentration, the higher advertising intensity. The third hypothesis reverses the direction of causality, arguing that advertising leads to higher concentration by virtue of advertising economies of scale. Finally, it is argued that at some critical level of concentration the gains to collusion on advertising lead to lower advertising. The collusion hypothesis implies a quadratic relationship; mutual increases in advertising and concentration initially and then a decline in advertising as concentration rises beyond the level where advertising collusion becomes feasible.

The first three hypotheses are clearly inconsistent with the last, and the net relationship – positive, zero, or negative – is unpredictable a priori. More specifically, the Dorfman–Steiner result for a profit maximizing monopolist predicts a relationship directly opposite to the advertising collusion hypothesis, so a cartel colluding on advertising would not be maximizing profits, according to the Dorfman–Steiner conditions; an unlikely situation. Similarly, to the extent that there are advertising barriers to entry, a cartel is unlikely to lower such barriers to forego advertising economies of scale. In short, why the advertising externality argument, the Dorfman–Steiner result, and advertising economies of scale should no longer apply or will be swamped by collusion on advertising beyond some critical concentration level has yet to be given a theoretical foundation. These types of contradictions are more likely in eclectic models, leading to ambiguous predictions on the signs of affected variables.

A second problem in eclectic model building is an incompatibility between empirical tests of individual linkages and macro-tests of the overall structure. To illustrate, a number of tests of individual elements of the model in figure 4.1 have been made. These include tests of advertising's relationship to brand loyalty and price elasticity, and tests for the existence of advertising economies of scale. These relationships comprise the core of the model. The evidence, on balance, does not support the purported effects of advertising. Marketers have been studying the causal determinants of brand loyalty for over 30 years and, to date, there is no strong evidence that advertising increases brand loyalty.[1] The little evidence that exists on advertising's relationship to price elasticity is somewhat mixed, but in general it indicates that advertising leads to increases in price elasticity, contrary to the conventional hypothesis.[2] The evidence on advertising economies of scale is somewhat controversial, but the overwhelming majority of studies find decreasing returns to advertising.[3]

This is not an imposing empirical foundation for testing the overall relationship between advertising, concentration, and price–cost margins. It is difficult to measure the basic causal factors: brand loyalty, price elasticities, and advertising economies of scale. But since advertising–sales ratios, concentration ratios, and price–cost margins are readily available, most studies have focused on these three variables. It is then argued that if positive relationships exist, they must be due to brand loyalty, advertising economies of scale, and barriers to entry. But the empirical basis for such inferences has not been demonstrated.

Of primary interest for this paper is that models, such as in figure 4.1, have been used to argue that single-equation models suffer from simultaneous equation bias. Attempts to correct for simultaneous equation bias, however, may be inappropriate in testing cross-section industrial organization models, as discussed below.

PROBLEMS IN THE USE AND ESTIMATION OF
SIMULTANEOUS EQUATION MODELS

Although in theory a limited or full information estimation procedure, such as 2SLS or 3SLS, appears required for the interactions outlined in figure 4.1, on closer examination this may not be so. First, lags in the system may allow OLS to suffice, and, second, the trade-off between consistency and efficiency inherent in OLS versus 2SLS may support using OLS even if estimators are inconsistent. The estimation of simultaneous equation models by a technique like 2SLS is most appropriate where the economic interactions between endogenous variables are truly contemporaneous in time. An example of the kind of simultaneity required is illustrated by demand and supply curves in financial markets, where, for example, interest rate changes are transmitted rapidly. In such a case simultaneous equation bias is clearly present and, in principle, needs to be purged from the system in order to obtain consistent estimators. But, in the absence of simultaneous interaction, the seriousness of simultaneous equation bias is called into question. If, for example, the endogenous variables are related by a lag structure, to the extent that the largest weights are given to the lagged terms, either initial or subsequent lags, then the extent of simultaneous equation bias is reduced. If there is no contemporaneous relationship, but only a lagged relationship, then simultaneous equation bias in theory is zero, since the lagged terms are assumed to be predetermined variables unrelated to the error term. In this case the model is in theory recursive.

The now common application of 2SLS or 3SLS estimation to simultaneous equation models of structure and performance do not address the issue of lags, and thus are generally misspecified. For the model in figure 4.1, advertising, concentration, and price–cost margins are assumed to interact simultaneously, with no lagged adjustments. But it is implausible to assume, for example, in the case of advertising and concentration that a change in one of these variables has a contemporaneous effect on the other. The underlying theory does not predict contemporaneous effects, but rather implies lags in adjustment: lower advertising costs due to economies of scale do not lead instantaneously to higher concentration and higher concentration does not lead immediately to collusion on advertising. And the nature of this lag structure is currently unknown. Studies of changes in advertising–sales ratios and concentration ratios using IRS data show no significant relationship between these variables (Telser, 1964). Studies relating an advertising intensity level to changes in concentration show mixed results depending on the time period tested; that is, some find a positive relationship and some find no relationship (Asch, 1979; Mueller and Rogers, 1980; Ornstein and Lustgarten, 1978; Scherer, 1979). Studies of a contemporaneous relationship between concentration and advertising–sales ratios show mixed results; about half find a positive relationship and about half find no relationship (Ornstein, 1977). In summary, if concentration and advertising intensity are related, it is unknown whether the relationship is contemporaneous or lagged and thus whether there is a serious simultaneous equation bias problem to be addressed or not.[4]

Of course, in the absence of time-series data, lags cannot be modeled. However, the fact that cross-section data is all that is available in this area does not justify treating the system as though the interactions are contemporaneous. To assume, as most studies limited to cross-section data do, that the data reflect long-run equilibrium in each industry, so dynamic adjustments can be ignored, is a convenient but absurd fiction since continual changes and disequilibria characterize most industries. Contrary to what most cross-section studies assume, disequilibrium is the rule, not the exception. This disequilibrium is evident in cross-section results on concentration, advertising, and profits which are unstable over time, and when measured as first differences give results that are inconsistent with cross-section results (Ornstein, 1984).

Another serious question, assuming the system is truly simultaneous, is whether a consistent estimation technique should be adopted. As Durbin (1954) pointed out long ago: "Since the use of an instrumental variable involves a certain loss of efficiency one should feel rather cautious about using it until the extent of the bias in the ordinary least-squares estimations has been investigated" (pp. 28–9). A variety of tests have been developed to see if simultaneous equation bias is serious enough to warrant the loss in efficiency inherent in 2SLS (Nakamura and Nakamura, 1981). Previous advertising, concentration, profit studies make no mention of having performed such tests.

The main econometric problem areas in 2SLS are: the fit in the first-stage regressions, and the extent of multicollinearity built into the second-stage regressions. The first-stage regressions, designed to eliminate the correlation between the error terms and right-hand side endogenous variables, can easily fail. The reason is that the reduced form equations are not necessarily specified well enough to obtain good instrumental variables. If the first stage explains little of the variation in an endogenous variable (with, for example, an R^2 of approximately 0.1 to 0.2), much useful information is being thrown away. The endogenous variable is replaced by essentially random noise, severely weakening the second-stage results, since the estimated endogenous variable's parameter in the second stage becomes meaningless. Conversely, if the first-stage R^2 is very high (say 0.8 or 0.9), then correlation with the error term has probably not been removed, so 2SLS will not produce consistent estimators (Intriligator, 1978, p. 392).

A second major econometric problem with 2SLS is its built-in tendency to exacerbate multicollinearity in the second-stage regression.[5] If an endogenous variable is fully explained by predetermined variables, that is, a high R^2, then the use of the estimated endogenous variable with its own regressors in the same second-stage regression will be strongly affected by multicollinearity. In such a case it is questionable whether the costs of increased multicollinearity are less than the benefits of gaining consistent estimators through 2SLS estimation, since the latter gain is extremely unlikely with high first-stage R^2.

TESTING FOR SIMULTANEOUS EQUATION PROBLEMS

The prototypical model tested in this area is that of Strickland and Weiss (1976). Because their model is the basis for most subsequent studies, a version of it was used to test for the econometric problems outlined above. Their model is:

$$Ad/S = a_0 + a_1 PCM + a_2 CD/S + a_3 CR + a_4 C^2 + a_5 GR + a_6 DUR + e_1$$
$$(4.1)$$

$$CR = b_0 + b_1 Ad/S + b_2 MES/S + e_2 \tag{4.2}$$

$$PCM = c_0 + c_1 K/S + c_2 GR + c_3 CR + c_4 GD + c_5 Ad/S + c_6 MES/S + e_3$$
$$(4.3)$$

where Ad/S is the advertising–sales ratio, PCM is the price–cost margin, CD/S is the ratio of consumption output to total output, CR is four-firm seller concentration, GR is the rate of growth in sales, DUR is a dummy variable for durable and nondurable goods, MES/S is the ratio of minimum efficient plant size to total sales, K/S is the capital–sales ratio, and GD is a dummy variable for geographic sales dispersion.

The merits of this and similar models can be questioned on numerous grounds: for example, their *ad hoc* nature (Geroski, 1982); the use of the PCM which has no relationship to economic rates of return (Liebowitz, 1982; Ornstein, 1975); or specification problems, such as the spurious relationship between CR and MES/S (Davies, 1983). My purpose, however, is not to justify and test another simultaneous equation structure-performance model, but to comment on the econometric problems inherent in such testing. For this purpose, and for comparison with prior results, the model is accepted on its own grounds.

THE SAMPLE AND VARIABLES USED

The sample tested was based on U.S. Census of Manufacturers' four-digit data for 1972. The sample included only four-digit industries for which there was a one-to-one correspondence between the Census and the input–output tables, the latter being the data source for Ad/S and CD/S.[6] This resulted in a sample of 229 industries.[7]

Concentration, minimum efficient plant size, and capital–output ratios are measured as in Strickland and Weiss. Price–cost margins are measured exclusive of advertising expenditures. The durability dummy variable and classification of industries into consumer and producer goods is based on the classifications in Ornstein (1977). Market growth for 1972 is measured as the percentage change in value of shipments from 1967 to 1972. Geographic dispersion is a dummy variable distinguishing between local (one) and national (zero) markets as classified by the Census (1967).

Three modifications to the Strickland and Weiss model were made. To correct for failure of the rank identification condition in equation (4.3), as pointed out by Martin (1979), a lagged PCM variable, the PCM in 1967, was added to equation (4.2), following Martin's approach. For purposes of a more complete specification, an import to sales ratio was added to equation (4.3), following the findings in recent studies by Marvel (1980) and Pagoulatos and Sorensen (1981). A final departure from the Strickland and Weiss model was the deletion of CR^2. This is justified on a number of grounds. First, whether there is strong empirical evidence of a quadratic relationship is subject to much dispute (Ornstein, 1977). Second, as noted above, there are strong contradictions between the collusion theory of advertising, purportedly tested by a quadratic function, and the other theories for a positive concentration–advertising relationship. Third, the correlation between CR and CR^2 for the samples tested was $+0.97$. The use of two highly collinear variables in the same regression equation leads to a negative correlation between the parameters, biasing the results in favor of the hypothesized quadratic relationship.[8] For each of these reasons the use of CR^2 is questionable, and it was deleted from the model tested.

EMPIRICAL RESULTS

Regressions were run separately for consumer and producer goods subsamples since F-tests for pooling rejected the null hypothesis of sample homogeneity. This resulted in samples of 72 consumer goods industries and 157 producer goods industries.

Starting with consumer goods, the first question is whether simultaneous equation bias is large enough to warrant consistent estimation and its attendant loss in efficiency. The Hausman (1978) regression test was used to answer this question. It consists of including as regressors the exogenous variables, the endogenous variable which may be correlated with the error term, and its instrumental variable, and testing whether the instrument is significantly different from zero. If there is correlation with the error term then the endogenous variable will reflect that correlation while its instrument will register the pure effects of the variable. If the variable is uncorrelated with the error term the instrument adds no new information and will be insignificant.

Using this test for consumer goods industries, in what amounts to reduced-form regressions, the instruments for Ad/S, CR, and PCM were, in each case, not significantly different from zero. The hypothesis of zero correlation between Ad/S, CR, and PCM and the respective error terms in equations (4.1)–(4.3) cannot be rejected, and, as a consequence, OLS is the correct estimation procedure.

Despite this result, regressions of 2SLS and 3SLS for consumer goods industries were also estimated in order to illustrate the consequences when such estimation procedures are misused. The first potential problem to address is the quality of the first-stage results. The values of R^2 for $\widehat{Ad/S}$, $\widehat{CR}$, and $\widehat{PCM}$ are 0.29, 0.60, and 0.89, respectively. Clearly, much of the information in Ad/S is being lost, resulting in possibly meaningless two- and three-stage results for Ad/S in equations (4.2) and (4.3). In contrast, the R^2 for $\widehat{PCM}$ is high, due largely to the presence of PCM67. If it were not for the Hausman test results, this would suggest that any bias due to PCM in equation (4.1) remains in the system. Only in the case of CR is R^2 in the acceptable range.

The OLS, 2SLS, and 3SLS results for consumer goods are presented in table 4.1. Results for equation (4.1) tend to be similar across estimation methods: PCM and GR are positive in each case with similar coefficients across regressions, while the durability variable is negative (advertising–sales is higher for nondurable consumer goods industries) and similar in results across regressions. The results for CR and CD/S, however, present problems. The coefficient and standard error for CR change sharply from OLS to 2SLS. Since the Hausman test shows no evidence of bias, this change for CR is probably not due to improved consistency. What accounts for this change is thus unclear. Concentration's lower standard error in 3SLS is expected if correlation across residuals exists, but the coefficients, in theory, should be identical between 2SLS and 3SLS, and they are not. These anomalies may reflect multicollinearity, which is discussed below. The lack of significance in CD/S, which is excluded in equations (4.2) and (4.3), indicates that equation (4.1) is not truly identified. However, since there is no apparent simultaneous equation bias this presents no problem here, but lack of attention to identifying variables may be a problem in other studies.

A similar unaccounted for result occurs in equation (4.2) where PCM67 inexplicably becomes significant in 3SLS. The main explanatory variable in this equation is MES/S which is expected because of its spurious relationship to CR (Davies, 1983).

The most glaring problems arise in estimation of equation (4.3) where no variable is significant in 2SLS and only CR becomes significant in 3SLS. Serious multicollinearity is immediately apparent. The coefficient of certain variables – MES/S, GD, and the intercept – blow up in 2SLS, a sign of severe multicollinearity. The lack of significance of any variable is also consistent with high multicollinearity. The extent of multicollinearity was investigated by regressing $\widehat{Ad/S}$ and $\widehat{CR}$ individually on the exogenous variables in equation (4.3). As a standard for comparison, that is, to indicate the extent to which 2SLS may worsen multicollinearity, this was also done in the OLS regression of equation (4.3) using Ad/S and CR. The relevant comparisons for Ad/S are an R^2 in OLS of 0.09 and in 2SLS of 0.76, while for CR the respective values of R^2 are 0.60 and 0.99.

Table 4.1 OLS, 2SLS, and 3SLS regression results for consumer goods industries, 1972

Estimation	Eq.	Intercept	CR	PCM	CD/S	GR	DUR	Ad/S	MES/S	PCM67	K/S	GD	IMP/S	R^2
OLS	4.1	-2.8211^c (−1.30)	0.0187 (0.99)	0.1617^a (3.24)	0.0185 (0.76)	0.0193^c (1.57)	-2.9914^a (−3.67)							0.31
2SLS	4.1	-3.0303^c (−1.33)	0.0351^c (1.35)	0.1282^b (2.26)	0.0229 (0.92)	0.0202^c (1.62)	-2.9352^a (−3.5681)							
3SLS	4.1	-2.4106 (−1.10)	0.0422^c (1.63)	0.1166^b (2.10)	0.0160 (0.70)	0.0162^c (1.38)	-2.8426^a (−3.52)							
OLS	4.2	24.4100^a (4.42)						0.4454 (0.86)	3.5379^a (7.95)	0.3009 (1.28)				0.56
2SLS	4.2	24.7486^a (4.37)						1.3213 (1.08)	3.4881^a (7.61)	0.1757 (0.61)				
3SLS	4.2	21.2351^a (5.10)						1.0200 (1.00)	3.3278^a (7.39)	0.3811^a (2.82)				
OLS	4.3	16.6557^a (4.6429)	0.0718 (1.12)			−0.0117 (−0.40)		0.6256^a (2.46)	0.2097 (0.60)		0.2105^b (2.07)	−2.0639 (−0.52)	0.0323 (−0.82)	0.31
2SLS	4.3	-75.2743 (−0.58)	2.8650 (0.71)			0.0941 (0.40)		−0.9247 (−0.18)	−10.1980 (−0.69)		−0.0487 (−0.08)	39.7609 (0.64)	0.3338 (0.63)	
3SLS	4.3	-42.5694^c (−0.73)	2.3227^c (1.30)			−0.0005 (−0.01)		−2.4694 (−0.75)	−7.7310 (−1.17)		−0.0139 (−0.06)	−9.3277 (−0.35)	−0.0089 (−0.04)	

[a] Significant at the 0.01 level
[b] Significant at the 0.05 level
[c] Significant at the 0.10 level

The problem is most acute for $\widehat{CR}$ since the variables that generate $\widehat{CR}$ – MES/S, K/S, etc. – are also in equation (4.3). Clearly, 2SLS can build substantial multicollinearity into a system of equations, severely weakening the results.[9]

The 3SLS results for equation (4.3) present further problems. The need for 3SLS can be determined by examining the matrix of correlations of residuals across equations. For consumer goods, the correlations are significant at the 0.01 level between equations (4.1) and (4.2) and (4.2) and (4.3). The latter two equations show an extremely high correlation across residuals of -0.93. This presents an interesting dilemma: the Hausman test results imply no loss in consistency using OLS, but the correlation across errors in 2SLS indicates gains in efficiency due to 3SLS. As a practical matter the Hausman test takes priority.[10]

Further problems are evident in 3SLS in equation (4.3). Some coefficients change drastically between 2SLS and 3SLS, for example, GR, Ad/S, MES/S, and GD, contrary to expectation between consistent estimators. Finally, the identifying variables in equation (4.3), IMP/S, GD, and K/S, are insignificant in 2SLS and 3SLS, indicating the system is not truly identified.

This detailed discussion provides the major points for an understanding of the econometric problems inherent in estimation by 2SLS and 3SLS. The problems, of course, are well known to econometricians, but industrial organization economists have shown little interest in these issues. They have presented results as if they were well grounded in econometric theory and testing. Results on 2SLS and 3SLS are presented with no strong justification or discussion of their empirical problems. The purpose of the analysis above is to outline, hopefully, a more careful set of procedures for future studies in this area.

Given the detailed analysis of consumer goods, the discussion of producer goods industries results, presented in table 4.2, can be much briefer. The Hausman test for specification error rejected the null hypothesis of no correlation with the error term in equation (4.1) for CR and in equation (4.3) for Ad/S. For PCM in equation (4.1) and Ad/S in equation (4.2) there is no basis to reject the null hypothesis. Accordingly, there is a basis for 2SLS in the producer goods sample, but not for the system as a whole.

The quality of the first-stage results mirrors that in consumer goods: the values of R^2 for $\widehat{Ad/S}$, $\widehat{CR}$, and $\widehat{PCM}$ are 0.20, 0.61, and 0.81 respectively, placing only CR in the acceptable range.

The coefficients and standard errors in certain equations once again shift across estimation methods without apparent cause. For example, the coefficient and standard error of CR in equation (4.1) change from OLS to 2SLS as expected, because of bias in OLS, but a similar shift occurs in equation (4.3) where bias was not found.

The correlations of residuals across equations in 2SLS are significant between each pair of equations. This explains the lower standard errors

Table 4.2   OLS, 2SLS, and 3SLS regression results for producer goods industries, 1972

Estimation	Eq.	Intercept	CR	PCM	CD/S	GR	DUR	Ad/S	MES/S	PCM67	K/S	GD	IMP/S	R^2
OLS	4.1	-0.0858 (-0.23)	0.0059[c] (1.42)	0.0173[c] (1.40)	0.0362[a] (4.19)	0.0023 (0.73)	-0.0748 (-0.36)							0.16
2SLS	4.1	-0.3134 (-0.75)	0.0153[a] (2.69)	0.0077 (0.53)	0.0364[a] (4.11)	0.0022 (0.68)	0.0681 (0.31)							
3SLS	4.1	-1.3588[a] (-3.69)	0.0173[a] (3.07)	0.0455[a] (3.55)	0.0213[a] (2.51)	0.0024 (0.83)	0.1243 (0.51)							
OLS	4.2	16.0098[a] (3.65)						-0.5512 (-0.51)	5.2864 (12.69)	0.4690 (2.87)				0.53
2SLS	4.2	16.1452[a] (3.58)						2.6934 (0.89)	4.9892[a] (9.98)	0.3899[b] (2.15)				
3SLS	4.2	9.3043[b] (2.13)						1.3700 (0.46)	5.1632[a] (10.41)	0.6867[a] (3.93)				
OLS	4.3	19.8617[a] (13.03)	0.0248 (0.63)			0.0597[a] (2.88)		1.3404[a] (2.67)	-0.2649 (-0.93)		0.0678[a] (3.37)	-0.9695 (-0.27)	-0.0356[b] (-1.74)	0.18
2SLS	4.3	12.3368[a] (2.59)	0.3200 (1.22)			-0.0099 (-0.23)		6.7924[a] (2.84)	-2.2264[b] (-1.75)		0.0337 (0.74)	6.2151 (0.78)	-0.0523[c] (-1.43)	
3SLS	4.3	7.6564[b] (1.70)	0.6146[b] (2.60)			-0.0182 (-0.46)		4.7191[b] (2.06)	-3.5916[a] (-3.07)		-0.0203 (-0.63)	6.9541 (1.12)	0.0012 (0.05)	

[a] Significant at the 0.01 level
[b] Significant at the 0.05 level
[c] Significant at the 0.10 level

under 3SLS, but the difference in coefficients between 3SLS and 2SLS remains an anomaly. In any event, there is a strong case for 3SLS in producer goods, which also highlights the structural differences between the two subsamples.

The problem of multicollinearity in equation (4.3) is again severe under 2SLS. Repeating the test on multicollinearity (regressing $\overline{Ad/S}$ and $\overline{CR}$ on the exogenous variables in equation (4.3)) the relevant values of R^2 for OLS and 2SLS are: 0.09 and 0.58 for Ad/S, and 0.59 and 0.97 for CR.

Various trade-offs are again presented to the investigator with no unambiguous way to choose among alternatives. When tests to choose between OLS, 2SLS, and 3SLS yield mixed or contradictory results, considerable judgement as to the most appropriate procedure must be exercised. The temptation to choose a procedure whose results support a priori hypotheses must always be guarded against.

CONCLUSIONS

There is obviously much more to good empirical research than the ready availability of data and the use of a more advanced statistical procedure than had heretofore been utilized. But ready data and more sophisticated estimation methods appear to have been the primary basis for a new generation of structure–performance model studies, particularly those explaining levels of industry advertising–sales, concentration, and price–cost margins. The theory underlying the monopoly view of advertising in such models is not well developed and its fundamental premises – advertising creates brand loyalty, there are large-scale advertising economies of scale, and advertising leads to lower price elasticity – are not supported by empirical evidence. Thus, how to interpret a positive advertising–profit relationship is not at all clear.

The switch from single to simultaneous equation models requiring consistent estimation has suffered from a lack of attention to whether the interactions are simultaneous or not and to whether bias exists or not. Tests of bias have not been reported in prior studies nor have the elements of the trade-off between efficiency and consistency been explored; specifically, the quality of the first-stage results, the extent of multicollinearity, and whether 3SLS is required or not. Using these procedures for a 1972 data set, serious problems with the use of 2SLS and 3SLS were found. As a consequence, the validity of prior studies remains in doubt.

Simultaneous equation models have not proven to be the panacea that was hoped for by some in the early 1970s. The findings of this study suggest that great care should be exercised before adopting a simultaneous equation framework. But once adopted, great care must also be exercised in choosing an estimation procedure, to ensure the estimation procedure does not introduce more econometric problems than it is designed to resolve.

NOTES

1 Massy and Frank (1965) found no difference in price and advertising elasticity between brand-loyal and nonloyal shoppers. Lambin's (1976) results show brand loyalty is primarily a function of product price, quality, and performance. Other tests of advertising's effects on brand loyalty have examined the relationship between advertising and market share stability (the greater stability the greater brand loyalty) and between advertising and the rate of new product entry (the less entry the greater brand loyalty). Studies by Telser (1964), Reekie (1974), and Lambin (1976) found the higher advertising intensity, the higher market share instability. Studies by Buzzell and Nourse (1967), Telser (1964), and Porter (1978) found new product introduction more likely in advertising intensive industries.

2 For an uncritical review of these studies see Albion and Farris (1981). Comanor and Wilson (1974) estimate long-run price elasticities for 33 IRS industries. Of these, 28 showed negative elasticities. The rank correlation between price elasticity and advertising to sales ratios for these 28 industries is $+0.44$ and significant. Lambin (1976) found mixed results. He found an insignificant negative correlation when advertising was measured as advertising share per brand, but a significant negative correlation when advertising per capita was used. Tests of individual brands at the retail advertising level typically find that advertising and price elasticity are positively related (Albion and Farris, 1981).

3 Reviews of advertising scale economies studies have come to different conclusions. Studies by Simon (1970), Schmalensee (1972), and Ferguson (1975) reviewed numerous tests of advertising scale economies and each concluded there is no evidence of such economies. Reviews of the advertising literature by Comanor and Wilson (1979) and Albion and Farris (1981) disagree, arguing that none of the studies used the correct methodology (for example, allowing all inputs to vary or using controlled experiments), so we do not know whether advertising economies of scale exist or not. Only one study to my knowledge, that of Brown (1978), has found evidence of advertising scale economies.

4 Recent studies by Geroski (1982) and others find that industry price–cost margins and concentration are both endogenous, determined by demand and supply conditions and firms' conjectural variation, requiring consistent estimation. Sawyer (1982) holds that OLS is sufficient despite this apparent simultaneity.

5 Strickland and Weiss (1976) recognized this problem but it has gone unmentioned in subsequent studies.

6 Strickland and Weiss use the full 1963 Census, but for 44 percent of their sample Ad/S and CD/S are at the two or three-digit level as compiled in the input–output tables. In such cases each four-digit industry within a two- or three-digit code is assigned the same Ad/S and CD/S ratios, resulting in large measurement errors. To avoid this problem only four-digit industries are used in this study.

7   There are 332 available industries for 1972, but the need to include lagged PCM back to 1967 reduced the sample size to 229 due to numerous industry definition changes between 1967 and 1972.

8   Taking the model, $Y = \alpha + \beta_1 X_1 + \beta_2 X_2 + \mu$
    Then

$$\text{Cov}(\beta_1, \beta_2) = \frac{-r_{12}}{1 - r_{12}^2} (\sigma_\mu^2)$$

So the higher r_{12} the more negatively correlated are the parameters.

9   The regression results are different from those of Strickland and Weiss and Martin who obtain stronger results in general, and in particular relative to equation (4.3). What accounts for this difference in results is unclear. One possibility is their estimation technique. Since their models include CR^2 they use Kelejian's (1971) technique for handling nonlinear variables, which involves the use of squared and cross-product terms in first-stage estimation. This may well lessen the severity of multicollinearity in their results.

10 One might consider a solution to be the use of seemingly-unrelated regressions, despite having endogenous variables on the right-hand side. But there is no compelling reason to expect significant correlations across residuals in OLS because they occur in 2SLS. This, in fact, is what occurred when seemingly-unrelated regressions were run: no significant correlations across equations for consumer goods industries.

BIBLIOGRAPHY

Albion, M. S. and Farris, P. W. 1981: *The Advertising Controversy*. Boston: Auburn House.

Asch, P. 1979: The role of advertising in changing concentration, 1963–1971. *Southern Economic Journal*, 46, July, 288–97.

Bain, J. S. 1951: The relation of profit rate to industry concentration, American manufacturing, 1933–1940. *Quarterly Journal of Economics*, 65, August, 293–324.

Brown, Randall S. 1978: Estimating advantages to large-scale advertising. *Review of Economics and Statistics*, 55, August, 428–37.

Brozen, Y. 1970: The antitrust task force deconcentration recommendation. *Journal of Law and Economics*, 13, October, 279–92.

Buzzell, R. D. and Nourse, R. E. M. 1967: *Product Innovation in Food Processing 1954–1964*. Division of Research, Graduate School of Business, Harvard University.

Caves, R., Porter, M., Spence, A. M. and Scott, J. T. 1980: *Competition in the Open Economy: A Model Applied to Canada*. Cambridge, Mass.: Harvard University Press.

Comanor, W. and Wilson, T. 1974: *Advertising and Monopoly Power*. Cambridge, Mass.: Harvard University Press.

Comanor, W. and Wilson, T. 1979: The effect of advertising on competition: A survey. *Journal of Economic Literature*, 17, June, 453–76.

Davies, S. W. 1983: Minimum efficient size and seller concentration: an empirical problem. *Journal of Industrial Economics*, 28, March, 287–301.

Dorfman, R. and Steiner, P. O. 1954: Optimal advertising and optimal quality. *American Economic Review*, 44, December, 820–36.

Durbin, J. 1954: Errors in variables. *Review of the International Statistical Institute*, 22, 23–32.

Ferguson, J. M. 1975: *Advertising and Competition: Theory, Measurement, Fact.* Cambridge Mass.: Ballinger.

Geroski, P. A. 1982: Interpreting a correlation between market structure and performance. *Journal of Industrial Economics*, 30, March, 319–26.

Hausman, J. A. 1978: Specification tests in econometrics. *Econometrica*, 46, November, 1251–71.

Intriligator, M. D. 1978: *Econometric Models, Techniques, and Applications.* Englewood Cliffs, New Jersey: Prentice-Hall.

Kelejian, H. H. 1971: Two-stage least squares and econometric systems linear in parameters but nonlinear in the endogenous variables. *Journal of the American Statistical Association*, 66, June, 373–4.

Lambin, J. J. 1976: *Competition, Advertising, and Market Conduct in Oligopoly Over Time: An Econometric Investigation in Western European Countries.* Amsterdam: North-Holland.

Leibowitz, S. J. 1982: What do census price-cost margins measure. *Journal of Law and Economics*, 25, October, 231–46.

Mann, H. M. 1966: Seller concentration, barriers to entry, and rates of return in thirty industries, 1950–1960. *Review of Economics and Statistics*, 48, August, 296–307.

Martin, S. 1979: Advertising, concentration, and profitability: the simultaneity problem. *Bell Journal of Economics*, 10, Autumn, 639–47.

Marvel, H. P. 1980: Foreign trade and domestic competition. *Economic Inquiry*, 18, January, 103–22.

Massy, W. F. and Frank, R. E. 1965: Short-term price and demand effects in selected market segments. *Journal of Marketing Research*, 2, May, 171–85.

Mueller, W. F. and Rogers, R. T. 1980: The role of advertising in changing concentration of manufacturing industries. *Review of Economics and Statistics*, 62, February, 89–96.

Nakamura, A. and Nakamura, M. 1981: On the relationship among several specification error tests presented by Durbin, Wu, and Hausman. *Econometrica*, November, 1583–8.

Ornstein, S. I. 1975: Empirical uses of the price–cost margin. *Journal of Industrial Economics*, 24, December, 105–17.

Ornstein, S. I. 1977: *Industrial Concentration and Advertising Intensity.* Washington, D.C.: American Enterprise Institute.

Ornstein, S. I. 1984: Explaining changes in price–cost margins. Working Paper.

Ornstein, S. I. and Lustgarten, S. 1978: Advertising intensity and industrial concentration: an empirical inquiry, 1947–1967. In D. G. Tuerck (ed.) *Issues in Advertising: The Economics of Persuasion.* Washington, D.C.: American Enterprise Institute, pp. 217–52.

Pagoulatos, E. and Sorensen, R. 1981: A simultaneous equation analysis of advertising, concentration, and profitability. *Southern Economic Journal*, 48, January, 728–41.

Porter, M. E. 1978: Optimal advertising: an intra-industry approach. In D. G. Tuerck (ed.) *Issues in Advertising: The Economics of Persuasion*. Washington, D.C., American Enterprise Institute, pp. 91–114.

Reekie, W. D. 1974: Advertising and market share mobility. *Scottish Journal of Political Economy*, 21, June, 143–58.

Saving, T. R. 1970: Concentration ratios and the degree of monopoly. *International Economic Review*, 11, February, 139–46.

Sawyer, Malcolm C. 1982: On the specification of structure–performance relationships. *European Economic Review*, 17, March, 295–306.

Scherer, F. M. 1979: The causes and consequences of rising industrial concentration: a comment. *Journal of Law and Economics*, 22, April, 191–208.

Schmalensee, R. 1972: *The Economics of Advertising*. Amsterdam: North-Holland.

Simon, J. L. 1970: *Issues in the Economics of Advertising*, Urbana, Illinois: University of Illinois Press.

Strickland, A. D. and Weiss, L. W. 1976: Advertising, concentration, and price–cost margins. *Journal of Political Economy*, 84, October, 1109–21.

Telser, L. 1964: Advertising and competition. *Journal of Political Economy*, 67, December, 537–62.

United States Bureau of the Census 1967: *Concentration Ratios in Manufacturing Industry, 1963*, Report for the Subcommittee on Antitrust and Monopoly of the United States Senate, Part II, Table 26, Washington.

Weiss, L. 1974: The concentration–profits relationship and antitrust. In H. J. Goldschmid, H. M. Mann, and J. F. Weston (eds) *Industrial Concentration: The New Learning*. Boston: Little, Brown and Company, pp. 184–233.

Part 2
Topics in Financial Economics

5
Empirical Evidence on Takeover Activity and Shareholder Wealth

RICHARD ROLL

PREFACE

J. Fred Weston's long-term work on mergers and corporate structure was an inspiration to a generation of researchers. I was a particular beneficiary of this inspiration both in preparing the chapter below and in preparing a related paper (The hubris hypothesis of corporate takeovers, Journal of Business, *April, 1986). I spent a lot of time talking to Fred and reading his papers, particularly some of his recent empirical papers with Kwang Chung. Fred's merger papers have always been full of hypotheses and implicitly open to opposing points of view. He takes the approach, both in print and in person, that the data will ultimately reveal the truth; and he has always been willing to change preconceived and cherished hypotheses if empirical evidence seems against them. The literature on mergers has been much enriched by Fred's work.*

As a colleague and friend, Fred is simply in a class by himself. Anyone who knows him is aware of three attributes of his character: first, Fred is physically present at the university seemingly around the clock. Second, despite an overcharged schedule, he is never too busy to give of his time. This applies to his faculty colleagues, of course, but it applies in equal measure to students and to anyone who simply drops by to talk. He is tireless in his encouragement and advice to research colleagues; he comments on most papers prepared by his colleagues at U.C.L.A. and

This paper also appears in *Takeovers and Contests for Corporate Control*, edited by Susan Rose-Ackerman, John C. Coffee, Jr. and Louis Lowenstein, published in 1987 by Oxford University Press, Inc., New York. Reprinted with permission.

on many from researchers around the world. He is an active attendee at the finance and economics workshops.

Third, Fred is one of those too-rare individuals who has a genuine concern for his fellow human beings. Most of us at U.C.L.A. are beneficiaries of Fred's investigations into such topics as ultraviolet radiation from fluorescent lights (Fred bought special low-emission bulbs for our offices), or getting around during power failures (Fred gives flashlights as Christmas presents). He is also an excellent dinner companion, theatre-goer, and bon vivant (especially when it comes to dancing at parties). As an amateur photographer, however, he could be better at getting the entire subject within the frame of the picture.

INTRODUCTION

The available empirical results about takeover activity can be summarized as follows: takeovers provide substantial economic benefits to shareholders of *target* firms. However, there is more doubt that takeovers, on average, provide gains to the shareholders of bidding firms, and there is similar doubt that gains accrue in aggregate and on average to all shareholders.

"Doubt" means simply that the evidence is insufficient to reach a definite conclusion. There have been takeovers in which the bidding firm's shareholders (and all shareholders) gained, but other cases have displayed the opposite pattern. Empirical studies have disagreed about the extent and sign of bidding firm and aggregate gains. Indeed, the measurement of gains is fraught with econometric difficulty. I believe that neither an unbiased statistician nor a policy maker could find much comfort in the empirical evidence to support any particular inference or action.

From the policy perspective, there is no empirical justification for limiting takeover activity because of potential damage to target firm shareholders. There is no empirical justification for restricting the activities of bidding firms, even for the paternalistic prevention of self-inflicted economic loss. Finally, the empirical evidence on private anti-takeover activity is not conclusive. At present, it could support no particular social policy.

In the following section, I will give a brief survey of the empirical results obtained on the takeover question over the last decade and will suggest an interpretation based on what a skeptical econometrician can read into them. The next section presents a discussion of takeover theories and, to the extent possible, interprets existing empirical results as confirmations or denials of those theories. The final section gives a summary and conclusion.

MARKET PRICE RESPONSE TO TAKEOVER ACTIVITY

Target Firms

Virtually *every* empirical study has found that target firms display statistically significant positive price response to the announcement of a takeover attempt. Jensen and Ruback (1983) averaged the results of about 20 scholarly papers and found an increase (over the pre-announcement market price), of 20 percent for mergers and 30 percent for tender offers, in the period around the takeover event.

In a more recent paper, Dennis and McConnell (1986) found that the average target firm's shares increase by 8.6 percent, adjusted for market movements, on the day of bid announcement and the previous trading day. This is an annualized return of several thousand percent!

Although there is a mystery about the motives of bidding firms in take-overs, there is absolutely no doubt that a bid is good economic news for the target. No matter what might happen to target firm shareholders subsequent to the original announcement bid, the bid *per se* is beneficial. If the target firm's shareholders were concerned about subsequent damaging action by the bidder (say in a two-tiered offer), they could simply sell at the prevailing price just after the bid. In doing so, they would realize a total return considerably higher than what would have obtained in the absence of a bid.

The empirical support for the value of receiving a bid is bolstered further by studies of target firms after the original bid. Perhaps the most dramatic and persuasive evidence was uncovered by Bradley *et al.* (1983) in a study of unsuccessful tender offers. When an unsuccessful tender offer is followed by another offer within a few years, the original price increase around the first bid is maintained permanently. However, when the original (unsuccessful) offer is not followed by a successful offer within five years, the entire market price increase associated with the original bid is reversed.

Before turning to the more complex issues surrounding the bidding firm, it is worth emphasizing that bids are apparently surprises to target firm shareholders. Most studies have found a large price increase in the few days surrounding the original bid announcement; and this announcement effect is much larger per unit of time than observed price movements either before or after. This result points to the essentially passive role played by the target firm, which is an important contrast to the active role of the bidding firm. It is much easier to ascribe price movements to the bid when the firm is surprised. The bidding firm is not surprised, and this complicates the attribution to price movements of *its* shares to the takeover event.

Bidding Firms

The empirical results for bidding firms permit a variety of interpretations. Different papers have found different results. Methods, time periods, and samples of firms vary across studies, making it difficult to draw conclusive inference. (Incidentally, the same factors differ across papers for target firms but, nevertheless, the results agree.) Just to mention a sample of papers, Asquith (1983), Bradley (1980), and Dennis and McConnell (1986) report positive price movements of bidding firms while Dodd (1980), Eger (1983), and Firth (1980) report negative price movements. Some papers, e.g. Malatesta (1983), report both, depending on the method and sample.

Whether bidding firm price movements are positive or negative on average, they are generally small in percentage terms (much smaller than target firm returns), and are less statistically significant. Again, just to give an example, Dennis and McConnell (1985) report a market-adjusted return in the equities of bidding firms of -0.12 percent on the day of the announcement and the previous trading day. This tiny negative two-day return is to be contrasted with the large positive 8.56 percent two-day return they found for target firms.

The return on the two-day announcement period is negative for bidders in the Dennis–McConnell sample, but it is not statistically significant. Interestingly, the authors conclude that the effect on bidders actually is positive, not negative, because of a positive price movement during a longer period around the announcement. The announcement day itself displays a negative return of -0.34 percent, which is marginally significant, but when the authors calculate returns for other periods (day -19 to -2, day -19 to 0, day -6 to $+6$), they find overall positive returns! Strangely, the greatest positive returns occur *after* the announcement.

The Dennis–McConnell paper is the most recent and one of the very best empirical papers on this subject, which is why I cite it extensively here. It seems to me that their results make something less than a persuasive case for the proposition that bidding firms' stockholders gain around merger events. Their paper is typical in this regard.

Dennis and McConnell also investigate the possibilities: (1) that total potential gains to bidding firms may be larger than gains to stockholders (e.g. bondholders may also benefit), and (2) that returns may be a less useful gauge of benefits than dollar price movements, particularly when assessing the relative gains of target and bidder firms, which generally differ substantially in size.

Results for other classes of stakeholders in the bidding firm are as follows: convertible preferred stockholders gain (even more than equity holders) in a wide period around the merger announcement, but the announcement day return is virtually zero; convertible bondholders gain over a wide period, but not by a statistically significant amount, and the announcement day return is negative (but insignificant); nonconvertible preferred stockholders receive no statistically reliable returns; nonconvertible bondholders have negative returns in all periods, but they are only marginally significant.

Dollar gains are reported only for a chosen period (for equities, the period is 20 days before until 20 days after the announcement). For all classes of stakeholders combined, target firms gain an average of $30 million and bidding firms an average of $40 million during this period. Keep in mind that the figure would be quite different for other periods around the announcement. For example, it would likely be negative for bidding firms on the announcement day itself.

The results for bidding firms reported in the Dennis–McConnell paper are typical of every empirical paper. Depending on the paper, the sample, the period, and the biases of the reader, widely differing conclusions can be reached. This state of affairs is possible, moreover, even ignoring what I believe is a more critical problem of interpretation of bidding firm market price reactions: the fact that the bid itself may convey information about the bidder unrelated to the takeover event.

To put this problem in perspective, one should remember that many types of public announcements by firms cause market prices to react. Dividend declarations, earnings results, splits, new products, personnel changes and so on, have been associated with market price movements. Any public announcement has this potential because it leads investors to revise their opinions about the value of the firm. The announcement of a takeover bid discloses at least two pieces of information: first, that the takeover will be attempted, and second, that the internal affairs of the bidding firm are in such a state that a takeover bid is possible. The second item is new information about the firm that is not necessarily related to whether a takeover will ever occur. It can signal good things; for example, that cash flow over the recent past has been higher than previously estimated and high enough to elicit a takeover attempt. It can also signal something less favorable; for example, that the managers are going to use the company's cash in pursuit of an expensive and elusive target, for which they may over-pay.

The problem is that the bid is a "polluted" information item. The bidding firm is an activist, unlike the target firm, and its actions can be interpreted in the market as conveying more than just information about the takeover *per se*.

THEORIES OF TAKEOVER ACTIVITY AND RELATED EMPIRICAL EVIDENCE

A number of distinct hypotheses have been advanced to explain the motivations in takeover activity. They are not mutually exclusive; different motives could explain different individual takeovers and more than one could be present in any particular case. Most takeover hypotheses make the natural presumption that economic benefits will flow from the corporate combination. Potential sources of gains include:

1 Monopoly – increased market power from a corporate combination.
2 Information – the current market price does not contain all relevant information about the value of the target. This information is revealed, and the revelation results in an upward market revaluation, during the process of a takeover.
3 Synergy–reductions in production or distribution costs.
4 Elimination of inferior management of the target firm.
5 Financial motivation – increased utilization of tax shields, lower expected bankruptcy costs, etc.

There are also existing hypotheses of takeover motivation which do not involve gains for shareholders:

6 Management self-interest – managers increase their remuneration and their psychic gratification by taking over other firms.
7 Hubris – bidders overvalue their targets and pay too much; thus, the takeover is merely a wealth transfer from bidder to target.

The Monopoly Hypothesis

The acquisition of market power is probably the most obvious "theory" of mergers. The (horizontal) merger of two large firms in the same industry brings an immediate increase in concentration; but whether this is translated into gains for shareholders remains in doubt.

In fact, based on the work of Stillman (1983) and Eckbo (1983), monopoly does not appear to be a significant motive. Both Stillman and Eckbo reach their conclusion from indirect evidence, the lack of market price reaction of competitor firms when two other rivals in the same industry announce a combination.

There is little direct evidence to the contrary. Furthermore, many corporate combinations simply could not be motivated by monopoly because they do not involve firms in the same or closely related industries. For example, the recent increase in the rate of leveraged buyouts could not be motivated by monopoly.

The Information Hypothesis

The information hypothesis is based on financial market inefficiency in the strong-form sense. The market price is too low because positive information about the target firm is not yet publicly known. Such information is obtained by the bidding firm who therefore regards the target as a bargain.

This hypothesis was given a substantial boost in papers by Dodd and Ruback (1977), Bradley (1980), and Firth (1980). The results presented there indicate that a tender offer, even if unsuccessful, causes a permanent upward revaluation in the target firm's market price. However, Bradley *et al.* (1983) question the information hypothesis because of a further examination of unsuccessful tender offers. Unsuccessful tenders are often followed by further (successful) bids. When an unsuccessful tender offer is not followed by a successful offer within five years, the original market price rise is completely reversed. It is only those targets of unsuccessful offers followed by later successful bids that experience permanent increases in value.

Based upon these results, and also on the stock price behavior of bidding firms, Bradley *et al.* argue against the information hypothesis and in favor of synergy. If information were revealed by a tender offer *per se*, they reason, the upward revaluation should be permanent even for firms which are never targets in subsequent successful tenders. To the contrary, the revaluation induced by synergy will accrue only when a corporate combination is actually effected. The price rise caused by potential synergy will be lost to shareholders of firms that never enter a combination.

This conclusion seems quite plausible but there is another, perhaps less palatable, possibility: what if the tender offer revealed the *probable* existence of private positive information about the target, not the certainty of such information? One would expect that those firms for which such information did exist might be more likely candidates for further bids. Since each bid has some chance of success, such firms would also be more likely to enter a subsequent combination. Firms for whom there was no private information in the first place would be less likely to elicit further bids since there would be little incentive for a potential acquiring firm to make a bid. Thus, firms which never enter a combination should experience a fall in price back to the original level. Information whose *possible* existence was revealed by the initial unsuccessful tender offer turns out not to exist in these cases.

The price behavior of unsuccessful bidding firms is advanced by Bradley *et al.* as further evidence against the information hypothesis. When an unsuccessful bid has been made for a firm which received no further bids, the bidding firm's price is virtually unchanged from its original level. But, when a bid is first announced by what turns out to be a successful rival, the first bidder's stock price drops by a statistically significant 2.84 percent (p. 203).[1] The authors argue, "the information hypothesis makes no prediction concerning the relation between the share-price behavior of unsuccessful bidding firms and the ultimate disposition of control of the target resources," (p. 203). While the synergy hypothesis implies "that when a firm loses the competition for a target firm to a rival bidding firm, the market perceives it to have lost an opportunity to acquire a valuable resource," (p. 203).

But doesn't the information hypothesis really imply the same thing? The appearance of a rival bid increases the probability that there exists positive nonpublic information about the target firm but it *decreases* both the probability that the initial bidder has exclusive possession of the information and the probability that the initial bid will succeed.

The Synergy Hypothesis

The hypothesis of synergy as an explanation for merger gains has considerable appeal. Jensen and Ruback (1983) support its possibility, "Some of the gains are also likely to result from . . . synergies in combining independent organizations," (p. 25).

Asquith (1983) argues that merger gains are caused by synergy, but he includes inefficient target firm management in the synergy category and he seems to be saying (p. 83) that the evidence really supports the inefficient management hypothesis. Bradley *et al.* (1983) conclude that, "the synergy hypothesis is a better description of the nature of tender offers than the information hypothesis," (p. 205) but they, too, include "more efficient management" (p. 184) under the synergy rubric.

The Jensen–Ruback characterization of synergy that excludes inefficient management is probably more useful for understanding the empirical results. Their concept of synergy is "potential reductions in production or distribution costs" (p. 23) through various devices available to the combined firm but not to the two firms operated separately. This is quite different from inefficient target firm management. Better management could bring the same gain in value if the target firm were operated independently. (The value gain in proxy contests, Dodd and Warner (1983), might be an appropriate measure of the gain to replacing inefficient managers, abstracting from any other information effect in the proxy contest announcement.)

Let us hereafter define synergy as something which causes an increase in value *only* if there is a successful corporate combination. Exclude from synergy new information, inefficient management, or anything else which could conceivably imply the same increase in value to the target firm *without* a successful takeover.

Many authors have presented evidence that the stockholders of acquired (target) firms obtain most and perhaps all of the economic benefits. Why should this occur if synergy is the cause? Synergy requires *both* firms in order to secure gains in value. On average over many takeovers, there is no reason to expect that most or all of these gains would go to the same side of the transaction. True, in some transactions, competition among bidding firms for a given target might result in the (apparently) observed asymmetry; the synergy would be available to several competing bidders but only in combination with a single target. But the opposite situation might be equally as likely; there could be instances of synergy available to a single bidder combining with several possible targets. In this case, competition among targets would assure that most of the gain accrued to the bidder. There might well be other cases, e.g. synergy available only to two *specific* firms and to no others, either target or bidder. The division of gains would then be determined by bargaining, not by competition.

On average over all observed takeovers, there seems to be no reason to think that synergy gains, as we have defined them, would be unevenly split. Rejection of the hypothesis on this basis is not possible, however, because there may be some reason, as yet undiscovered, why bidding firms are more frequently at a competitive disadvantage relative to target firms.

If the gains in takeovers actually are positive and if they turn out under further study to be approximately evenly divided, synergy would be a strong candidate for explaining the takeover phenomenon. The recent Dennis and McConnell (1985) paper does find a roughly even dollar division; so synergy is, in my opinion, a hypothesis that is empirically viable.

One puzzle remaining about synergy is why these firms undertook the combination at the observed time rather than at an earlier date when the synergy may also have been available? Perhaps synergy arises suddenly or perhaps managers discover its existence according to some random process. The synergy hypothesis could be further developed to explain why synergy elicits a takeover bid at a particular time.

The Inefficient Management Hypothesis

Inefficient management could be replaced by a variety of devices, not just by a takeover. Perhaps takeover costs are lower than the costs of alternatives such as proxy fights, replacement of operating managers by the board of directors, or simply replacement of directors by stockholder vote.

But if most target firm stockholders agreed with the bidding firm that incumbent management was inefficient, there would be no necessity to incur the expense of a takeover bid. Disgreement between bidding firm managers and a voting majority of target firm stockholders could necessitate a takeover as the method of target firm management replacement. Rather than convincing target firm shareholders by newspaper advertisements, speeches at the annual meeting, or by direct mail, the bidding firm offers the more persuasive argument of a higher price for the target firm's shares.

An interesting experiment concerning the synergy and management inefficiency hypotheses was conducted by Dodd and Ruback (1977). In conjunction with their broader study of tender offers, they collected results for a sample of 19 "clean-up" tender offers, offers by bidding firms who already owned over 50 percent of the target. As Dodd and Ruback note, "since bidders already had control of the target firm, these abnormal returns (around the bid announcement) cannot reflect synergy, monopoly, or internal efficiency gains," (p. 371). Yet the returns observed in the announcement month were similar in magnitude to those observed in their

Table 5.1

	Abnormal % return in announcement month	
	Bidder	Target
Clean-up offers	2.71	17.41
(*t*-statistic)	(1.89)	(6.68)
Ordinary offers	2.83	20.58
(*t*-statistic)	(2.16)	(25.8)

Source: Dodd and Ruback, (1977, pp. 368, 371).

sample of ordinary successful tender offers (consisting of 124 bidders and 136 targets) as shown in table 5.1. (The smaller sample size explains the smaller *t*-statistics in the "clean-up" sample.) Dodd and Ruback argue that the premium paid to "clean-up" target shareholders "include(s) the savings in litigation costs to the majority stockholder." Perhaps so; but there is remarkable similarity between the two samples, one of which cannot be subject to either synergy or efficiency gains. The elimination of litigation costs might just happen to bring about the same empirical results as, say, synergy, but this would indeed be fortuitous.

The Tax Hypothesis

The final hypothesis of gains is that tax benefits of some kind accrue to corporate combinations. The tax law offers many possible merger motives; Ginsburg (1983) requires 142 pages to discuss recent changes in the relevant code. One prominent scenario involves a firm with sizeable embedded losses that would bring valuable tax deductions to any firm with sufficient earnings. There are few reported empirical results about this scenario even though direct evidence on tax benefits would seem easier to uncover than evidence about, say, synergy or inefficient management.

An indirect implication of this particular tax hypothesis is that mergers should be more frequent during and just after business contractions when more firms have generated tax-deductible losses. Of course, at such times it may be difficult to find a merger partner with positive earnings against which losses can be deducted. Perhaps this explains why Chung and Weston (1982) find a positive relation between the dollar amount of merger activity and the real growth rate in GNP from 1957 to 1977. The general frequency of mergers appears to be higher since the early 1950s; the only other comparable period was 1927–31. There were relatively few mergers in the 1930s and 1940s regardless of the market's performance.

A further indirect implication of the tax hypothesis is that the Federal tax law change in 1981 which allowed firms to sell tax depreciation and investment tax credits directly and without merging, should have caused a reduction in the rate of merger activity, *ceteris paribus*, since it reduced the tax incentives for merging. This change was in effect for only about sixteen months, so its impact may be hard to spot. It is certainly not evident in time series of the extent of merger activity.

Another tax scenario is the allegation that tax-depreciated but still valuable assets constitute a tempting target; see Weston and Chung (1983) and Dertouzous and Thorpe (1982). The latter authors conclude that this motive in conjunction with estate taxes explains many acquisitions in the newspaper industry. The acquirer is supposedly willing to pay a premium in order to "step up" the basis of the depreciated assets, thereby obtaining a further tax shield in the combined firm that would not have been available to the target firm operating alone. However, the actual advantage is complicated by the liability created for target shareholders by the recognized capital gain.[2]

Another possible financial motivation for a corporate combination is reduction in bankruptcy costs through diversification (Jensen and Ruback, 1983, p. 24). This has been termed the "co-insurance hypothesis" by Lewellen (1971). Presumably, diversification allows the use of more debt capital, thereby bringing larger tax deductions from interest. Reduction of direct bankruptcy costs cannot alone explain large gains in takeovers because even the perfect certainty of realizing such costs would result in only a small change in value, at least according to the empirical evidence in Warner (1977), but indirect bankruptcy costs of the type discussed in Titman (1984) may be material.

An indirect test supporting diversification as a merger motive is provided by Marshall *et al.* (1984). They find that mergers are more likely between partners in less-correlated manufacturing industries and that conglomerate firms are more likely to be composed of industry divisions that are less correlated than the average pair of industries.

The diversification motive has been directly tested by Kim and McConnell (1977), Asquith and Kim (1982), Dennis and McConnell (1983), Eger (1983), and Settle *et al.* (1984). The first of these five papers finds that "merged firms do make greater use of financial leverage," (Kim and McConnell, 1977, p. 362) but, consistent with the co-insurance hypothesis, bondholders do not lose value from increased leverage, presumably because the probability of default is reduced by the combination. Asquith and Kim (1982), however, using different methods and data, find no evidence to support a "diversification effect." Dennis and McConnell (1983) conclude that the evidence is "partially consistent with the co-insurance hypothesis," because the abnormal returns to senior security holders are "negatively correlated with the correlation coefficient between the returns on the mergings companies' common stocks," (p. 27). This result indicates that bondholders gain when the risk of default decreases. Eger (1983) finds direct evidence of bondholder gains at the expense of stockholders in "pure" stock exchange mergers (mergers which involve an exchange of shares only with no increase in leverage). This is consistent with the "co-insurance" hypothesis in that default risk is reduced by the merger but it raises another puzzle in that shareholders allow bondholders to obtain part of the resulting gain. The results of Settle *et al.* (1984) also indicate significant gains to bond-holders, but *prior* to the merger announcement month. In private correspondence, the authors showed me further results which seem to suggest that part of the bond price increase could be attributed to nonmerger related positive news about acquiring firms. The results do not eliminate the possibility that news about the merger leaked out before the announcement and that this leak caused the bonds to react positively. However, the peak price occurred three months prior to the month of the first public announcement; this may be a rather long time in advance for a leak to occur.

There is a peculiar theoretical problem in interpreting price movements around a takeover event when the firms involved have outstanding debt. Shastri (1983) proves that stock price increases do not necessarily imply increases in the economic value of the total firm nor does a lack of stock price increase imply that no economic value has been created by the corporate combination. The reason for this involves the complex interaction of the options implicit in the corporate debt, and the opportunities these options offer for redistributing wealth from bondholders to stockholders, or vice versa, during a takeover event. (Dennis and McConnell (1986) do provide information about all classes of stakeholders.)

Finally, another tax-related motive for takeovers involves cash-rich bidding firms who might acquire other firms instead of paying dividends, provided that there is an effective personal tax differential between dividends and capital gains (but see Miller and Scholes, 1978). This particular tax explanation implies that bidding firms would receive most of the takeover gain because the personal tax savings would accrue regardless of the target's identity. It also implies more merger activity with higher *personal* tax rates, which does seem consistent with the post-war increase in merger frequency.

Management Self-Interest

The management self-interest explanation of takeovers is based on the strong positive empirical relation between firm size and management compensation. Penrose (1959), Williamson (1964), and many others have argued that the connection between executive rewards and the size of the firm provides an incentive for growth, including growth by takeover, even when there is no anticipated gain for the shareholders. The idea is sometimes referred to as the "size maximization hypothesis" (see, for example, Malatesta, 1983, p. 157).

There are both logical and empirical difficulties here. Perhaps the most apparent conceptual problem is that a correlation (between size and management compensation) does not imply causation *for a* given manager. Larger enterprises undoubtedly require more management skill, but making an enterprise larger does not make its manager more skillful. Thus, a manager with a known level of skill could not expect to improve his financial remuneration by taking over another firm provided that his compensation was already at a level commensurate with his talent.

A rescue of the concept might be attempted either by making managers' utilities depend on nonfinancial reward (e.g. "power"), or by arguing that managers signal their skill levels through bids and that some skillful managers move into more appropriate positions by effecting corporate combinations. The latter possibility is merely a variant of the synergy hypothesis; a manager with unexploited skills is a wasted resource whose more efficient use would bring gains to someone. Presumably, the unrecognized manager would not obtain all of the gain in every case.

The spirit of the management self-interest hypothesis is that there really are *no* gains and that stockholders confuse correlation with causation. However, even admitting to the existence of such confusion or to the possibility that managers are motivated by psychic rewards, there are unexplained empirical phenomena around takeover events. The most anomalous is that target firms receive unambiguously large premia. If takeovers were motivated purely by manager self-aggrandizement, there would be no necessity for such payments. The target firm could be acquired by open market purchases or by offering a very modest premium. Even a manager motivated exclusively by size maximization would see no necessity to squander resources currently in hand, not to mention any hesitation induced by possible *ex-post* penalties (such as unemployment) which might be imposed by disgruntled shareholders.

The Hubris Hypothesis

A recent paper by the present author (Roll, 1986) advances a behavioral explanation for the takeover phenomenon. Roll's argument is that bidding firm managers intend to profit by taking over other firms, possibly because they *believe* that synergy is present, that the target has inefficient management, etc. Their intentions are not fulfilled, however, because the market price already reflects the full value of the firm (i.e. there is actually no synergy nor inefficient management involved). Why then do bidding firms persist in their pursuit of the target? Because the *individual* decision makers in the bidding firm are infected by overweening pride and arrogance (hubris), and thus persist in a belief that their own valuation of the target is correct, despite objective information that the target's true economic value is lower.

The hubris explanation is heavily dependent on improper recognition of the "winner's curse," a concept familiar to scholars of bidding theory. The idea of the winner's curse is simple: whoever makes the winning bid for a valuable object is likely to be a bidder with a positive valuation error. In auctions with only a few bidders, the winner is likely to have made the biggest (positive) error. Optimal bidding theory recognizes this problem and prescribes a lower bid than the valuation in general. The extent of downward bias in the bid depends on the variability in the bidder's distribution of values, perhaps subjectively determined, and the number of competitors.

Roll points out that all takeover bids are preceded by an independent valuation of the target. Although the valuation is often quite formal and extensive it can be rudimentary. If the market price fully reflects value, only positive valuation errors will be observed because a valuation below the market price will not elicit a bid. This implies that takeover activity results in a straightforward wealth transfer from bidding firm shareholders to target firm shareholders, and that there is a slight aggregate net loss due to the expenses of the takeover. Target firm prices should increase when a bid is announced while bidding firm prices should decrease.

After the initial bid, there is an interim period when the outcome of the takeover is in doubt. The hubris hypothesis predicts that the prices of ultimately successful bidding firms will decline during this period as the probability moves to 100 percent that the offer will succeed. Evidence from mergers (Asquith, 1983) seems to support this prediction but evidence from tender offers (Bradley, 1980) does not. In both mergers and tender offers, the statistical reliability of the interim period price movement is low.

Another prediction of hubris is that the premium paid for the target (above the initial market price), should be negatively related to the price movement of the bidding firm's shares on the announcement date. Evidence by Firth (1980) and Varaiya (1985) strongly supports this prediction. Varaiya's empirical work also supports the presence of the winner's curse among bidders. The empirical test is too complicated to describe here, but involves measures of the quantity of information about the target available in the market. Less information is accompanied by bigger valuation errors by bidders.

Hubris cannot be the sole explanation of the takeover phenomenon because it implies that *every* bid announcement should elicit a price decline in the bidding firm's shares. Some papers have even found an average increase. Furthermore, if all bids were inspired by hubris, stockholders could easily stop them by the simple expedient of a prohibition in the corporate charter. On the other hand, a strict prohibition would be irrelevant to a fully diversified shareholder since a hubris-driven takeover is a wealth transfer, from one of his issues to another (ignoring the deadweight takeover costs). We do not observe such stringent anti-bid charter provisions, which must imply that stockholders must at least believe that an occasional bid by a firm might have positive individual and aggregate benefits.

SUMMARY AND CONCLUSION

The empirical evidence indicates that target firm shareholders are materially benefited by a takeover attempt. There is a positive price reaction in the few days surrounding the bid. It is statistically significant in all studies and amounts to 8 to 30 percent, depending on the study. The fact that the price reaction occurs in the few days around the bid announcement indicates that the market is surprised, at least to some extent, by the bid.

The empirical results for bidding firms are much less conclusive. Depending on the method, sample period, and data, different authors have reached differing conclusions. Some have found small positive price reactions while others have found price declines. In all cases, the absolute magnitude and the statistical significance of the price reaction are smaller for bidding firms than for target firms. It is also more difficult to ascribe the price reaction of a bidding firm to the takeover *per se*. Simply by issuing a bid, the bidding firm may be disclosing other information about itself, information unrelated to the takeover.

A few studies have examined the relation between the price reaction of the target and the price reaction of the bidder. In all cases, they are strongly negatively related. This probably indicates that the market interprets high bids to be *too* high, thereby transferring wealth from the bidding firm's shareholders to the target shareholders.

There have been at least seven distinct theories of takeovers advanced in the financial economics literature. They are not mutually exclusive, so different theories could conceivably account for different takeovers. The available empirical results provide no support for the theory that monopoly is a takeover motive nor for the theory that information about the target firm is available to the bidding firm but not to other market participants. The other theories, ranging from tax effects, synergy, and elimination of inferior management to noneconomic motives such as management self-interest and hubris seem to be consistent with the empirical evidence (however, the extent of formal statistical testing is still quite limited).

In conclusion, takeovers provide a significant economic benefit to target firm shareholders. It is not yet clear whether bidding firm shareholders benefit as well; the effect on them is relatively small, and its sign is still in doubt. There are a number of competing theories to explain the motives in takeovers and much empirical analysis remains to be done before the truth or falsity of each theory is proved.

NOTES

1 It is interesting to note that the first bidder's stock price drops on average despite the fact that sizeable positions are often taken in the target's stock by the first bidder. One might have thought that the first bidder's own stock price would increase upon the announcement of a rival bid, merely because those shares of the target already owned would increase in value; yet this effect is apparently more than offset by other factors.

2 For example, consider a sale for cash of depreciated assets. Let G be the difference between the cash sale price and the seller's tax basis and let x be the ordinary tax rate; for simplicity, assume $x/2$ is the capital gains rate. The buyer can deduct G in increments over time depending on a depreciation schedule; the value to the buyer of a "stepped-up basis" is the discounted present value of these deductions. For example, using the sum of the years' digits method, a useful life of n years, and a discount rate r, the benefit to the buyer is

$$\frac{2xG}{n(n+1)} \sum_{t=1}^{n} \frac{n+1-t}{(1+r)^t}$$

while the tax cost to the seller is $xG/2$. There is no net benefit when

$$\frac{4}{n(n+1)} \sum_{t=1}^{n} \frac{n+1-t}{(1+r)^t} < 1$$

Remembering that the tax deduction to the buyer is risky (it is available in any period only to the extent of pre-deduction income), the discount rate should be fairly large. For $r = 20$ percent, for instance, the condition above is satisfied for $n > 11$; i.e. for useful lives beyond eleven years, there is no net tax benefit in a stepped-up basis. Even for much shorter useful lives, the benefit is only a fraction of the capital gain; for example, with a tax rate of 46 percent, the net benefit is only 7.8 percent of G when the useful life is five years. For a lower interest rate, e.g. $r = 10$ percent, the benefit is only 14.1 percent of G, *ceteris paribus*.

The analysis above applies to either the corporate or the personal taxpayer but it probably understates the true tax advantage of a change in ownership because corporations can sometimes avoid immediate tax liability by structuring "stock-for-stock" deals. The overall net benefit is complex and clearly deserves further analysis. There is also one other wrinkle to consider: Dertouzous and Thorpe (1982) argue that estate taxes often "force" a sale because the heir has no cash. However, this argument can be criticized on the ground that an heir can borrow to pay the tax, pledging the inherited firm's assets as collateral, thus obviating the necessity of sale.

BIBLIOGRAPHY

Asquith, P. 1983: Merger bids, uncertainty, and stockholder returns. *Journal of Financial Economics*, 11, April, 51–83.

Asquith, P. and Kim, E. H. 1982: The impact of merger bids on the participating firm's security holders. *Journal of Finance*, 37, December, 1209–28.

Asquith, P., Bruner, R. F. and Mullins, D. W. Jr. 1983: The gains to bidding firms from merger. *Journal of Financial Economics*, 11, April, 121–39.

Bradley, M. 1980: Interfirm tender offers and the market for corporate control. *Journal of Business*, 53, October, 345–76.

Bradley, M. and Wakeman, L. M. 1983: The wealth effects of targeted share repurchases. *Journal of Financial Economics*, 11, April, 301–28.

Bradley, M., Desai, A. and Kim, E. H. 1982: Specialized resources and competition in the market for corporate control, unpublished Working Paper, University of Michigan, September.

Bradley, M., Desai A. and Kim, E. H. 1983: The rationale behind interfirm tender offers: information or synergy? *Journal of Financial Economics*, 11, April, 183–206.

Chung, K. S. and Weston, J. F. 1982: Diversification and mergers in a strategic long-range planning framework. In M. Keenan and L. I. White (eds) *Mergers and Acquisitions*, Lexington, MA: D.C. Heath, ch. 13.

Dennis, D. K. and McConnell, J. J. 1983: Corporate merger and security-holder returns: tests of the investment hypothesis, the incentive hypothesis, and the co-insurance hypothesis, unpublished paper, Texas A & M, or Purdue, August.

Dennis, D. K. and McConnell, J. J. 1986: Corporate mergers and security returns. *Journal of Financial Economics*, 16, June, 143–87.

Dertouzous, J. N. and Thorpe, K. E. 1982: Newspaper groups: economics of scale, tax laws, and merger incentives, Publication R-2878-SBS, Rand Corporation, June.

Dodd, P. 1980: Merger proposals, managerial discretion and stockholder wealth. *Journal of Financial Economics*, 8, June, 105–38.

Dodd, P. and Ruback, R. 1977: Tender offers and stockholder returns: an empirical analysis. *Journal of Financial Economics*, 5, December, 351–74.

Eckbo, B. E. 1983: Horizontal mergers, collusion, and stockholder wealth. *Journal of Financial Economics*, 11, April, 241–73.

Eger, C. E. 1983: An empirical test of the redistribution effect in pure exchange mergers. *Journal of Financial and Quantitative Analysis*, 18, December, 547–72.

Firth, M. 1980: Takeovers, shareholder returns and the theory of the firm. *Quarterly Journal of Economics*, March, 235–60.

Ginsburg, M. D. 1983: Taxing corporate acquisitions, *NYU Tax Law Review*, 38, 177–319.

Jensen, M. C. and Ruback, R. S. 1983: The market for corporate control. *Journal of Financial Economics*, 11, April, 5–50.

Kim, E. H. and McConnell, J. J. 1977: Corporate merger and the co-insurance of corporate debt. *Journal of Finance*, May, 349–63.

Lewellen, W. G. 1971: A pure financial rationale for the conglomerate merger. *Journal of Finance*, May, 521–37.

Malatesta, P. H. 1983: The wealth effect of merger activity and the objective functions of merging firms. *Journal of Financial Economics*, 11, April, 155–81.

Marshall, W. J., Yawitz, J. B. and Greenberg, E. 1984: Incentives for diversification and the structure of the conglomerate firm, Working Paper 12–80, National Bureau of Economic Research, February.

Miller, M. H. and Scholes, M. S. 1978: Dividends and taxes. *Journal of Financial Economics*, 6, December, 333–64.

Penrose, E. T. 1959: *The Theory of the Growth of the Firm*, Oxford: Blackwell.

Roll, R. 1986: The hubris hypothesis of corporate takeovers, (*Journal of Business*, 59, April, 197–216).

Settle, J. W., Petry, G. H. and Hsia, Chi-Cheng 1984: Synergy, diversification, and incentive effects of corporate merger on bondholder wealth: some evidence. *Journal of Financial Research*, Winter.

Shastri, K. 1983: The differential effects of mergers on corporate security values, unpublished paper, University of Pittsburgh, Graduate School of Business, November.

Stillman, R. S. 1980: Examining antitrust policy towards horizontal mergers, Ph.D. dissertation, University of California, Los Angeles.

Titman, S. 1984: The effect of capital structure on a firm's liquidation decision. *Journal of Financial Economics*, 13, March, 137–51.

Varaiya, V. 1985: A test of Roll's hubris hypothesis of corporate takeovers, Working Paper, SMU.

Warner, J. B. 1977: Bankruptcy costs: some evidence. *Journal of Finance*, 32, May, 337–47.

Weston, J. F. and Chung, K. S. 1983: Some aspects of merger theory. *Journal of the Midwest Finance Association*, 12, Annual, 1–33.

Williamson, O. E. 1964: *The Economics of Discretionary Behavior: Mangerial Objectives in a Theory of the Firm*, Englewood Cliffs, N.J.: Prentice Hall.

6

Management Buyouts of Publicly Traded Corporations

HARRY DeANGELO and LINDA DeANGELO

PREFACE
by HARRY DeANGELO

Fred Weston's most obvious influence on my career came from the major contribution he made to my Ph.D. training at U.C.L.A. during 1973–1977. I served as Fred's research assistant during my entire time in the program and, with the benefit of hindsight, I can see that he carefully tailored my work assignments to complement my academic interests and particular stage of development. For example, my first assignment was to read and critique one of Fred's books that dealt with – and gave me exposure to – basic issues in corporate finance. Shortly thereafter, he assigned me to work on an empirical project when I was showing a strong interest in econometrics. As my interests evolved toward theory, he had me read and discuss with him mainstream articles in the theory of corporate finance. And, after a substantial period of study, he supervised Larry Dann and myself as we jointly taught a Ph.D. theory seminar. I am convinced that these experiences – coupled with almost daily discussions with Fred, other faculty members, and fellow Ph.D. students – provided me with a strong foundation to conduct research in finance.

Research-oriented graduate study is particularly difficult because the student often encounters problems with no obvious solutions. Fred often helped me work around such roadblocks by listening to alternative possible solutions and by telling me that other (eventually successful) students had found themselves in similar situations. More generally, Fred was a constant source of encouragement and motivation – I still have a collection of brief notes of praise he sent me when he thought I had performed well. The

Partial financial support for this project was provided by the Managerial Economics Research Center of the University of Rochester.

harshest criticism I ever received from Fred was on my answer to a comprehensive exam question that dealt with a topic we had studied together in some detail. Fred gave my answer a score of nine (out of ten possible) and told me that, while my answer was quite good, someone – perhaps God – could have done a bit better! Clearly, Fred's approach to reward structures leans heavily toward carrots (and away from sticks) and, importantly, it makes one feel appreciated and work that much harder.

Fred's most subtle influence on my career came from the pure joy he communicated about mastering new ideas. I recall with great fondness the many hours we spent together in his office trying to figure out why a particular model worked or how a new set of findings fit with extant results. Through this study, I came to appreciate how much enjoyment there can be in the process of fitting together pieces of the puzzle, only to have the new understanding point you toward additional unanswered questions. An experience that I recently shared with Larry Dann underscores Fred's strong commitment to this process. Shortly after completing the first draft of a paper on takeover defenses, Larry and I received from Fred a long letter that advanced a number of sensible suggestions for the next revision together with a thorough and clear outline of what we had accomplished in the first draft. We were both in awe that someone at Fred's level of success and stage of career would still have such a strong interest in the process of learning to make a significant investment in providing us with a substantive critique of our working paper.

Finally, Fred's most important influence on my life has nothing to do with finance. Simply put, he is the kindest and most considerate individual I have ever met and he serves as an outstanding role model for the kind of person I would like to be.

INTRODUCTION

In 1980, Congoleum Corporation, an N.Y.S.E.-listed company with nearly $600 million in annual sales revenue, was acquired by a newly formed shell corporation in which Congoleum managers owned 16 percent of the common stock. The remaining stock in the new corporation was held by a small group of institutional investors and by the financial adviser that arranged the acquisition. Debt financing constituted 87 percent of the new corporation's total capitalization. Public stockholders received $38 per share cash and Congoleum was effectively transformed from a dispersed-ownership corporation into a privately held firm in which top management held a significant equity stake.

In 1983, Dan River Inc., a textile manufacturer that faced a hostile takeover bid by investor Carl Icahn, merged into a newly formed and closely held company. The equity securities of the new (acquiring) company were owned by Dan River management (25 percent), a Dan River Employee Stock Ownership Plan (70 percent), and the financial specialist that arranged the transaction (5 percent). Debt financing totaled 93 percent of the privately held firm's total capitalization, and the debt proceeds enabled the management group to outbid Carl Icahn and successfully acquire the shares owned by Dan River's public stockholders.

The Congoleum and Dan River transactions are examples of management buyouts of publicly traded corporations. Both transactions replaced dispersed (public) stock ownership with concentrated (private) ownership by an incumbent management group. In both cases, managers and a small group of third-party investors purchased all the publicly held common stock with funds obtained to a large degree by additional corporate borrowing. Management buyout transactions with third-party equity participants are commonly called leveraged buyouts (L.B.O.s) because of the substantial increase in corporate debt financing that they typically engender. In other buyouts, incumbent managers have sufficient financial resources to purchase the public stock interest without taking on nonmanagement equity partners and without materially increasing the level of corporate debt.

In this paper, we present an introduction to management buyouts of publicly traded corporations. Our goal is to provide a synthesis that clarifies the essential institutional features of these buyouts and that also identifies some potentially important economic considerations in the decision to go private. We begin by summarizing some general financial characteristics of 64 New York and American Stock Exchange listed corporations whose managers proposed a buyout of public stockholders during 1973–1982. The subsequent section discusses the basic characteristics of leveraged buyout financing arrangements and describes the role played by the L.B.O. specialist in these transactions. We then outline some potential trade-offs involved in managers' decision to acquire all shares held by public stockholders. The next section describes the constraints dictated by the current regulatory and judicial environment on incumbent managers' ability to buy out public stockholders. The final section provides some brief concluding observations.

CHARACTERISTICS OF PUBLIC CORPORATIONS
THAT GO PRIVATE: AN OVERVIEW

The past decade has witnessed a dramatic increase in the number of management buyouts of public corporations, as well as several important innovations in the transactional and financial structure of these acquisitions. By our count of transactions that were announced in *The Wall Street Journal* during 1973–1982, managers of 64 New York and American Stock Exchange listed firms revealed buyout proposals that were

Table 6.1   Characteristics of 64 New York and American Stock Exchange firms that proposed management buyouts during 1973–1982 and had filed a proxy statement for the proposed plan to go private by July 1983

	33 leveraged buyouts (with third-party equity participants) mean (median)	31 other buyouts (no third-party equity participants) mean (median)
1 Total revenues	366,099	151,376
($000s)	(204,390)	(60,947)
2 Total assets	232,791	191,411
($000s)	(87,993)	(52,052)
3 Market value of equity	90,477	42,832
($000s)	(60,202)	(7,539)
4 Number of firms listed on N.Y.S.E. and A.M.E.X. at time of buyout proposal (N.Y.S.E.:A.M.E.X.)	18:15	8:23
5 Book value of long term debt to total assets	0.169 (0.129)	0.193 (0.150)
6 Market value to net tangible book value of common stock	0.920 (0.860)	0.937 (0.730)
7 Managerial stock ownership in the public firm	24.5% (15.4%)	50.1% (51.7%)

sufficiently serious to have resulted in a proxy statement mailing to stockholders by mid-1983. All but four of these 64 proposed acquisitions were completed.[1] Eighteen buyouts were instigated in the first half of our sample period (1973–1977), while 46 buyouts were proposed during the second half of the period, which represents an increase of about 2½ times. This increase is largely attributable to a greater incidence of leveraged buyouts (which we define here and throughout the paper as buyouts that include third-party equity investors). For example, leveraged buyouts constituted nearly 60 percent of the sample transactions proposed during 1978–1982, versus only 33 percent during the prior five-year period. In 1982, which is the last year of our sample period, the sample contains 13 leveraged buyouts and only two buyouts that did not include third-party equity investors.

Table 6.1 summarizes company size, stock ownership, and financial leverage attributes of the 64 publicly traded firms in our sample of management buyouts. There are significant differences across public firms, depending on whether the privately held company would have equity participants other than current management. Accordingly, the table reports financial characteristics separately for the 33 leveraged buyouts and for the 31 other buyouts in the sample. By all size measures – total revenues, total assets, market value of equity – the public corporations whose managers proposed a leveraged buyout tend to be considerably larger than those whose managers sought to go private without third-party equity partners. This substantial size difference is also reflected in the public firms' exchange-listing – the leveraged buyout companies are more frequently listed on the New York than on the American Stock Exchange, whereas the opposite holds for the remaining sample companies.

The typical firm in each subsample employed moderate levels of financial leverage while a publicly traded corporation, with mean and median ratios of long-term debt to total assets that were less than 20 percent. However, pro forma financial statements contained in proxy disclosures reveal a significant planned increase in corporate borrowing (to an average 86 percent of total capitalization) for firms in the leveraged buyout subsample. Pro forma financial statements are infrequently included in proxy disclosures by companies that go private without third-party equity investors. Analysis of a limited sample of such disclosures revealed that managers of these companies typically planned only a small increase in corporate borrowing. Hence, another major difference between transactions involving third-party equityholders and the other buyouts is the material increase in corporate debt that tends to accompany the former transactions (and this empirical regularity explains why the label "leveraged buyout" is assigned to the former).

Managers who proposed a leveraged buyout typically owned a much smaller fraction of the common stock of the publicly traded corporation than did managers who proposed a buyout with no third-party equity participation. For the leveraged buyout subsample, managers owned an average 24.5 percent of the common stock in the public corporation (median 15.4 percent), which contrasts markedly with the average 50.1 percent stake (median 51.7 percent) held by managers of the remaining sample firms. The median is likely to be a better measure of pre-offer managerial ownership, since it is less sensitive to the inclusion of some early, small leveraged buyouts in which managers held a large fraction of the public company's equity. In any case, both the mean and median figures reflect a general tendency for management groups of the larger sample firms (i.e. those that undertook leveraged buyouts) to own smaller fractions of the publicly traded corporation's common stock.[2]

These company size and managerial stock ownership statistics suggest that limited managerial wealth may be an important determinant of whether a given management group proposes to go private via a leveraged or nonleveraged buyout. Specifically, the data suggest that leveraged buyouts tend to be undertaken when managers' personal resources are especially small relative to the size (value) of the public stock interest. In such cases, managers by themselves are unable (or unwilling) to buy all publicly held shares and, consequently, a closely held equity ownership structure can be attained only if managers take on equity partners and materially leverage the firm. By this interpretation, the leveraged buyout financing vehicle represents a contractual innovation which makes it possible to obtain the advantages of private ownership (discussed later in the paper) when limited managerial wealth would otherwise make it impossible or undesirable to go private.

LEVERAGED BUYOUT FINANCING ARRANGEMENTS

The transformation from public to private ownership via a leveraged buyout typically entails the creation of a complex ownership structure with several layers of debt and equity claims. These claims are owned to various degrees by incumbent managers, the buyout specialist that arranged the acquisition, banks, insurance companies, pension funds, and other private investors. The ownership structure of the newly private firm is designed both (1) to protect the interests of nonmanagement parties that have supplied capital to buy out public stockholders, and (2) to improve the incentives and hence performance of a management group that commonly retains the same individuals who operated the company while it was publicly traded. To illustrate the change in ownership structure effected through a leveraged buyout, we briefly describe the buyout of Norris Industries, an N.Y.S.E.-listed firm that went private in December 1981. The Norris transaction was arranged by Kohlberg, Kravis, Roberts & Co., a firm which played a key role in the development of the leveraged buyout as a financing vehicle and which today represents the most well-known leveraged buyout specialist.

Table 6.2 provides details of the capital structure of Norris Industries, first as a publicly traded company (column (1)), and then pro forma after it became a closely held corporation (column (2)). The most striking feature of Norris' capital structure data is the substantial increase in long term borrowing engendered by the management buyout. In absolute dollar terms, Norris' debt obligations increased by a factor of thirteen – from $23 million to $297 million – in the transition from public to private ownership. And when measured in relative terms, Norris' long term debt obligations increased from a conservative 7.7 percent of total assets under public ownership to a substantial 88.1 percent of total capitalization under private ownership. The immediate post-buyout debt ratio, while it clearly represents a significant increase in leverage, is not markedly different from the post-buyout debt ratio of 86 percent for the average leveraged buyout company in our sample.

Table 6.2   Capitalization of Norris Industries, Inc.

	(1) Norris as a public company ($000s)	(2) Pro forma following the leveraged buyout ($000s)
Long-term debt		
6.3–7.5% industrial revenue bonds due through 2004	22,990	22,990
Bank revolving credit loans	—	275,000
Senior bank notes due 1990	—	12,800
19.5% subordinated notes due through 1992	—	39,900
Total long-term debt	22,990	350,690
Shareholders' equity		
Common stock – Norris	5,090	—
Voting common stock – buyer	—	6,683
Nonvoting common stock – buyer	—	1,925
Additional paid in capital	8,528	38,732
Retained earnings	260,238	—
Total shareholders' equity	273,856	47,340
Total capitalization	296,846	398,030
Long-term debt as a percentage of total capitalization	7.7%	88.1%

Claimant group	Percentage of voting shares to be purchased at the closing	Fully diluted percentage of total voting stock[a]
Banks	– %	4.5%
Subordinated note purchasers	53.4	46.8
Affiliates of and investors associated with Kohlberg, Kravis & Roberts	40.6	38.5
Norris management	6.0	10.2

[a] Assumes exercise of all options and warrants outstanding at the closing date and expected to be granted after January 1, 1982, and the conversion of all nonvoting common stock into voting common stock.
Source: Proxy Statement dated November 11, 1981.

At least three complementary aspects of Norris' new ownership structure contributed to the corporation's ability to carry a substantially higher debt load as a private company. First, as discussed in more detail below, the new ownership structure gave managers a materially larger equity stake which, in turn, strengthened their incentives to effect profitable changes in corporate policy. Hence, lenders could rationally expect an increase in cash flows under private ownership which would provide better coverage – or a deeper equity cushion – for their debt claims. By this logic, the effective leverage engendered by the buyout is not as great as it appears on the surface – i.e. the 88.1 percent debt-to-assets ratio probably overstates the private company's effective leverage position because the total assets figure is unlikely to reflect the full value of Norris' equity after the buyout.

A second factor that helped protect the lenders' collateral position, and that thereby enabled the company to carry a substantially increased debt load, was the inclusion of numerous covenants (that constrained the company's future indebtedness, types of business activities, sale-leaseback transactions, future capital expenditures, etc.) in the $275 million bank revolving credit loans. These loans, which constituted most of Norris' new debt financing, also stipulated a mandatory schedule of principal reductions that would begin four years after the buyout. Under this schedule, complete repayment of the debt was required by the ninth year. In essence, the management group gave the lenders a contractual guarantee that reduction of corporate debt – and hence of the lenders' risk exposure – would be a primary managerial objective after the buyout. In other words, the substantial post-buyout debt level portrayed in table 6.2 does not represent a permanent capital structure for the private company. Rather, it represents a transitional policy which raised sufficient capital to buy out public stockholders, but which generated a level of debt that would intentionally be reduced over the intermediate term through, e.g., additional cash flows generated by the restructuring of corporate operations.

The lenders' position was also protected through their simultaneous ownership of residual claim securities issued by the newly private Norris. For example, the same banks that granted the revolving credit loans held the senior bank notes, and common stock warrants were issued in conjunction with those notes. If these warrants were exercised, the banks would own 4.5 percent of the equity. Holders of the $39.9 million of subordinated notes – the so-called "mezzanine" layer of financing – were also protected by equity ownership position. For Norris, the mezzanine layer of subordinated debt was held by institutional investors who also held 53.4 percent of the common stock after the buyout (46.8 percent of the equity on a fully diluted basis). This substantial equity ownership by lenders is consistent with the argument (advanced, for example, by Jensen and Meckling (1976)) that such ownership is designed to mitigate the incentives of other equityholders to undercut the collateral position of lenders through opportunistic adjustments in corporate asset or financial structure.

The remaining equity of the new Norris was held by the partners and affiliates of Kohlberg, Kravis, Roberts & Co. and by members of Norris management. These parties, respectively, acquired 40.6 percent and 6.0 percent of the common stock of the private company (38.5 percent and 10.2 percent on a fully diluted basis). Incumbent managers had owned less than 3/10 of 1 percent of the common stock of Norris prior to the buyout (less than 1.5 percent after the exercise of stock options). Hence, one effect of the leveraged buyout was to increase managers' percentage holdings of common stock by a factor of about 20 times (7 times on a fully diluted basis). The common stock held by management was restricted by stock subscription agreements that precluded or limited their right of transfer for five years after the date the transaction was closed. Such constraints on transfer effectively tie managers' personal wealth to the future profitability of the company. Accordingly, they give incumbent management stronger incentives to remain affiliated with the newly private corporation and to take actions that enhance its overall profitability.

We have described the details of the capital structure of Norris Industries because it is reasonably representative of the larger, more recent buyouts in our sample. It is, however, a bit misleading to speak of the representative buyout since different companies obviously have different borrowing capacities that depend, in principle, on earnings risk, asset securability, potential for managerial opportunism, etc. Moreover, the structure of leveraged buyout financing arrangements has evolved over time, as buyout specialists have adapted the details of these transactions to reflect new opportunities and experience from previous management buyouts. Two relatively recent innovations seem worth noting here – buyouts financed partially by an Employee Stock Ownership Plan (E.S.O.P.) and the accumulation by buyout specialists of equity pools that provide a ready source of funds to effect management buyouts.

E.S.O.P. financing is a technique that is usually associated with Kelso & Co., the firm that pioneered this approach. For example, in the 1983 Dan River buyout arranged by Kelso, 70 percent of the equity in the privately held company was purchased by the E.S.O.P. for a nominal cash payment and a $110 million note payable to Dan River. Simultaneously, Dan River took out a term loan which it planned to repay through a series of transactions with the E.S.O.P. that would effectively convert the principal on the term loan into a federal income tax deduction. As part of this agreement, Dan River promised to make a series of fully deductible future contributions to the E.S.O.P. on behalf of its employees. Each "cash" contribution is in essence a paper transaction that yields a tax shield, since each will be immediately returned to Dan River (as interest and *nontaxable* principal) to satisfy the E.S.O.P.'s obligation under its note payable to Dan River. Dan River will make actual cash payments to satisfy its interest and principal obligations under the term loan. (In the calculation of Dan River's future tax bills, interest payments under the term loan represent deductions that offset interest income from the E.S.O.P.'s note payable.) E.S.O.P. financing arrangements can be especially attractive to wealth-constrained managers because they provide substantial cash which can be used to buy out the public stockholders, and employees potentially benefit because they receive an equity interest in the firm with no immediate tax obligation.[3]

The second important development in buyout financing is the formation of equity pools by Kohlberg, Kravis, Roberts, & Co. (K.K.R.) and by other buyout specialists. These pools bring together large amounts of capital which the specialists can invest in the equity of buyouts they judge to be attractive. Pool investors are willing to accord substantial discretion to specialist firms because of their demonstrated success in previous leveraged buyouts. The formation of equity pools may help explain why substantially larger public companies have completed leveraged buyouts in recent years. (In 1982, for example, public stockholders received an average of $136.6 million in the leveraged buyouts in our sample for which the compensation was entirely cash. The average value of these later buyouts is considerably larger than the $14.5 million average payment to public stockholders in the three leveraged buyouts in our sample that were proposed in 1976.)

Leveraged buyout specialists (such as K.K.R.) perform two general functions in the buyout of a publicly traded corporation. Their first, and most visible role is to arrange the debt and equity financing necessary to purchase the common stock held by the public. A second, and ongoing role is to serve as financial adviser and director of the post-buyout private corporation. For example, the post-buyout board of directors of Norris Industries consisted of the chief executive officer of Norris, Messrs. Kohlberg, Kravis, and Roberts, and an associate of K.K.R. The buyout specialist's role here is the same as that of any corporate director, namely to monitor managers to ensure that they follow strategies which are in the best interests of stockholders. An evident advantage of the leveraged buyout ownership structure is that the specialist usually owns a large percentage of the stock and thus has a correspondingly strong incentive to monitor management diligently.

The reputation of a buyout specialist plays a key role in its ability to raise the financing necessary to effect a leveraged buyout. For example, substantial reliance on debt financing places lenders in a potentially risky situation and the reputation of the buyout specialist serves as a guarantee that the company's post-buyout investment and financing decisions will protect the lenders' interests. Since specialists are repeat players in the market for leveraged buyout financing, they have clear incentives to safeguard the interests of debtholders in their current buyouts. Such protection can be accomplished by the general post-buyout strategy of streamlining company operations to generate additional cash flows that will help reduce the amount of debt outstanding and, with it, the risk exposure of lenders. Should this strategy fail and the company encounter financial difficulties after the buyout, the specialist has an incentive to cooperate with lenders to restructure the firm (e.g. to alter the management team and/or to modify aspects of operating policy) so that lenders' interests are protected.

At any given time, a buyout specialist typically holds an equity stake in (and actively monitors the management of) a number of privately held companies. In the period following a particular buyout, the specialist's contribution to firm value is apparently attributable to an ability to ensure that management effects a profitable realignment of company operations. At some point in time, the operations of a given company will have largely been restructured to yield whatever increase in profitability is feasible. At this point, the buyout specialist has a corresponding incentive to sell its ownership interest in this firm in order to redeploy efforts and equity capital in a new buyout, where its incremental contribution to value will be greater. Specialists commonly say they plan to sell their equity interest in a given firm within 5–10 years following a buyout of public stockholders, with the precise horizon depending on the specific attributes of the company in question.

In any case, a firm's post-buyout equity ownership structure – like its immediate post-buyout debt level – is properly viewed as temporary or transitional. In other words, public corporations that go private via a leveraged buyout can typically expect (another) major restructuring of equity ownership some years after the management buyout. This restructuring can take a variety of forms. For example, third-party investors may sell their shares directly to management, or to the corporation or an E.S.O.P., leaving the firm wholly-owned by management (perhaps in partnership with the employees). Should managers be unwilling to purchase the shares held by third-party investors, or be unable to obtain the necessary financing, these investors might sell their shares to another group of outside investors. Alternatively, managers and third-party investors might agree to merge the privately held firm into another corporation, one that is either publicly traded or privately held. Yet another possibility is for third-party investors to dispose of their stock through a public offering which would, in effect, return the corporation to public ownership.

Three of the 64 firms in our sample, all of which went private via a leveraged buyout, have since returned to public ownership status. For example, N.I. Industries, the corporate successor to Norris Industries, which went private in December 1981, went public again in October 1983, and was subsequently acquired by Masco Corporation. In the Masco acquisition, K.K.R. and other insiders who controlled two-thirds of N.I.'s stock agreed to receive $20 per share, while they simultaneously negotiated a price of $22 per share for the shares held by the public. The Masco acquisition serves to illustrate the apparent importance of the L.B.O. specialist's reputation in these transactions. In particular, K.K.R.

apparently negotiated the premium for the minority stockholders so that the public would receive more than the $20 per share they had paid in the 1983 public stock offering. The long-term confidence of the public, who will undoubtedly be offered the opportunity to buy shares in future K.K.R. stock sales, was apparently more important to K.K.R. than the opportunity to earn a greater return on one particular transaction.

SOME CONSIDERATIONS IN THE DECISION TO GO PRIVATE[4]

One potential benefit of a management buyout is the expected increase in company profitability associated with the change to a new equity ownership structure that more closely links managers' personal rewards to their performance. Managers of a publicly-traded corporation divide the residual profits (net rewards) of managerial decisions with a dispersed group of public stockholders. Consequently, as Jensen and Meckling (1976) point out, managers have incentives to operate the enterprise in ways that generate perquisites (e.g. excess support staff and large expense accounts) or otherwise direct resources to themselves at the cost of some reduction in overall corporate profitability. The larger is the managers' holding of the firm's common stock – or, more precisely, their share of residual profits – the smaller is their incentive to sacrifice profitability to advance their narrow self-interest. For example, a larger equity stake gives managers stronger incentives to cut their support staff, to pare inventories, and to implement other improvements in operating policy. A buyout through which managers acquire 100 percent of the equity obviously increases their ownership stake and hence strengthens their incentives to operate the company efficiently.

Managers' profit-seeking incentives should also be strengthened by a leveraged buyout with third-party equity participants because managers' post-buyout equity percentage typically exceeds their holdings under public ownership. Moreover, since third-party equity investors represent a small group with a relatively large share in company profits, they are likely to monitor managers more closely than did dispersed stockholders under public ownership. Another reason to expect greater operating efficiency after a leveraged buyout is that (risk-averse) managers may find the private company's debt level to be uncomfortably high and thus may work to generate additional cash flows so that their personal portfolios can be returned to less risky (lower leverage) positions. Finally, the increased flexibility of a private company can enable it to adopt innovative compensation packages that tie an individual manager's income more closely to his or her personal productivity, but that would be unattractive for a public corporation (e.g. because they appear overly generous to managers and hence could engender public stockholder litigation).

A public corporation that goes private can avoid the costs associated with the dissemination of information about the company's past performance and future prospects to a large number of dispersed investors. For example, the firm can avoid the costs of printing and mailing financial reports, proxy statements, and other communications to public stockholders. It can also save the additional auditing, accounting, and legal fees necessary to satisfy S.E.C. reporting requirements that apply to publicly-traded firms. And some of these firms may enhance their competitive positions because managers no longer must disclose potentially sensitive financial information to the public, and hence to product market competitors. The cost savings from going private also include salaries and overheads for stockholder relations departments, as well as management time spent dealing with public stockholders, financial analysts, and the financial press. For some companies, the additional time available to top management may be the most valuable – albeit difficult to estimate – cost savings from going private.

Excluding management time, estimates of the direct costs of public ownership range from $75,000 to $200,000 per year for an average American Stock Exchange firm, and more should special problems arise. These cost figures are probably understated because they are based on estimates compiled by Borden (1974) over twelve years ago. Furthermore, the costs of public ownership can be significantly higher for the relatively large public corporations that have gone private in recent years since these companies typically have a greater number of stockholders, each of whom must be provided with financial reports, proxy statements, dividend checks, dividend tax reporting forms, etc. Estimates of the incremental (variable) cost necessary to service one additional public stockholder range from $5 to $25 per year, depending on firm characteristics. Importantly, all these cost figures understate the possible savings from going private, since the relevant cost for managerial decision making is the capitalized value of the stream of costs that could be avoided by going private.

Public companies whose managers own relatively little common stock also face another potential cost of public ownership – the potential disruption associated with a hostile takeover attempt. This factor seems to be empirically important in so far as fourteen (22 percent) of our 64 sample firms went private within one year of a hostile takeover attempt or an explicit threat thereof. Corporate profitability can suffer if managers spend a great deal of time (and other resources) defending against a hostile takeover. Moreover, the prospect of an unwanted takeover can make it more difficult to attract and retain competent managers and employees, who will be more reluctant to invest in firm-specific human capital if they perceive an especially high likelihood that a corporate control transfer will endanger their jobs. Finally, the threat of hostile takeover can detrimentally affect the company's operating performance if it induces managers to adjust investment and financing policy in ways that make the firm less attractive to potential hostile bidders, but that sacrifice overall profitability in the process. Whether such defensive actions are justified for public corporations is a controversial issue that is well beyond the scope of our inquiry. Our point is simply that, whether justified or not, these takeover defenses represent a potential (real resource) cost of public stock ownership and hence are a relevant consideration in the decision to effect a management buyout.

Like other corporate acquisitions, a management buyout can be attractive because the transaction itself generates additional corporate tax savings. Most obviously, a leveraged buyout can generate additional interest tax shields for as long as the incremental debt remains outstanding. Additionally, when properly structured to satisfy the requirements of the tax code, a buyout can generate a step-up in the basis of assets currently held by the publicly traded firm. The higher basis translates into greater future depreciation deductions and hence a lower corporate tax bill than would otherwise prevail.[5] (The future advantage of a stepped-up basis at the corporate level will be partially offset by the immediate tax consequences of capital gains realization for stockholders who sell their equity interest.) In any case, one would expect that a firm would, other things equal, be a more attractive buyout candidate if its assets have been depreciated substantially for tax purposes.

An important disadvantage of a management buyout is that the new ownership structure implies reduced access to the public equity market and the ready sources of capital and marketability it provides. For example, access to the public equity market can enable the firm to raise capital at more attractive terms because investors will be better able to diversify away the firm's unique risk and hence will accept a lower expected return on their stock investments. Moreover, for private firms, new investment is limited by (1) the availability of senior claim financing at acceptable terms, (2) the amount of funds generated by company operations, and (3) the ability and willingness of current stockholders to contribute equity capital. Hence, the post-buyout private corporation faces implied limits on new capital investment, with the corresponding prospect that managers may have to forego otherwise profitable projects so that the corporation can remain closely held.

Reduced marketability of the post-buyout corporation's common stock can also impose direct costs on managers, forcing them to hold personal portfolios that are poorly diversified or otherwise not well-suited to their own financial objectives. These costs of reduced marketability are relevant not only for the incumbent managers that initially take the firm private, but also for any managers hired in future periods. Moreover, to the extent that these costs impair the company's future ability to hire and retain qualified managers, they are relevant to the current decision to effect a management buyout. The reason is simply that the post-buyout private corporation will have to compensate managerial personnel on other dimensions (e.g. with higher salaries) if competitor firms that are publicly traded can offer a compensation package that better accommodates the preferences of individual managers, because, for example, it includes common stock claims that offer greater liquidity.

Finally, standard Fisherian analysis indicates that the absence of a ready market for a private company's stock makes it more difficult to resolve disagreements among stockholders over corporate policy issues. When they have access to a well-functioning capital market, all stockholders agree that value maximization is the optimal corporate policy. In essence, a well-functioning equity trading market harmonizes the interests of stockholders – those for whom a particular publicly traded company's risk profile or dividend policy is suboptimal can simply sell their shares and find an investment better suited to their preferences. Under private ownership, stockholders cannot readily sell their shares and, consequently, can dissipate resources in costly disagreements that arise because each stockholder wants corporate policy to be tailored to suit his or her specific consumption preferences. For example, stockholders who are especially averse to risk may want the company to operate with lower leverage and to select less risky investment projects (and are willing to sacrifice some expected profitability in the process) so that their personal investment portfolios are less risky.

The compatibility of prospective equityholders' individual preferences (for portfolio risk versus return, timing of cash distributions, liquidity of investment, etc.) can be an important consideration in the decision to effect a management buyout, since widely divergent personal objectives among prospective residual claimants reduce the attractiveness of private equity ownership. For example, different personal preferences for risk versus return can make managers reluctant to undertake a buyout if they forecast extensive disagreement about the private company's optimal set of risky projects. The compatibility issue is especially important in leveraged buyouts, not only because of heterogeneous risk–return preferences, but also because the investment horizons of outside equityholders are likely to differ from those of operating managers. As noted earlier, buyout specialists typically expect to sell their equity after 5–10 years and, while this horizon may suit the desires of managers near retirement age, it may well conflict with the objectives of managers in earlier stages of their careers.

In sum, the discussion in this section identifies the following eight factors as important considerations in the decision to effect a management buyout:

1 potential improvements in the incentives of the management group when a corporation becomes privately held;
2 savings in the transactions costs of disseminating information to a dispersed group of public stockholders;
3 potential improvements in a firm's competitive position because sensitive

information about company strategy need not be disclosed to product market rivals when the firm becomes privately held;

4 tax savings from additional interest tax shields and from an asset value "write-up" in a buyout transaction that is properly structured to satisfy the requirements of the tax code;

5 avoidance of the threat of hostile takeover which can prove costly because, for example, it makes managers and employees especially reluctant to invest in firm-specific human capital;

6 potential difficulties for a privately held firm to raise sufficient capital (from sources other than the public equity market) to finance otherwise profitable projects, should they arise in the future;

7 potential costs – such as greater difficulty in attracting competent managerial personnel – that can arise when managers' personal portfolios are poorly diversified or illiquid because of reduced share marketability under private ownership;

8 increased potential for costly disagreements among stockholders over corporate policy issues, which are more likely because company value (stockholder wealth) is insufficient to rank stockholder preferences absent a well-functioning trading market for the company's shares.

The foregoing analysis does not, by itself, enable one to determine whether a particular publicly traded firm will on balance find it economically attractive to go private. None the less, it does serve to identify some factors – each of which ultimately must be assessed empirically and weighed against one another on a case-by-case basis – that are relevant to the decision to effect a management buyout. Moreover, the decision to go private should reflect not only the company-specific tradeoffs identified here, but should also take into consideration some difficulties that are particular to the process of contracting for a return to private ownership status – a subject to which we next turn.

THE TRANSITION FROM PUBLIC TO PRIVATE OWNERSHIP

The transition from public to private ownership is complicated by the fact that a management buyout is a nonarm's length acquisition in which incumbent managers face a potential conflict between their own interests and those of the public stockholders. In terms of narrow self-interest, managers would prefer to acquire the publicly held stock at the lowest possible price. At the same time, they have a fiduciary obligation to negotiate fair compensation for the publicly held shares. This inherent conflict of interest tends to make public stockholders suspicious that a management buyout proposal represents a self-interested attempt by managers to acquire outsiders' shares at an unfairly low price, a suspicion that is reinforced because managers possess inside information about future firm profitability. The practical consequences are that (1) management buyouts generate a great deal of litigation by public stockholders who charge that the compensation offered by managers is "unfair," (2) these transactions are subject to special regulations promulgated by (and come under the close scrutiny of) the Securities and Exchange Commission, and (3) management groups apparently go to great lengths to structure a buyout transaction in ways that mitigate their conflict of interest and hence that reduce their potential exposure to legal and regulatory challenge.

Legal challenge to a management buyout could take two basic avenues during our sample period (1973–1982) for firms incorporated in Delaware which, of course, is the primary state of incorporation for publicly held firms. First, public stockholders could seek to enjoin the transaction itself on the grounds that it lacked a proper business purpose or that it was unfair. Alternatively, they could dissent to the acquisition and pursue their right to have the courts set the value of their stock under the appraisal statutes. The latter avenue will likely become more important due to the 1983 Delaware Supreme Court decision in *Weinberger* v. *UOP, Inc.* which held that, except in cases of fraud or misrepresentation, appraisal is the exclusive remedy available to dissenting stockholders.

The appraisal remedy provides public stockholders with an independent valuation of their shares, and thus reduces the potential for management to unilaterally dictate the terms of these nonarm's length acquisitions. Managers can either structure the buyout transaction to trigger statutory appraisal rights or they can provide them by contract as a means of assuring that public stockholders are not exploited by the acquisition. In our sample of 64 management buyouts, 48 transactions were structured in ways that triggered statutory appraisal rights, and 16 were not. In the latter 16 buyouts, managers of five firms voluntarily subjected the transaction to an appraisal proceeding, in the event that public stockholders objected to the proposed buyout terms. This observation would seem to suggest both that (1) appraisal rights provide sufficient net benefits for some firms (e.g. a credible guarantee against self-dealing) that managers find it in their interest to provide them, and (2) appraisal rights have some "teeth" to them, or one would expect managers of all sample firms to grant them, either by private contract or by structuring the transaction to trigger such rights under state law.

The Securities and Exchange Commission, which has evidenced concern about managerial conflicts of interest in going-private transactions since at least the mid-1970s, has promulgated special disclosure requirements for management buyouts. In 1975 and again in 1977, the S.E.C. proposed rules that were designed to curtail the perceived abuses engendered by these acquisitions. Rule 13e–3, the rule finally adopted in 1979, requires that managers state whether they believe the proposed transaction is fair or unfair to public stockholders, and provide a list of factors upon which that judgment is based. In essence, the S.E.C. requires managers to address three separate questions. First, who besides management approved the transaction – was it put to a separate vote of the public stockholders, and did it receive majority approval of the public corporation's outside directors? Second, did an independent party negotiate with management on behalf of the public stockholders? Finally, is the proposed compensation "fair" to public stockholders, not only in management's view, but in the opinion of one or more independent financial experts? In effect, these questions require managers to take a public position about the extent to which they have structured a buyout to mitigate their inherent conflict of interest.

As an empirical matter, managers who own a substantial fraction of the common stock almost unanimously ask the public stockholders to approve the acquisition by a separate vote. Such a managerial vote waiver becomes especially important when managers control sufficient voting stock to unilaterally approve the transaction under state statutes for arm's length acquisitions. Our sample of 64 management buyouts includes only three acquisitions in which managers held enough votes to approve the transaction and failed to cede veto power to the minority through the voting mechanism. All three proposals were initiated around 1975, and only two of these buyouts were successfully completed. Public corporations whose managers own only a trivial fraction of the common stock typically do not provide for a separate vote of the public stockholders because outsiders already have the ability to deny approval of the buyout, should they so desire. For example, the managers of Signode Corporation owned only about 0.1 percent of the common stock before their 1983 buyout proposal, and they did not structure the transaction to require separate approval of the public stockholders.

The buyout of Signode Corporation provides a good illustration of how management buyout negotiations are structured to minimize the potential for, and appearance of, managerial self-dealing. Merrill Lynch initially suggested the transaction to the senior management of Signode. The Signode board of directors appointed a Special Advisory Committee (of three outside directors and the Chairman of the Board, who had retired from active management) to consider the proposal. The Special Advisory Committee engaged Goldman Sachs as its financial adviser and Signode's legal counsel as its legal adviser. The Special Committee and its advisers received Merrill Lynch's offer and directed Goldman Sachs to negotiate an increase in the offer price. After the price was increased, the Committee recommended that Signode's board accept the revised offer. The revised offer was approved by Signode's board of directors, all of whom advised the company that they would vote their shares in favor of the merger. The proxy material for the buyout states that the terms of the merger were negotiated at arm's length between Merrill Lynch and the Special Advisory Committee. Goldman Sachs, in its capacity as independent financial expert, delivered a "fairness opinion" to the board which stated that the proposed transaction was fair, from a financial point of view, to the outside stockholders of Signode.

In virtually all management buyouts, the incumbent board of directors hires at least one – and sometimes two – investment banking firms to express independent opinions on the fairness of the transaction. The magnitude of the compensation managers offer to public stockholders, which typically includes a substantial premium above the pre-offer open market stock price, is obviously an important consideration in these independent assessments of the fairness of a management buyout. (DeAngelo *et al.* (1984a) document an average cash offer premium of about 56 percent above the market price that prevailed two months before the initial buyout proposal.) The investment banker's fairness opinion, moreover, does not simply "rubber-stamp" management's offer, at least in so far as bankers do sometimes express an opinion that a given offer price is unfair. In response to an adverse opinion, managers generally increase the offer price, and they often do so for other reasons as well, for example, to settle litigation brought by public stockholders. Twenty-six of the 64 firms in our sample (40.6 percent) raised the price they initially proposed to public stockholders, and none subsequently lowered it.

Despite the various precautions designed to protect public stockholders in management buyouts, these stockholders generally go to court in attempts to extract additional compensation for their shares. The courts consider several factors when evaluating whether the terms of a given transaction are fair from a financial perspective. For example, they compare the magnitude of the current offer premium to that offered in other, similar transactions. Investment bankers and other expert witnesses also typically generate independent estimates of fair value by capitalizing the firm's earnings at an average price-earnings multiple for comparable companies. (For our sample, the typical cash buyout involved per-share payment to public stockholders of about 10 or 11 times the previous year's per-share earnings.) They also consider and sometimes explicitly weigh other factors – such as the book value of equity or the firm's total asset value – in their assessment of whether the offer represents fair compensation for the publicly held shares.

Since accounting-based measures of value can influence the price managers must pay to take a firm private, managers have an evident incentive to exercise their discretion over reported accounting numbers to make the firm appear less valuable to outsiders. However, the available evidence indicates that managers do not systematically engage in such accounting manipulations.[6] The most plausible explanation for this finding is that, because going-private transactions are characterized by substantial inherent conflicts of interest between managers and outside stockholders, outsiders closely examine managers' accounting choices in the reporting periods prior to the buyout. Such close scrutiny, in turn, makes it more difficult for managers to selectively present accounting numbers that portray the firm in a less favorable light, and hence that lower the price they must pay for the publicly held shares. The evident consequence is that managers who propose a buyout must be able to justify the offer price not only in terms of the premiums paid in other acquisitions, but also in relation to their corporation's previously reported accounting income.

Another consideration in setting the offer price is the fact that a buyout proposal can implicitly reveal to other potential bidders that managers view the firm as an especially attractive acquisition candidate. And, if managers own less than a majority of the public firm's equity, a buyout proposal at a low price can generate a competing offer from another company. Hence, potential competition from outside bidders, like scrutiny by the courts and the S.E.C., helps ensure that public stockholders are compensated adequately for their shares. As an empirical matter, public stockholders do appear to gain significantly from the typical management buyout since, as noted above, they usually receive substantial premiums over the pre-offer market price. Moreover, stock prices generally increase dramatically when a buyout proposal is announced.[7] While a management buyout proposal is outstanding, the market price tends to remain somewhat below the offer price as a hedge against the possibility that the acquisition might not succeed (with an attendant fall in stock price). And when management buyout proposals are withdrawn, stock prices do tend to decrease significantly. All of this evidence suggests that the typical management buyout does not simply benefit corporate management, but also makes public stockholders better off.

SOME CONCLUDING OBSERVATIONS

This paper provided a descriptive analysis of management buyouts of publicly traded corporations, acquisitions through which dispersed public stock ownership is replaced by concentrated equity ownership by an incumbent management group. Our discussion emphasized various institutional features – such as the leveraged buyout financing vehicle and the role played therein by the L.B.O. specialist – that have emerged to facilitate the purchase by wealth-constrained managers of substantial amounts of equity owned by outside stockholders of publicly traded firms. We also outlined a variety of underlying economic considerations that, in principle, affect the decision to convert from a public to a private equity ownership structure. These considerations include, for example, the effect of the ownership structure change on managers' incentives to implement profitable policies, the value of any projects foregone because the company no longer has access to public equity capital, and some legal and regulatory obstacles designed to mitigate the managerial conflicts of interest inherent in these buyouts. The question of whether – or the extent to which – the factors outlined here represent important determinants of the choice between public and private ownership remains an interesting issue for future research.

NOTES

1 The statistics we quote here and throughout this article are based on the samples in DeAngelo (1986) and DeAngelo *et al.* (1984a). The sample of 64 buyouts described in this section is identical to that employed in the former study and differs from that of the latter study by (1) its coverage of two additional sample years (1981 and 1982), and (2) its restriction to proposals that were sufficiently serious to reach the proxy statement stage by mid-1983.
2 In the years following our 1973–82 sample period, an increasing number of very large public corporations have been taken private through leveraged buyouts. A reasonable conjecture is that a sample drawn from recent buyouts would exhibit a larger total equity value and a smaller management ownership percentage than the current sample.
3 Provisions in the Tax Reform Act of 1984 significantly increased the attractiveness of E.S.O.P. financing arrangements. For example, interest received on loans to an E.S.O.P. for the purpose of acquiring the employer's securities is now given a 50 percent exclusion from the gross income of the lender. Moreover, cash dividends on such securities now result in a special corporate deduction to the employer. These tax provisions increased the attractiveness of E.S.O.P. financing of leveraged buyouts and, as one would expect, the number of E.S.O.P. buyout proposals seems to have increased in response.
4 This section contains material that was initially developed in DeAngelo *et al.* (1984a; 1984b) and, in part, represents an elaboration and extension of that material.
5 Recently proposed changes in the tax law would severely curtail the tax benefits of a management buyout, as outlined in Collinson and Fitzsimmons (1986).
6 For presentation of the evidence and discussion of some forces that constrain managers' ability to engage in self-interested accounting manipulations before a management buyout, see DeAngelo (1986).
7 For more details on the premiums offered by managers and on the average share price reaction to these offers, see DeAngelo *et al.* (1984a; 1984b).

BIBLIOGRAPHY

Borden, A. 1974: Going private – old tort, new tort, or no tort? *New York University Law Review*, 49, 987–1042.
Collinson, D. S. and Fitzsimmons, J. D. 1986: Tax revision vs. takeovers. *The Wall Street Journal*, April 16, 32.
DeAngelo, H., DeAngelo, L. and Rice, E. M. 1984a: Going private: minority freezeouts and stockholder wealth. *Journal of Law and Economics*, October, 307–401.

DeAngelo, H., DeAngelo, L. and Rice, E. M. 1984b: Going private: the effects of a change in corporate ownership structure. *Midland Corporate Finance Journal*, Summer, 35–43.

DeAngelo, L. 1986: Accounting numbers as market valuation substitutes: a study of management buyouts of public stockholders. *The Accounting Review*, July, 400–20.

Jensen, M. C. and Meckling, W. H. 1976: Theory of the firm: managerial behavior, agency costs and ownership structure. *Journal of Financial Economics*, October, 305–60.

7

Corporate Spinoffs: Multiple Announcement and Ex-Date Abnormal Performance

THOMAS E. COPELAND,
EDUARDO F. LEMGRUBER,
and DAVID MAYERS

PREFACE

by THOMAS E. COPELAND and DAVID MAYERS

This paper relates to Fred's research in the merger and acquisition area. If there are benefits arising from merger, then it is logical to wonder whether there are also benefits from splitting up, as in a spinoff. Both are significant corporate restructuring events. And it is not surprising that there are, indeed, increases in shareholder wealth from both. In fact, our chapter (with Eduardo Lemgruber) shows that earlier papers on the topic have underestimated the value of completed spinoffs by as much as 50 percent.

Fred has been an inspiration to us throughout our careers at U.C.L.A. We have never known anyone as energetic and enthusiastic as he. He was instrumental in recruiting us, and has served as a mentor. In the days when summer support was virtually nonexistent, he took us on a visit to see Bernie Cantor. The result was funding by the Cantor–Fitzgerald Foundation which helped finance our research on portfolio performance, culminating in "The Value Line Enigma." It is a pleasure to work with Fred because he does not suffer from the senior colleague syndrome. All that counts for him is the discussion of ideas in the scientific tradition – an ideal which we try to emulate.

Mr Lemgruber is grateful for financial support received from the *CAPES*/Ministerio de Educacao, Brasil.

INTRODUCTION

A spinoff splits the assets of the corporation into two parts. Shareholders of the original company receive equity claims in the newly created entity. Thus, shareholders of the parent company find themselves to be owners of two companies after the spinoff. There are a variety of possible motivations for spinoffs. Some are involuntary, being mandated by court action. Others are intended to avoid regulatory constraints by separating a regulated subsidiary from an unregulated parent. Some spinoffs are taxable distributions to shareholders while others are not (and may even have tax benefits, e.g. the formation of real estate or oil royalty trusts). Additionally, the anergy hypothesis postulates that the value of the separated parts of the corporation will be greater than the whole because of improved managerial incentives when division managers are on their own, or because the market can better evaluate the separated parts of the firm.

Schipper and Smith (1983) find a statistically significant 2.84 percent abnormal return on the spinoff announcement date for 93 voluntary spinoffs between 1963 and 1981. They also find that the size of the announcement effect is positively related to the relative size of the entity being spun off, the average size of the spinoff being 19.7 percent of the original firm. Larger abnormal returns are found for the set of voluntary spinoffs which are motivated by regulation avoidance (5.07 percent versus 2.29 percent for the rest of the sample). Examples of the benefits of avoiding regulation are that labor contracts are not necessarily binding with the spunoff firm, that parent cash flows need no longer subsidize a regulated utility subsidary, and that multinationals which spinoff a foreign subsidiary can free the subsidiary of restrictions imposed by Congress. Hite and Owers (1983) find abnormal returns of 3.8 percent around the spinoff announcement date for a sample of 123 voluntary spinoffs by 116 firms between 1962 and 1981. They confirm the relationship between spinoff size and the announcement effect. Neither Schipper and Smith nor Hite and Owers find any evidence of abnormal returns for bondholders. Thus expropriation of bondholder wealth is apparently not a motivation for spinoffs.

The aforementioned spinoff studies examine the first public announcements of spinoffs using samples drawn from a list of completed spinoffs. Our study is based on two samples. The first, and smaller sample, is a sample of announced spinoffs that is constructed to have no post-selection bias. We find that 11 percent of the announced spinoffs are never completed. Given an informationally efficient market, the implication is that first announcements underestimate the full value of completed spinoffs. To capture the full effect, we study successive announcements and find significant positive abnormal returns. A second expanded sample, which is subject to post-selection bias, confirms the significance of successive announcements and allows us to estimate the full wealth effect of a completed spinoff. We also study ex-date effects and find significant positive abnormal performance on the ex-date as well. The ex-date abnormal performance is puzzling and we attempt (unsuccessfully) to explain it. Finally, our expanded sample is partitioned into taxable and non-taxable spinoffs, and we find a significant difference, but when we control for the relative size of the spunoff entity the difference vanishes.

The second part of the chapter describes our sample selection criteria, the third part outlines the empirical methodology, the fourth provides results, and the final part summarizes and concludes the chapter.

SAMPLE SELECTION CRITERIA

We collected two samples. The smaller (small sample) has no post-selection bias and was developed as follows. For the 1962–1981 calendar interval, the "Dividend News" section of the *Wall Street Journal* was examined for spinoff announcements by New York, American, and Over-the-Counter listed parent firms. This search yielded 156 spinoff notices. The *Wall Street Journal Index* was then consulted to be sure that the "Dividend News" section was actually the first announcement. For 65 cases the "Dividend News" proved to contain a second (or later) announcement. We concluded that 18 other notices were second announcements from the language used in the "Dividend News." Thus, our final sample is 73 first announcement plans by 70 different parent companies.[1] Of these only 65 were successfully completed.[2] Fully 11 percent of the first announcements were never completed. Other studies (Miles and Rosenfeld, 1983; Hite and Owers, 1983, 1984; Schipper and Smith, 1983) use only successfully completed spinoffs in their samples, hence, their first announcement results are affected by post-selection bias.

For our sample of 65 completed spinoffs, the ex-date was obtained from *Standard and Poor's Corporate Record*. Companies were excluded from our ex-date sample if daily returns for the parent corporation were not available for 310 trading days prior to the first announcement and 310 days after the ex-date, or if the market value of the spunoff firm's equity was not available. These conditions reduced our ex-date sample to 54 firms.

We also collected intermediate and last day announcement dates. The last announcement day is defined as the last day, after the initial announcement and prior to the ex-day, that the *Wall Street Journal* carried a notice mentioning any information about the spinoff plan. Intermediate announcement dates are those that fall between the initial and last announcements. For the small sample, 40 last announcements preceded the 54 ex-dates.

Table 7.1   Decile distribution of trading days (small sample) between the first
announcement, last announcement and ex-date

Decile	First announcement to ex-date	Last announcement to ex-date	First announcement to last
1	3.0– 10.4	1.0– 2.0	4.0– 8.5
2	10.5– 32.4	2.1– 3.0	8.6– 37.5
3	32.5– 41.6	3.1– 4.0	37.6– 73.0
4	41.7– 63.4	4.1– 6.0	73.1– 96.0
5	63.5–100.0	6.1– 7.0	96.1–114.5
6	100.1–122.8	7.1– 10.0	114.6–146.5
7	122.9–158.0	10.1– 14.0	146.6–164.5
8	158.1–194.4	14.1– 27.5	164.6–205.0
9	194.5–275.8	27.6– 35.5	205.1–305.5
10	275.9–572.0	35.6–107.0	305.6–565.0
No. of companies	54	40	40

Table 7.1 shows the decile distribution of trading days between the first announcement, last announcement and ex-date. The median time between the last announcement and the ex-date is only 6.5 trading days (the average was 21.7 days), while the median time between the first announcement and the ex-date is relatively long – 81 days, as is the median length of time between the first and last announcements – 105 days. The 14 companies which made only one announcement were expeditious in completing their announced spinoffs.

An expanded sample (large sample) of spinoffs was obtained by searching the *Standard and Poor's Annual Dividend Record*. This search yielded a list of all completed spinoffs by N.Y.S.E. and A.M.E.X. listed firms between 1962 and 1983 which we added to the small sample. After eliminating those with insufficient data, and those which did not have their first announcement in the *Wall Street Journal Index*, we were left with 191 firms. We were unable to find a first announcement for 3 firms in the sample of 191. Thus, we report results for 188 first announcements. Our ex-date search in the *Standard and Poor's Corporate Record* identified 160 ex-dates (three ex-dates have no corresponding first announcement). We also identified 127 last announcements preceding the ex-dates. This sample provides 3.5 times as many observations as the small sample, but it is subject to post-selection bias for first announcement analysis. Table 7.2 shows the decile distribution between the first announcement, last announcement and ex-date for all firms in the large sample.

As with the small sample, the median time between the last announcement and the ex-date is relatively short (29 days), while median time between

Table 7.2 Decile distribution of trading days (large sample) between the first announcement, last announcement and ex-date

Decile	First announcement to ex-date	Last announcement to ex-date	First announcement to last
1	1.0– 7.5	1.0– 4.5	1.0– 4.6
2	7.6– 13.5	4.6– 10.0	4.7– 21.5
3	13.6– 25.0	10.1– 15.0	21.6– 38.0
4	25.1– 44.5	15.1– 21.0	38.1– 61.0
5	44.6– 66.5	21.1– 37.0	61.1– 80.0
6	66.6– 97.5	37.1– 51.0	80.1– 97.0
7	97.6–111.0	51.1– 57.3	97.1–112.0
8	111.1–150.5	57.4– 67.5	112.1–154.5
9	150.6–233.5	67.6– 78.5	154.6–225.1
10	233.6–572.0	78.5–190.0	225.2–565.0
No. of companies	160	160	127

the first and last announcements (for those companies which had more than one announcement) is 70.6 days, and the median time between the first announcement and the ex-date is 81.8 days.

Table 7.3 shows the break-down of spinoff companies by their listing location, the year of the spinoff first announcement, and the year of the spinoff ex-date. As can be seen, from the small sample data, the frequency of spinoffs is similar across listing locations with some dominance being shown for N.Y.S.E. listed companies. There also does not appear to be any great degree of concentration or bunching of spinoffs in particular years – from the large sample data the distribution of announcement date totals is relatively uniform across time with some evidence of spinoffs being recently more popular.

METHODOLOGY

Our basic methodology is that of the standard event study as pioneered by Fama *et al.* (1969). Event dates are defined as day 0, with surrounding trading days numbered relative to the particular event date. Because *Wall Street Journal* announcements normally occur the day after news is made public, we include days 0 and +1 as the announcement interval for the first, intermediate and last announcements. The ex-date, however, is known in advance, and consequently, we use only day 0 as the relevant ex-date interval.

Table 7.3 Spinoff frequency by listing location and years for announcement and ex-dates

Year	Small sample data announcement date					Large sample data announcement date				
	N.Y.S.E.	A.M.E.X.	O.T.C.	Total	Ex-date Total	N.Y.S.E.	A.M.E.X.	O.T.C.	Total	Ex-date Total
1962	0	0	0	0	0	—	—	—	—	—
1963	0	0	0	0	0	2	2	0	4	3
1964	0	0	0	0	0	3	2	0	5	4
1965	1	0	0	1	1	3	2	0	5	5
1966	1	0	0	1	0	3	3	0	6	6
1967	0	1	0	1	1	4	5	0	9	6
1968	2	3	0	5	3	3	9	0	12	12
1969	1	1	0	2	2	4	14	0	18	16
1970	0	3	1	4	1	2	6	1	9	5
1971	1	0	2	3	0	2	5	2	9	6
1972	3	0	0	3	2	5	4	0	9	7
1973	3	2	1	6	2	5	3	1	9	6
1974	0	2	0	2	2	5	4	0	9	8
1975	3	1	1	5	4	4	2	1	7	6
1976	1	1	0	2	3	5	3	0	8	7
1977	2	2	1	5	2	7	4	1	12	8
1978	5	2	6	13	5	6	3	6	15	6
1979	2	1	5	8	10	8	4	5	17	14
1980	1	5	2	8	9	9	5	2	16	17
1981	3	0	1	4	7	10	1	1	12	16
1982	0	0	0	0	0	0	0	0	0	2
Total	29	24	20	73	54	90	81	20	191	160

One parent company changed from the O.T.C. to the N.Y.S.E. after the spinoff announcement but before the ex-date.

Time series of two-day stock returns were created for plus or minus 60 trading days around each announcement event. Daily returns were used for ex-date events. For those firms which had less than 60 days between the last announcement and the ex-date, the ex-date time series is truncated by excluding data prior to the second trading day after the last announcement date. This procedure eliminates any bias in the pre-ex-date residuals due to potentially significant last announcement returns.

Daily stock rates of return were retrieved from the University of Chicago, Center for Research in Security Prices (C.R.S.P.) Daily Returns File for N.Y.S.E. and A.M.E.X. listed firms, and the average of daily closing bid-ask prices were obtained from the *Standard and Poor's Daily Stock Price Record* to compute daily returns for O.T.C. traded stocks. Computed O.T.C. rates of return were corrected for all identified distributions (e.g. cash or stock dividends, stock splits, and spinoffs).

The ex-date rate of return for shareholders of the ith parent company is defined as

$$R_{i,0} = \frac{P_{i,0} + v_i}{P_{i,-1}} \tag{7.1}$$

where $P_{i,0}$ is the parent company stock price on the ex-date, $P_{i,-1}$ is the parent company stock price on the day prior to the ex-date, v_i is the value of the spinoff distribution in dollars per share, and

$$v_i = F_i[P_s] \tag{7.2}$$

where F_i is the number of shares of the new company distributed for each share of the parent and P_s is the ex-date price per share of the newly created company. Share ratios, F_i, were obtained from the *Capital Changes Reporter*.[3]

Abnormal returns for the ith company, $AR_{i,t}$, (also called residual or excess returns) are estimated by subtracting an estimated expected return, $E(R_{i,t})$, from the actual observed return, $R_{i,t}$.

$$AR_{i,t} = R_{i,t} - E[R_{i,t}] \tag{7.3}$$

Expected returns are estimated with a market model

$$E[R_{i,t}] = a_i + b_i[R_{m,t}] \tag{7.4}$$

estimated using out-of-period returns.[4] The benchmark interval -310 to -60 days before the first announcement was used for the first and last announcement events, and the benchmark interval $+61$ to $+310$ days after the ex-date was used for the ex-date event.[5]

Average abnormal returns for the equally-weighted portfolio of spinoffs are defined as

$$\text{AAR}_{p,t} = (1/N_i) \sum_{i=1}^{N_i} (\text{AR}_{i,t}) \tag{7.5}$$

where N_i is the number of securities in the sample at time t.

Cumulative average abnormal returns for a portfolio of firms to date D, CAAR(D), are calculated as

$$\text{CAAR}(D) = \sum_{t=d}^{D} \text{AAR}_{p,t} \tag{7.6}$$

where d is the beginning date for calculation of the CAAR, and D is the ending date for calculation of the CAAR.

To test the null hypothesis that the event date average abnormal returns are not significantly different from zero we employ a standard t-test. The t-statistic is

$$t = \frac{\text{AAR}_{p,t} - \text{AAR}_p}{\text{SE}_p} \tag{7.7}$$

where AAR_p and SE_p are the mean and standard deviation of average abnormal returns in the 120 days surrounding the event date. The standard error, SE_p, is calculated as

$$\text{SE}_p = [\ \frac{1}{59} \sum_{t=1}^{60} (\text{AAR}_{p,t} - \text{AAR}_p)^2]^{1/2}$$

using two-day rates of return. The t-statistic has 59 degrees of freedom.

EMPIRICAL RESULTS

The empirical results are divided into two parts. The first presents abnormal returns for announcement dates: the first announcement, the last announcement, and intermediate announcements. We also discuss ex-date effects and estimate the total abnormal return associated with a completed spinoff. In the second part we present evidence on the effect of the taxability of spinoff distributions on abnormal returns. This analysis includes our assessment of the effect of the size of the spinoff on abnormal returns.

Announcement and Ex-Date Effects

First announcement. Table 7.4 contains the time series of two-day average and cumulative average abnormal returns around the first announcement event for both of our samples. Figure 7.1 contains plots of the cumulative average abnormal returns. For the smaller sample, the two-day

Table 7.4 Two-day market model abnormal returns around the first announcement day, both samples

Relative date	Small sample				Large sample			
	A.A.R.	C.A.A.R.	%>0	No. of firms	A.A.R.	C.A.A.R.	%>0	No. of firms
−59	0.0019	0.0019	0.506	73	0.0027	0.0027	0.495	188
−49	−0.0027	0.0076	0.534	73	−0.0030	0.0012	0.420	188
−39	−0.0012	0.0305	0.466	73	−0.0008	0.0067	0.442	188
−29	0.0031	0.0264	0.507	73	−0.0026	−0.0013	0.404	188
−19	−0.0006	0.0360	0.452	73	0.0033	0.0016	0.473	188
−9	−0.0067	0.0413	0.397	73	0.0000	0.0015	0.431	188
−7	0.0005	0.0418	0.466	73	−0.0030	0.0111	0.426	188
−5	−0.0019	0.0398	0.397	73	0.0049	0.0160	0.473	188
−3	0.0053	0.0454	0.493	73	0.0063	0.0224	0.521	188
−1	0.0012	0.0466	0.480	73	0.0090	0.0316	0.516	188
1	0.0249	0.0726	0.630	73	0.0303	0.0629	0.617	188
3	0.0066	0.0797	0.616	73	0.0003	0.0632	0.479	188
5	−0.0015	0.0781	0.507	73	−0.0045	0.0584	0.436	188
7	−0.0080	0.0694	0.398	73	−0.0025	0.0557	0.394	188
9	0.0026	0.0721	0.480	73	−0.0033	0.0522	0.420	188
19	−0.0060	0.0825	0.411	73	−0.0020	0.0572	0.378	188
29	−0.0037	0.0612	0.411	73	−0.0021	0.0444	0.452	188
39	−0.0011	0.0519	0.493	73	0.0049	0.0465	0.516	188
49	0.0070	0.0782	0.486	72	0.0048	0.0565	0.489	188
59	0.0036	0.0864	0.514	72	−0.0001	0.0594	0.457	188

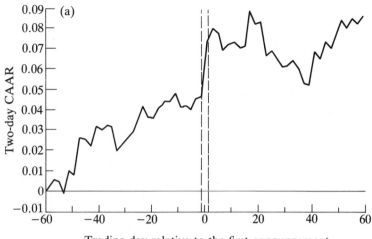

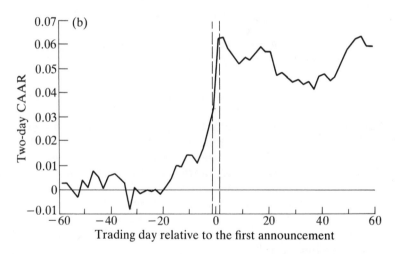

*Figure 7.1 Cumulative average abnormal returns around the first announcement:
(a) smaller sample (73 companies), (b) larger sample (188 companies)*

announcement return is 2.49 percent with a significant (0.001 level) *t*-value of 4.08.[6] 63 percent of the spinoffs have positive residuals on the announcement date. This is the largest percentage of positive residuals for any two-day period during the test period, and provides evidence that the results are not being driven by a few large outliers. For the larger sample of 188 spinoffs, the two-day average abnormal return in the first announcement period is 3.03 percent with a *t*-value of 7.46. Fully 61.7 percent of the residuals are positive on the announcement date. The patterns of cumulative abnormal returns (figure 7.1) are similar for

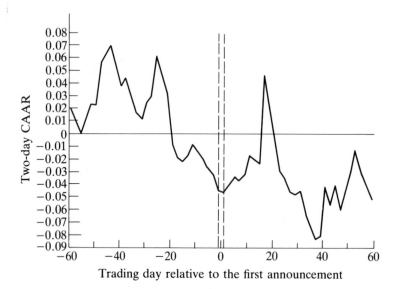

Figure 7.2　Cumulative average abnormal returns around the first announcement for the sample of eight parent companies that did not spin off

both samples. There is no apparent drift following the announcement date.

There is always the possibility that spinoff announcements may be coincident with other announcements. To eliminate this possibility, we removed, from our smaller sample, any firm which had another announcement of any type during the two-day announcement period. This reduces our small sample from 73 to a "clean" sample of 64.[7] The announcement period average abnormal return for the "clean" sample is essentially the same as that for the entire sample. The two-day announcement period average abnormal return is 2.60 percent with a significant *t*-value of 4.06.

A subsample of special interest is the eight firms which announced spinoffs that were never consummated. Their two-day average abnormal rate of return is an insignificant −0.15 percent. However, the average abnormal return on the cancellation of the spinoff, for the four firms for which we found cancellation announcements, is −5.9 percent. This number is also insignificantly different from zero (*t*-value of −1.22), but the power of the test is obviously low. Figure 7.2 presents a plot of the cumulative average abnormal returns around the spinoff announcement date for the eight firms that announced spinoffs but never completed them.

Last announcement. Our smaller sample, which has no post-selection bias, indicates that approximately 11 percent of announced spinoffs are never

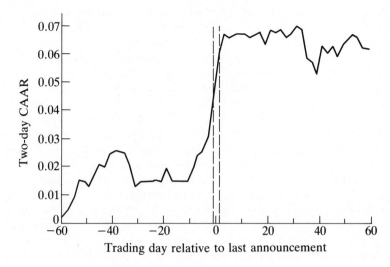

*Figure 7.3   Cumulative average abnormal returns around the last announcement
date for 127 events*

*Table 7.5   Two-day market model abnormal returns around the last announcement
date (larger sample)*

Relative date	A.A.R.	C.A.A.R.	% > 0	No. of firms
− 59	0.0028	0.0028	0.464	127
− 49	− 0.0019	0.0131	0.456	127
− 39	0.0012	0.0256	0.520	127
− 29	0.0016	0.0147	0.456	127
− 19	0.0048	0.0193	0.488	127
− 9	0.0037	0.0186	0.576	127
− 7	0.0056	0.0243	0.504	127
− 5	0.0014	0.0257	0.448	127
− 3	0.0040	0.0297	0.480	127
− 1	0.0014	0.0415	0.552	127
1	0.0162	0.0582	0.640	127
3	0.0085	0.0671	0.504	127
5	− 0.0012	0.0659	0.424	127
7	0.0010	0.0669	0.480	127
9	0.0001	0.0670	0.456	127
19	− 0.0039	0.0638	0.440	127
29	0.0014	0.0673	0.480	127
39	− 0.0034	0.0532	0.395	126
49	0.0039	0.0633	0.532	126
59	0.0002	0.0620	0.419	126

completed. Thus, not all information is contained in the first announcement. Not only is there a significant probability that the spinoff will never be completed, but also the first announcement does not usually provide information about the tax status of the spinoff, the timing of the ex-date, or the number of shares of the spinoff company to be received by each shareholder of record. In order to determine the total effect of completed spinoffs on shareholders' wealth, it is necessary to study the abnormal returns (if any) on all spinoff-related announcement dates.

Our analysis from this point utilizes the larger sample. There are 127 last announcements that we were able to identify in our original larger sample of 188. Table 7.5 contains the average abnormal returns and cumulative average abnormal returns around the last announcement date. Figure 7.3 plots the cumulative average returns. The two-day last announcement average abnormal return is a significant 1.62 percent (t-value of 4.24); 64 percent of the estimated two-day abnormal returns are positive. These results confirm our suspicion that there is significant favorable information in successive announcements.

*Intermediate announcements.*One company in our larger sample has a total of 13 spinoff announcements prior to the ex-date. Table 7.6 summarizes the intermediate announcement date abnormal returns and their statistical significance, for all announcement dates, starting with 188 first announcements. The first, second, and third announcements are all positive and significant at the 5 percent confidence level. This evidence confirms that the first announcement effects reported earlier in this chapter and

Table 7.6 Abnormal return summary for large sample (188 spinoff announcements) all announcement dates

Announcement	A.A.R.	No. of firms	t-value[a]	5% confidence
first	0.0303	188	5.33	1.96
2nd	0.0160	127	3.51	1.96
3rd	0.0178	71	2.88	1.96
4th	0.0081	37	1.21	1.96
5th	0.0133	16	0.90	2.13
6th	0.0210	8	2.05	2.36
7th	−0.0368	3	−2.93	4.30
8th	−0.0248	2	−2.52	12.71
9th	0.0049	1	—	—
10th	−0.0139	1	—	—
11th	−0.0319	1	—	—
12th	0.0294	1	—	—
13th	−0.0053	1	—	—
last	0.0176	188	4.03	1.96

[a] The t-values calculated are based on the cross-sectional standard errors.

Table 7.7 Two-day average abnormal returns for the ith announcement given that there were i announcements

No. of announ.	1st	2nd	3rd	4th	5th	6th	7th	8th	9th	10th	11th	12th	13th	All	No. of cos.
1	0.0204													0.0204	61
2	0.0194	0.0135												0.0329	56
3	0.0371	0.0255	0.0250											0.0876	34
4	0.0454	0.0028	0.0008	0.0185										0.0675	21
5	0.0839	0.0234	0.0140	-0.0199	0.0134									0.1148	8
6	0.0724	0.0476	0.0431	-0.0108	0.0179	0.0140								0.1842	5
7	0.0513	-0.0428	0.0011	0.0423	0.0261	0.0408	-0.0674							0.0514	1
8	0.0090	-0.0248	-0.0177	0.0266	-0.0190	0.0669	-0.0246	-0.0307						-0.0143	1
9	0	0	0	0	0	0	0	0						0	0
10	0	0	0	0	0	0	0	0						0	0
11	0	0	0	0	0	0	0	0						0	0
12	0	0	0	0	0	0	0	0						0	0
13	0.0645	-0.0830	0.0869	0.0569	0.0009	-0.0098	-0.0185	-0.0109	0.0049	-0.0139	-0.0319	0.0294	-0.0053	0.0702	1
Avg. rtn.	0.0303	0.0160	0.0178	0.0081	0.0133	0.0210	-0.0368	-0.0248							
No. of cos.	188	127	71	37	16	8	3	2							

by other authors, are an underestimate of the value increment to shareholders from completed spinoffs.

Table 7.7 shows the two-day abnormal returns for the ith announcement, given that there were only i announcements for the jth company. Reading across rows gives the average abnormal return for successive announcements. The first announcement usually has the largest effect, followed on average by successively smaller announcement effects. One of the surprises, at least for us, was that firms with fewer total announcements had smaller initial first announcement effects. Apparently firms with more announcements also had more significant spinoff events.[8] The next to last column in table 7.7 gives the sum of all announcement effects given that there were i announcements. This sum becomes progressively larger (at least until we run into samples of one company with 7, 8, and 13 announcements respectively). Later on, after having discussed ex-date effects, we shall be able to estimate the total return for those firms which completed spinoffs.

Ex-dates. Spinoffs are concluded on the ex-date when shares of the new firm are distributed to shareholders of record of the parent firm. No new information is released on the ex-date and its calendar date is known in advance. One would expect, therefore, that there would be no abnormal returns on the ex-date. However, our results reveal a significantly positive ex-date effect larger in magnitude than reported by Eades *et al.* (1984)

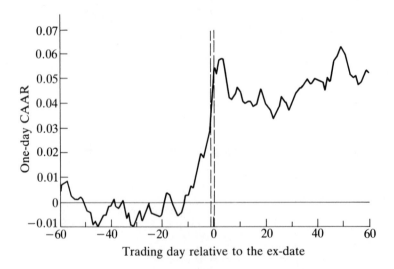

Figure 7.4 Cumulative average abnormal returns around the spinoff ex-date for 160 events

for dividend and split ex-days and similar in magnitude to the ex-days of stock dividends as reported by Grinblatt *et al.* (1984).

Table 7.8 and figure 7.4 contain the one-day market model abnormal ex-date returns. The sample consists of 160 events. In order to avoid contamination by earlier announcements, returns for each event are included in the ex-date portfolio beginning two days after the last announcement date.

The ex-date average abnormal return is a significant 2.19 percent with a *t*-value of 7.62 (59 degrees of freedom). As mentioned above, this effect is similar in magnitude to that reported by Grinblatt *et al.* for stock dividends, but the abnormal performance appears more concentrated than in their study where the day prior to the ex-date appears important. We have no good explanation for this ex-date effect. Ohlson and Penman (1985) observe significant increases in stock rate of return variances following stock split ex-dates. Subsequently, Cornell (1984) suggests that this might explain positive ex-date abnormal returns for stock splits because

Table 7.8   One-day average abnormal returns around the ex-date (larger sample)

Relative date	A.A.R.	C.A.A.R.	% > 0	No. of firms
− 59	0.0021	0.0021	0.539	78
− 49	− 0.0030	− 0.0036	0.427	89
− 39	0.0024	0.0013	0.474	95
− 29	0.0035	− 0.0030	0.481	104
− 19	0.0056	0.0013	0.478	113
− 9	0.0040	0.0068	0.449	132
− 7	0.0047	0.0107	0.471	136
− 5	0.0054	0.0201	0.503	144
− 4	− 0.0018	0.0183	0.473	146
− 3	0.0050	0.0234	0.571	149
− 2	0.0031	0.0265	0.480	152
− 1	0.0065	0.0332	0.566	156
0	0.0219	0.0559	0.688	160
1	− 0.0032	0.0524	0.406	160
2	0.0053	0.0580	0.475	160
3	0.0001	0.0582	0.450	160
4	− 0.0010	0.0571	0.456	160
5	− 0.0072	0.0495	0.388	160
7	− 0.0012	0.0412	0.413	160
9	0.0033	0.0469	0.494	160
19	− 0.0029	0.0429	0.406	160
29	− 0.0024	0.0371	0.463	160
39	0.0020	0.0502	0.525	160
49	0.0032	0.0632	0.506	160
59	0.0026	0.0536	0.453	160

of the greater value of the tax-timing option implicit in stock prices as suggested by Constantinides (1983). Spinoffs are capital distributions which reduce the price level of the parent corporation as do stock splits. We test for changes in rate of return variance of the parent corporations following spinoff ex-dates using the Ohlson and Penman (1985) methodology and our small sample. We find no evidence suggesting rate of return variance is higher following the spinoff ex-date.[9] Another tack that we follow is to test for the possibility that the ex-date effect is a bid-ask spread phenomenon.[10] We regress the ex-date abnormal returns on a proxy for the bid-ask spread. The proxy we use is the reciprocal of the parent company closing price on the day prior to the ex-date.[11] Our regression results indicate a positive coefficient on the reciprocal of price, consistent with the bid-ask spread hypothesis, but the *t*-statistic is 1.032 indicating only weak support.

At a minimum the ex-date evidence reinforces other similar evidence that implies ex-date returns for cash dividends should be interpreted with caution when trying to infer tax effects.

Total average abnormal returns. It is possible to estimate the total returns to shareholders of completed spinoffs, if we assume (1) that all relevant returns are captured during the announcement and spinoff periods, and (2) that the ex-date effects for the 28 firms in the announcement sample but not in the ex-date sample are similar to the 160 firms which were in the ex-date sample. Table 7.9 shows the sum of all announcement abnormal returns and the ex-date returns broken down by the number of announcements.

Table 7.9 Total returns for completed spinoffs organized by the number of announcements

Announ. no.	Sum of announ. rtns.	Ex-date rtn.	Total	No. of firms
1	0.0204	0.0124	0.0328	61
2	0.0329	0.0199	0.0528	56
3	0.0876	0.0192	0.0876	34
4	0.0675	0.0110	0.0785	21
5	0.1148	0.0187	0.1335	8
6	0.1842	0.0150	0.1992	5
7	0.0514	− 0.0546	− 0.0032	1
8	− 0.0143	0.0037	− 0.0106	1
9	0	0	0	0
10	0	0	0	0
11	0	0	0	0
12	0	0	0	0
13	0.0702	− 0.0384	0.0399	1

A weighted average of the total abnormal returns in column four of table 7.9 (where the weights are the number of firms) is an estimate of the expected total abnormal return for a firm which actually completes a spinoff. The estimated return is 7.30 percent. This number must be too high because only approximately 11 percent of announced spinoffs fail to be executed. Excluding the ex-date from the estimate (i.e. averaging the announcement returns), yields an estimated expected abnormal return for a firm which actually completes a spinoff of 5.02 percent.[12] This estimate seems more reasonable given the evidence we have presented concerning the expected number of noncompletions (11 percent) and the weak evidence on the wealth effect of an announcement to cancel a spinoff (-5.9 percent). There is also the possibility (as in Eades *et al.* (1985) and Kalay and Lowenstein (1985)) that the market's responses to the announcements of a spinoff are positively biased.

Although the first announcement return is an unbiased estimate of the effect of a spinoff announcement on shareholders' wealth, it is not a good estimate of the effect of a completed spinoff, because not all spinoffs are completed. Hence, earlier empirical studies have underestimated the wealth effect of a completed spinoff.

Taxability of Spinoff Distributions

The taxability of spinoffs is governed by section 355 of the 1954 Tax Code which covers the "Distribution of Stock and Securities of a Controlled Corporation."[13] Roughly speaking, spinoffs are nontaxable events for shareholders if the entity which was spunoff was (at least 50 percent) controlled by the parent corporation. However, it is taxed at the capital gains rate if the spinoff was a minority interest. Partial taxability is also possible. We divided our large sample into three groups: taxable spinoffs (where the event was at least 90 percent taxable), nontaxable spinoffs (where the event was less than 10 percent taxable), and a mixed group where the tax status was either undetermined, or between 10 and 90 percent. The average abnormal returns for the first announcements and

Table 7.10 Summary of announcement and ex-date effects for taxable and nontaxable spinoffs

	Taxable	Nontaxable	Mixed
First announcement			
A.A.R.	1.88%	3.76%	2.96%
t-value	1.99	10.07	3.68
No. of firms	62	101	25
Ex-date			
A.A.R.	0.72%	3.12%	1.93%
t-value	1.04	8.96	1.65
No. of firms	57	93	10

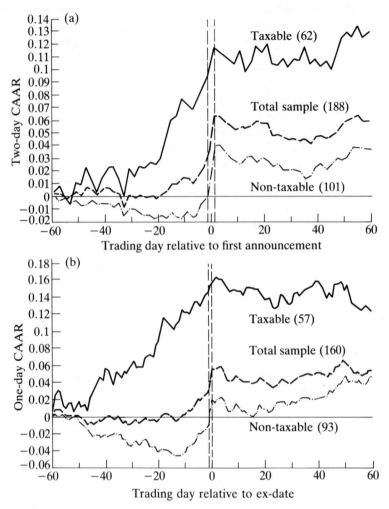

Figure 7.5   Cumulative average abnormal returns around the first announcement and ex-dates by tax status: (a) first announcement; (b) ex-date

the ex-dates are presented in table 7.10. Figure 7.5 presents plots of the cumulative average abnormal returns.

Average abnormal returns are not significant for taxable spinoffs either on the first announcement date or on the ex-date. Nontaxable spinoffs have significant average abnormal returns larger than those presented earlier as representative of the sample as a whole.[14] Thus, there appears to be a difference between taxable and nontaxable distributions. We also know from the work of Hite and Owers (1983) and Schipper and Smith (1983) that the relative size of the spunoff entity is important for the size

Table 7.11 Decile distribution of
spunoff company size as a percentage
of parent company size

Decile	Large sample
1	0.01– 1.10
2	1.11– 2.17
3	2.18– 3.39
4	3.40– 4.81
5	4.82– 6.62
6	6.63– 9.79
7	9.80–15.75
8	15.76–30.75
9	30.76–49.68
10	49.69–95.10

of the average abnormal returns. Before concluding that the tax status of the spinoff is important we must control for size.

The size of a spinoff is defined as the ratio of the market value of the new spinoff company on the ex-date to the market value of the parent company one day before the ex-date. Table 7.11 shows the decile distribution of size.

To test for the size relationship and also to test for the taxability relationship while controlling for size we estimate cross-sectional regressions. For the large sample, a linear regression of the two-day first announcement average abnormal returns against size confirms the results of Hite and Owers (1983) and Schipper and Smith (1983) (t-statistics in parentheses):

$$\text{Announcement AR} = 0.00665 + 0.14095 \text{ size} \quad r^2 = 0.18, \text{ df} = 155$$
$$(5.81) \quad\quad\quad\quad F = 33.80$$

Thus the announcement average abnormal return is significantly related to size. A regression of the one-day ex-date average abnormal returns on size shows similar, but weaker, results:

$$\text{Ex-date AR} = 0.01272 + 0.03576 \text{ size} \quad r^2 = 0.03; \text{ df} = 158$$
$$(1.92) \quad\quad\quad\quad F = 3.68$$

To control for size and test the taxability relationship we use multiple regressions with an added tax status dummy variable to determine the marginal effects of the tax status of the spinoff. The results for the two-day first announcement average abnormal returns are

$$AR = 0.00914 + 0.14734 \text{ size} - 0.00749 \text{ Tdummy} \qquad r^2 = 0.19, \text{ df} = 145$$
$$\qquad\qquad (5.56) \qquad\quad (-0.577) \qquad\qquad F = 16.77$$

where Tdummy is the tax status dummy variable which takes the value 1 if a spinoff is nontaxable and 0 if it is taxable. The results for the one-day ex-date abnormal returns are

$$AR = 0.00504 + 0.02557 \text{ size} + 0.01348 \text{ Tdummy} \qquad r^2 = 0.04, \text{ df} = 145$$
$$\qquad\qquad (1.25) \qquad\quad (1.35) \qquad\qquad\quad F = 2.71$$

These results show that the tax status of the spinoff does not have an important effect on either the announcement or ex-date abnormal returns once size is taken into account. Taxable spinoffs are also small spinoffs.

SUMMARY AND CONCLUSIONS

This chapter adds to the empirical literature on spinoffs in several ways. First, we select a sample of spinoff announcements which is not subject to post-selection bias, and find that 11 percent of announced spinoffs are never completed. Hence, the first announcement average abnormal return of 2.49 percent measured by our small sample is an unbiased estimate of the expected increase in shareholder wealth from a spinoff announcement. An expanded sample of completed spinoffs has a higher 3.03 percent average abnormal first announcement return.

Successive announcements carry relevant information regarding the probability of completion of the spinoff and the terms of the spinoff. The majority of our spinoffs have more than one announcement, and one firm had 13 announcements. These later spinoff announcements also indicate significant positive abnormal performance. Combining the first and following announcement abnormal returns we estimate the expected abnormal return for a completed spinoff as 5.02 percent. We also find that spinoff ex-date abnormal returns are significantly positive. We doubt that the ex-date performance reflects the revelation of new information. Thus we exclude the ex-date performance from our estimate of the expected abnormal return for a completed spinoff. We find weak evidence relating the ex-date performance to the bid-ask spread.

Confirming the results of other papers, we find that first announcement abnormal returns are positively related to the relative size of the spunoff entity. Similar, but weaker results, are reported for the ex-date abnormal returns. When spinoffs are partitioned by tax status, the abnormal returns for taxable spinoffs are not significantly different from zero, while those for the nontaxable partition are higher than the average for the entire sample. However, when the relative size of the spunoff entity is controlled for, the tax effect vanishes.

NOTES

1 Three companies attempted more than one spinoff. Two tried to spin off different assets at different times and (by coincidence) were unsuccessful in their first attempts. The other firm performed two distinct distributions of shares of the company's stock interest in the same subsidiary within a period of two years. No company tried to spin off the same assets more than one time.

2 Of the eight uncompleted spinoffs, four later announced that they were dropping their plan to spinoff, two merged prior to spinoff and two had no notice of completion in either the *Wall Street Journal Index* or in the *Capital Changes Reporter*.

3 This ratio was known at the time of the first announcement for some, but not all, spinoffs. The spinoff stock price, P_s, was available on the ex-date for 23 of the 54 ex-date companies in our small sample. For another 24, the information was found in the *Capital Changes Reporter*. For the remaining seven, the first available trading day price was used. Three had prices four trading days after the ex-date, and the others had prices available 7, 14, 21, and 22 trading days after the trading date. For our larger sample, which added only N.Y.S.E. and A.M.E.X. listed companies, we had ex-date information for 160 out of 188 first announcements.

4 All experiments were repeated using a mean return model in place of the market model. All results are qualitatively the same as the ones reported.

5 For the group of completed spinoffs in our smaller sample, the average beta increased by 8.66 percent from 1.107 during the pre-announcement benchmark period to 1.2029 during the post-announcement benchmark period; and the average alpha (see equation (7.5)) decreased by 204 percent from 0.000695 to -0.000726. Neither difference is statistically significant at the 5 percent level.

6 A cross-sectional t-statistic for the announcement period is also calculated. The value is 2.67 which is significant.

7 Simultaneous announcements included stock dividends (1), cash dividend announcements (2), dividend changes (1), earnings announcements (4), and a change in the board of directors (1).

8 As will be shown, the relative size of the spinoff is important for the size of the announcement abnormal return. Moreover, relative size and the number of announcements are positively correlated. The simple correlation between relative size and the number of announcements is 0.364.

9 There is still the possibility that the tax-timing option could be important for the ex-date effect. This follows because the sum of tax-timing options on the separate shareholdings will have greater value than a tax-timing option on the combined shares, as long as rates of return on the separate companies are less than perfectly correlated.

10 A larger than average number of buy orders on the ex-date would increase the probability that the observed closing price is executed at the ask price. This could account for a large unexpected average abnormal return on the ex-date. If buying activity returns to normal on the following day, or when it does, we should observe a lower than expected average abnormal return. We do observe a slight negative average abnormal return on the day after the ex-date.

11 Branch and Freed (1977) indicate that the reciprocal of price is a highly significant explanatory variable in their study of the bid-ask spreads of N.Y.S.E. and A.M.E.X. stocks.

12 Excluding the ex-date effect seems reasonable given that there should be little new information associated with the ex-date itself, as the ex-date is usually announced in advance. Moreover, there is a precedent for excluding the ex-date. Eades *et al.* (1985) find that excluding the ex-date from dividend announcement studies solves the sluggish price adjustment problem noted in earlier studies (e.g. Charest, 1978).

13 Our source is Part III of "Corporate Organization and Reorganizations" contained in the 1954 Tax Code. This was the code applicable for spinoffs during our entire sample period.

14 There can, of course, be a tax motivation for spinoffs, e.g. the creation of oil royalty trusts or real estate investment trusts. In an oil royalty trust, the oil company spins off some assets, giving its shareholders direct ownership in the property. The company still manages the wells and the acreage. But if the Internal Revenue Service approves (and it almost always does) the shareholders, because of their direct ownership, receive tax deductions usually reserved for corporations that own depleting assets. The shareholders also figure to receive bigger dividends than they got as shareholders in the company alone because a trust, unlike a corporation, doesn't pay income taxes. An oil royalty trust does not spend cash on drilling or exploration, and it stops paying dividends when the reserves are depleted. Real estate investment trusts usually occur in the later years of an income-producing property, after rapid depreciation write-offs have diminished. If a corporation has no other losses to shelter the real-estate income, it is better to spin off the assets to shareholders to avoid the double taxation of dividends. A spinoff can also avoid the payment of capital gains taxes and/or recapture of depreciation which might result from outright sale of the property.

BIBLIOGRAPHY

Allen, P. 1984: An economic analysis of voluntary corporate spinoffs. Working Paper, College of Business Administration, Louisiana State University, Baton Rouge, LA.

Branch, B. and Freed, W. 1977: Bid-asked spreads on the AMEX and the big board. *Journal of Finance*, March, 159–63.

Charest, G. 1978: Dividend information, stock returns, and market efficiency. *Journal of Financial Economics*, June/September, 297–330.

Choi, D. and Philippatos, G. 1983: On the economic rationale for corporate divestitures and spinoffs. Paper presented at the Western Finance Association Meetings.

Constantinides, G. 1983: Capital market equilibrium with personal tax. *Econometrica*, May, 611–36.

Cornell, B. 1984: Testing the tax-timing option theory: a new approach. Working Paper No. 5–84, Graduate School of Management, U.C.L.A.

Eades, K., Hess, P. and Kim, E. H. 1984: On interpreting security returns during the ex-dividend period. *Journal of Financial Economics*, March, 3–34.

Eades, K., Hess, P. and Kim, E. H. 1985: Market rationality and dividend announcements. *Journal of Financial Economics*, December, 581–604.

Fama, E., Fisher, L., Jensen, M. and Roll R. 1969: The adjustment of stock prices to new information. *International Economic Review*, February, 1–21.

Grinblatt, M., Masulis, R. and Titman, S. 1984: The valuation effects of stock splits and stock dividends. *Journal of Financial Economics*, December, 461–90.

Hite, G. and Owers, J. 1983: Security price reactions around corporate spin-off announcements. *Journal of Financial Economics*, December, 409–36.

Hite, G., Owers, J. and Rogers, R. 1984: The separation of real-estate operations by spin-off. *AREUEA Journal*, Fall, 318–32.

Kalay, A. and Lowenstein, U. 1985: Predictable events and excess returns: the case of dividend announcements. *Journal of Financial Economics*, September, 423–50.

Klein, A. 1982: Financial, informational, and empirical implications of major voluntary corporate divestitures. Working Paper, University of Chicago.

Linn, S. and Rozeff, M. 1984: The effects of voluntary spinoffs on stock prices: the anergy hypothesis. Working Paper, The College of Business Administration, The University of Iowa.

Miles, J. and Rosenfeld, J. 1983: The effect of voluntary spin-off announcements on shareholder wealth. *Journal of Finance*, December, 1597–1606.

Ohlson, J. and Penman, S. 1985: Volatility increases subsequent to stock splits: an empirical aberration. *Journal of Financial Economics*, June, 251–66.

Schipper, K. and Smith, A. 1983: Effects of recontracting on shareholder wealth: the case of voluntary spinoffs. *Journal of Financial Economics*, December.

8

Risk and the Optimal Debt Level

JEFFREY F. JAFFE
and RANDOLPH WESTERFIELD

PREFACE
by RANDOLPH WESTERFIELD

As a graduate student at U.C.L.A. in the late 1960s, nothing puzzled me more than the Modigliani–Miller (MM) hypothesis that a firm's value is not dependent upon its financial structure. I remember very clearly, in Fred Weston's graduate finance theory course, our attempts to think of new ways to test the MM hypothesis. These attempts followed Fred's own attempt ("A Test of Cost of Capital Proposition," Southern Economic Review, *October 1963).*

What has emerged since the early 1970s is the basic textbook theory that there is a static trade-off between the tax benefits and financial distress costs of debt. This trade-off produces an "optimal finance structure." Because of financial distress costs, it has been presumed that the riskier the firm's operating activities, the less debt the firm would employ (in the optimum).

Our chapter shows that this presumed negative relation between risk and debt does not always follow. In our comparative static analysis (under one set of assumptions) the opposite occurs. This is counterintuitive and the opposite of what most textbooks claim is the prediction of the static theory of financial structure.

INTRODUCTION

Perhaps one of the most widely held beliefs in finance is that the optimal amount of debt for a firm is negatively related to the variability of firm value. This basic argument is repeated in many recent textbooks. Two examples are[1] Brealey and Myers (1981): "With or without bankruptcy, financial distress is costly. Therefore firms try to limit the probability of distress. Risky firms, therefore, should borrow less than the average," (p. 374), and Levy and Sarnat (1983): "The more stable a firm's sales and earnings, the greater is the probability that it will be able to meet its fixed charges out of operating income. Hence we expect such a firm to finance a relatively larger proportion of its assets out of debt," (p. 347), "The degree to which leverage is employed depends inversely on the firm's underlying economic risk: the greater the economic risk the smaller will be the financial leverage ratio," (p. 902).

These beliefs appear to follow from the theory that, with corporate income taxes and corporate bankruptcy costs, there exists a value-maximizing amount of corporate debt for each firm. As a firm's variability increases, the probability of bankruptcy increases and the value-maximizing amount of debt decreases.

Recent empirical work is sparse and ambiguous on the relationship between debt and risk. Flath and Knoeber (1980) suggest no relationship between the variation in firm income, measured in several ways, and firm debt. Castanias (1983) reports that firms in lines of business that tend to have high failure rates also tend to have less debt in their capital structures.[2]

We present a simple model, incorporating both corporate taxes and bankruptcy costs, that shows that neither the face value of debt, the market value of debt, nor the ratio of the market value of debt to the market value of equity need be a negative function of the firm's variability. Indeed, under plausible assumptions, the face amount of debt and the market value of debt may be *increasing* functions of the variability of the firm.

THE BASIC MODEL

A simple two-date, one-firm model is employed. The firm's pre-tax value at date 1 is denoted by random variable, $\tilde{X}$, where $\tilde{X}$ is uniformly distributed between $\bar{X} - Q$ and $\bar{X} + Q$. The firm is valued at date 0.

As mentioned above, our results can be stated as counterexamples to previous thinking on the topic. We choose the uniform distribution since it is a particularly tractable and intuitive one (if a counterexample exists for one distribution, previous ideas cannot be correct for all distributions).

The value of the firm is

$$V = \frac{1}{2Q} \int_{\bar{X}-Q}^{B} (\tilde{X} - K) \, dX + \frac{1}{2Q} \int_{B}^{\bar{X}+Q} [B + (\tilde{X} - B)(1 - t)] \, dX \qquad (8.1)$$

where K is a lump-sum bankruptcy cost, t is the corporate tax rate, and B is the face amount of the firm's debt payments of principal and interest.[3] As with a number of other models, debt payments (and not just interest payments) are tax deductible. In setting up equation (8.1), we assume that all investors are risk neutral and the interest rate is zero. As should be clear, relaxation of any of these simplifying assumptions will not change our conclusions.

To determine the firm's optimal amount of debt, we set

$$\frac{dV}{dB} = \frac{1}{2Q}[-K+(\bar{X}+Q-B)t] = 0 \qquad (8.2)$$

implying that:[4]

$$B = \bar{X} - \frac{K}{t} + Q \qquad (8.3)$$

From equation (8.3), we have

$$\frac{dB}{dQ} = 1 \qquad (8.4)$$

The parameter, Q, is an unambiguous measure of variability in our uniform distribution. Thus, (8.4) implies that the face amount of the debt is an *increasing* function of the variability of the firm. This is a rather surprising result since, as mentioned earlier, much of the received literature has argued that debt is always a decreasing function of a firm's variability.

Though surprising, our result can be explained intuitively. The firm optimizes its level of debt by trading off two deadweight costs. Bankruptcy costs are incurred if $\tilde{X} < B$, while taxes are paid if $\tilde{X} > B$. However, these two costs are not symmetric. If $\tilde{X} < B$, the cost of bankruptcy, K, is *not* a function of the shortfall of cash flow, $B - \tilde{X}$. Conversely, if $\tilde{X} > B$, the corporate tax payment *is* a positive function of the firm's pre-tax cash flow, $\tilde{X} - B$.

This asymmetry can be seen in (8.2). Here , $K/2Q$ can be viewed as the firm's expected cost increase from raising its level of debt. The expected benefit increase, i.e. tax reduction, from raising its debt level is $[(\bar{X}+Q-B)t]/2Q$. A consequence of the asymmetry is that Q appears in the numerator of this marginal expected gain but not in the numerator of the marginal expected cost. In other words, a previously optimizing firm where Q rises unexpectedly now finds the marginal bankruptcy costs from a debt increase smaller than the marginal tax benefit. Thus, debt rises.[5]

Our main point above is that the face value of the debt is *always* positively related to firm variability in our model. It is worthwhile to examine the present value of the debt as well. For a given B, the debt of a firm is equal to

$$V_B = \frac{1}{2Q} \int_{\bar{X}-Q}^{B} (\tilde{X}-K) \, dX + \frac{1}{2Q} \int_{B}^{\bar{X}+Q} B \, dX \tag{8.5}$$

which simplifies to[6]

$$V_B = \bar{X} - K + \frac{\left[\dfrac{K^2}{t} - \dfrac{\left(\dfrac{K}{t}\right)^2}{2} \right]}{2Q} \tag{8.6}$$

From (8.6), it follows that

$$\frac{dV_B}{dQ} = \frac{K^2}{2(Qt)^2} \left(\frac{1}{2} - t \right) \tag{8.7}$$

Equation (8.7) is positive (negative) if $t < \frac{1}{2}$ ($t > \frac{1}{2}$). This result is in line with our earlier finding, though this latter result is not as strong. In our model, the face value of debt always rises with an increase in firm variability while the market value of debt rises only when the corporate tax rate is below 50 percent.[7]

The effect of variability on the market value of the firm can be determined from equation (8.1). After simplifying this equation, we have

$$\frac{dV}{dQ} = -\frac{K^2}{4tQ^2} \tag{8.8}$$

which is always negative. This result is, of course, not surprising. Given risk neutrality, variability should have no effect on firm value in a world with neither taxes nor bankruptcy costs. However, as mentioned earlier, these deadweight costs come into play in our model whenever the realization of $\tilde{X}$ differs from B. The firm must pay bankruptcy costs when $\tilde{X} < B$ and must pay taxes when $\tilde{X} > B$. Thus, the firm's deadweight losses are inversely related to its ability to forecast $\tilde{X}$. This forecasting ability is, in turn, inversely related to Q.

Because the market value of debt may be positively related to firm variability while the market value of the firm is always negatively related to variability in our model, the ratio of market value of debt to market value of equity may be positively related to variability.

AN EXTENSION

Our purpose has been to show that the firm's optimal amount of debt is not necessarily negatively related to the firm's variability. We presented an example where the face value of debt is always positively related to firm variability. In order to avoid leaving the reader with the impression that this relationship is always positive, we close our note by generalizing equation (8.1) slightly.

Some researchers (see Kraus and Litzenberger, 1973; Turnbull, 1979) have assumed that bankruptcy costs are unrelated to the extent of bankruptcy. Our model, where the sum of these costs is set equal to K, is in this spirit. Others have assumed that bankruptcy costs are positively related to the extent of the bankruptcy (see Kim, 1978; DeAngelo and Masulis, 1980). We employ both approaches in the following model:

$$V = \frac{1}{2Q} \int_{\bar{X}-Q}^{B} [\tilde{X} - K + (\tilde{X} - B)c] \, dX + \frac{1}{2Q} \int_{B}^{\bar{X}+Q} [B + (\tilde{X} - B)(1 - t)] \, dX \tag{8.9}$$

In (8.9), bankruptcy costs, $-K + (\tilde{X} - B)c$, are linearly related to the extent of the default.[8]

The firm's value is maximized when

$$\frac{dV}{dB} = -\frac{(B - \bar{X} + Q)c}{2Q} + \frac{(\bar{X} + Q - B)t}{2Q} - \frac{K}{2Q} = 0 \tag{8.10}$$

implying that

$$B = \bar{X} + Q \left(\frac{t - c}{t + c} \right) - \frac{K}{t + c} \tag{8.11}$$

Thus, B is positively related to Q whenever $t > c$.

This result can easily be explained intuitively.[9] We stated earlier that the unusual results for our previous model were caused by an asymmetry. There, when $\tilde{X} < B$, the cost of bankruptcy was not a function of the shortfall, $B - \tilde{X}$. Conversely, when $\tilde{X} > B$, the corporate tax payment was a function of pre-tax cash flow, $\tilde{X} - B$. This asymmetry is reduced, but not eliminated, in our new model. Here, both bankruptcy costs and corporate taxes are functions of the difference between $\tilde{X}$ and B. However, the functions are equal only when $c = t$.

This asymmetry can most easily be seen by examining (8.10) when $K = 0$. Here, $[(B - \bar{X} + Q)/2Q]c$, is the firm's expected bankruptcy cost increase from raising its debt, where $(B - \bar{X} + Q)/2Q$ is the probability of bankruptcy. The offsetting expected tax reduction from increasing debt is $[(\bar{X}+Q-B)/2Q]t$, where $(\bar{X}+Q-B)/2Q$ is the probability of no default. Thus, a previously optimizing firm where Q rises unexpectedly now finds the marginal bankruptcy costs from a debt increase less (greater) than the marginal tax benefit if $t>c\,(t<c)$.[10] The level of debt rises (falls) if $t>c\,(t<c)$.

CONCLUSIONS

Financial economists have generally asserted that, in a world of corporate taxes and bankruptcy costs, the debt level of a firm is negatively related to its risk. Surprisingly, our note shows that neither the face value of debt, the market value of debt, nor the ratio of market value of debt to market value of equity need be a negative function of a firm's variability.

NOTES

1   In addition, Van Horne (1982) argues that: "The greater and more stable the expected future cash flows of the firm, the greater the debt capacity of the company" (p. 285). Weston and Brigham (1982, p. 579) conclude that:

> Sales stability and debt ratios are directly related. With greater stability in sales and earnings, a firm can incur the fixed charges of debt with less risk than when its sales and earnings are subject to periodic declines; in the latter instance it will have difficulty meeting its obligations. The stability of the utility industry, combined with relatively favorable growth prospects, has resulted in high leverage ratios in that industry.

Carleton and Silberman (1977) posit: "the higher the variability is in rate of return on invested capital, *ceteris paribus*, the lower will be the degree of financial leverage adopted," (p. 811) and Ferri and Jones (1979, p. 632) state:

> The third hypothesis concerns the impact of business risk . . . on the firm's use of fixed payment funding. The variability of the firm's future income is the chief factor in *ex ante* estimates of its ability to meet fixed charges. As a result, one may anticipate that business risk is negatively correlated with the percentage of debt in a firm's financial structure.

2   Castanias (1983) presents a theoretical model that shows that under one set of assumptions the optimal book debt level and risk can be negatively related.
3   (a) This model is in the spirit of Kraus and Litzenberger (1973), who also use a lump-sum cost of bankruptcy and a flat corporate tax rate. However, they employ a discrete states of the world approach rather than a continuous probability distribution. It is also similar to Kim (1978), though he uses a more general function of bankruptcy cost.
    The trade-off between taxes and deadweight costs has been explored in more complex worlds. For example, in a paper critically examining the

Miller (1977) model, DeAngelo and Masulis (1980) consider the firm's capital structure decision in a world with bankruptcy costs and both corporate and personal taxes. Jensen and Meckling (1976) point out that bankruptcy costs are only a portion of the agency costs of debt. Brennan (1978) shows that an interior leverage optimum occurs in a world where tax credits are lost in bankruptcy, even when bankruptcy costs and other agency costs are ignored. Our simple model could be expanded to consider these complexities as well.
(b) Since both stockholders and bondholders have limited liability, $\bar{X} - K$ must be positive. One easy way to ensure this is to set $\bar{X}$ high enough so that $\bar{X} - Q \geqslant K$.
(c) Equation (8.1) is applicable only if $\bar{X} - Q \leqslant B \leqslant \bar{X} + Q$. If $B < \bar{X} + Q$, equation (8.1) should be rewritten as

$$V = B + \frac{1}{2Q} \int_{\bar{X}-Q}^{\bar{X}+Q} (\tilde{X} - B)(1 - t)\mathrm{d}X = \bar{X}(1 - t) + tB \qquad (8.1')$$

which is simply the Modigliani and Miller (1963) formula for riskless debt in a world with corporate taxes but no bankruptcy costs. However, (8.1') is of minimal importance in our framework since it can easily be shown that $\bar{X} - Q \leqslant B \leqslant \bar{X} + Q$ always holds if the firm optimizes its debt.
4   Equation (8.3) yields the optimal amount of debt only if $\bar{X} - Q \leqslant B \leqslant \bar{X} + Q$, i.e. $K/t \leqslant 2Q$. Equation (8.3) is not applicable under other conditions because equation (8.1) is not applicable under other conditions (*supra* note 3(a)). When $K/t > 2Q$, the optimal amount of debt is equal to $\bar{X} - Q$, not the lesser amount given in (8.3). That is, a firm would never set B below $\bar{X} - Q$ since debt is still completely riskless if $B = \bar{X} - Q$.
    We focus only on the case where $K/t \leqslant 2Q$, since results contradicting the previous literature occur here. We do not examine the case where $K/t > 2Q$ because it is an uninteresting, corner situation where only riskless debt is issued. We can, of course, choose our focus since K, t and Q are all exogenous.
5   It is best to assume that, while the debt *decision* had been made prior to the change in Q, no debt had actually been issued. Otherwise, the managers might consider maximizing stockholder wealth rather than firm wealth when changing the level of debt. The problems arising here have been discussed at length in Jensen and Meckling (1976), Galai and Masulis (1976), and Kim and McConnell (1977). We ignore this coinsurance problem since it is not germane to our discussion. After all, our purpose is to compare debt levels *across* firms when variability differs across them.
6   The reader may initially feel uneasy with (8.6) because $V_B \rightarrow \infty$ as $Q \rightarrow 0$. However, as pointed out in note 3(b) above, our preceding work is predicated on the assumption that $2Q > K/t$.
7   Currently, the maximum tax on corporate income is 46 percent.
8   As in our earlier model, we want stockholders and bondholders to have limited liability. This always occurs in (8.9) if $\bar{X} - Q - K + (X - Q - B)c \geqslant 0$. Using (8.11), we can rewrite this inequality as

$$\bar{X} - Q - Qc \left(\frac{2t}{t+c} \right) - \frac{t}{t+c} K \geqslant 0$$

Since t, K, c, and Q are exogenous parameters, one can always choose a value of $\bar{X}$ large enough to insure the inequality.
9 These results may be sensitive to the assumption of a uniform probability distribution since, with a similar model, Castanias (1983) finds a negative relationship between the face value of debt and risk using a normal distribution.
10 The direct cost of bankruptcy has been established by Warner (1977) to be 5.3 percent of the market value of a sample of railroads, estimated just before bankruptcy. See also note 3(c) above.

BIBLIOGRAPHY

Brealey, R. and Myers, S. 1981: *Principles of Corporate Finance*, New York: McGraw-Hill.
Brennan, M. 1978: Corporate income taxes, valuation, and the problem of optimal capital structure. *Journal of Business*, 103–14.
Carleton, W. and Silberman, I. 1977: Joint determination of rate of return and capital structure: an econometric analysis. *Journal of Finance*, 811–21.
Castanias, R. 1983: Bankruptcy risk and optimal capital structure. *Journal of Finance*, 1617–35.
Copeland, T. and Weston, J. 1983: *Finance Theory and Corporate Policy*, Reading, Mass.: Addison Wesley.
DeAngelo, H. and Masulis, R. 1980: Optimal capital structure under corporate and personal taxation. *Journal of Financial Economics*, 3–30.
Ferri, M. and Jones, W. 1979: Determinants of financial structure: a new methodological approach. *Journal of Finance*, 631–44.
Flath, D. and Knoeber, C. 1980: Taxes, failure costs, and optimal industry capital structure: an empirical test. *Journal of Finance*, 99–117.
Galai, D. and Masulis, R. 1976: The option pricing model and the risk factor of stock. *Journal of Financial Economics*, 53–82.
Jensen, M. and Meckling, W. 1976: Theory of the firm: managerial behavior, agency costs and ownership structure. *Journal of Financial Economics*, 305–60.
Kim, E. 1978: A mean variance theory of optimal capital structure and corporate debt capacity. *Journal of Finance*, 45–64.
Kim, E. and McConnell, J. 1977: Corporate mergers and the co-insurance of corporate debt. *Journal of Finance*, 349–65.
Kraus, A. and Litzenberger, R. 1973: A state-preference model of optimal financial leverage. *Journal of Finance*, 911–22.
Levy, H. and Sarnat, M. 1983: *Capital Investment and Financial Decisions*, Englewood Cliffs, N.J.: Prentice Hall.
Miller, M. 1977: Debt and taxes. *Journal of Finance*, 261–75.
Modigliani, F. and Miller, M. 1963: Corporate income taxes and the cost of capital: a correction. *American Economic Review*, 433–43.
Turnbull, S. 1979: Debt capacity. *Journal of Finance*, 931–40.
Van Horne, J. 1982: Financial management and policy. Englewood Cliffs, N.J.: Prentice Hall.
Warner, J. 1977: Bankruptcy costs: some evidence. *Journal of Finance*, 337–47.
Weston, J. and Brigham, E. 1982: Managerial Finance, Hinsdale, Ill: Dryden Press.

9

Product Quality, Nonsalvageable Capital Investment and the Cost of Financial Leverage

KWANG S. CHUNG and RICHARD L. SMITH II

PREFACE

The traditional corporate finance literature has been developed largely around the assumption that capital markets are perfect except for taxes. The firm, in that literature, is an abstraction, stripped of such intangible assets as reputation and with no distinction made between the profit objective of investors and the utility maximization objective of agent managers. Only recently has finance theory begun to incorporate information costs and informational asymmetries between investors, managers, and customers. With these developments the finance profession is gradually moving toward a comprehensive theory of the firm.

This chapter is part of this emerging new literature. The topic area is motivated by Professor Weston who, while recognizing and contributing immensely to the development and acceptance of the traditional literature, has steadfastly focused attention on the limitations to "real world" application of the "irrelevance" theorems around which that literature has grown. Professor Weston's research and teaching reflect his reluctance to accept the proposition that financial fine-tuning efforts of corporate managers are largely misdirected. His questioning posture stems from overlapping interests in corporate finance and the economics of industrial

Financial support for this research was provided by the Research Program in Competition and Business Policy, U.C.L.A. and by a Civitas Grant made through the Foundation for Research in Economic Education. The authors are grateful to C. Hsia, B. Klein, D. Levy, L. Senbet, J. Smith, and S. Titman and especially to an anonymous referee for helpful comments and suggestions.

organization, a field mainly concerned with the behavior of the firm in a real world setting. It is quite natural that many of Fred Weston's students are trained in both finance and industrial organization and that their research topics often tend to bridge the two disciplines.

In this chapter we depart from the traditional perfect markets approach to corporate finance and employ the theory of the firm to explain capital structure decisions. We observe that a firm is not merely a collection of tangible factors of production. Rather, we contend that firm reputation ("brandname capital") and firm-specific informational assets give rise to the creation of human and organizational capital beyond the value of tangible assets. The chapter recognizes an important role of capital structure in protecting the value of such reputational capital.

We employ the idea that adverse selection arises in markets where product quality is difficult to determine prior to purchase. This problem is solved by corporate investments in reputation. However, since bankruptcy can result in a loss of the value of reputational capital, the incentive of the firm (owners or managers) to honor its implicit commitment to maintain the expected quality of its product is influenced by capital structure. There are times when the owners of a levered firm would rationally want to cash in the firm's reputation (i.e. cheat customers by lowering product quality) whereas the owners of an unlevered firm would not. This occurs when the levered firm is in, or on the verge of, financial distress. The incentive of the levered firm to depreciate product quality can be anticipated by customers through such things as news of the possibility of impending bankruptcy so that the firm's reputation can be lost even before it could depreciate quality. This risk of loss of reputation is an indirect cost of financial leverage and will be reflected in the capital structure decision.

INTRODUCTION

The early theoretical studies of capital structure by Modigliani and Miller (1963; see also Barnea *et al.*, 1981) suggest that in the presence of a corporate income tax, extreme financial leverage is consistent with firm value maximization. Since the conclusion is at odds with actual capital structures of firms, subsequent research has focused on identifying costs associated with financial leverage.[1] Specifically, both direct and indirect costs of bankruptcy have been offered as explanations to resolve the discrepancy between theory and practice. However, evidence by Baxter (1967) and Warner (1977) suggests that, at least for large firms, the direct costs of bankruptcy are small and not sufficient to explain the actual choice of capital structure. Further, an important recent contribution by Haugen and Senbet (1978) has cast doubt on the relevance of indirect costs for explaining capital structure.[2] They contend that the so-called indirect costs of bankruptcy are actually costs of liquidation and "however large their expected value might be, these costs are independent of the capital structure decision." Their position turns on the point that the liquidation decision depends on a comparison of the liquidation value of corporate assets with their value in use. They argue that the relative values are independent of capital structure. Thus, they conclude that the liquidation decision is separate from bankruptcy and, consequently, that liquidation costs have no bearing on the capital structure decision.

The argument by Haugen and Senbet reflects the lack of theoretical treatment of the nature of so-called indirect costs of bankruptcy. In particular, the ability of corporate assets to generate cash flows from continued current use is assumed to be independent of bankruptcy. If this assumption does not hold, then the possibility of bankruptcy may cause liquidation. If so, the two will not be separable and consequently capital structure will reflect the indirect costs of bankruptcy.

The purpose of this chapter is to show that there are situations in which prospective bankruptcy may cause liquidation. We show further, that even if liquidation does not result, the firm will be unable to avoid a related decline in firm value during a period of financial distress. While the analysis may be construed as a "bankruptcy cost" argument, it will become clear that the cost arises not from bankruptcy *per se* but from the agency relationship between equityholders and debtholders.

To begin, we note that the quality of a firm's products is not perfectly observable prior to purchase and use by customers. If information about product quality cannot be acquired prior to purchase, Akerlof (1970) has shown that only the lowest quality level (minimum cost) will be supplied. Klein and Leffler (1981) suggest that in such cases a firm may signal its commitment to a higher level of quality by provision of a "bond" in the form of nonsalvageable investment. The bond functions as a quality guarantee to consumers if the cost to the firm of depreciating quality (the lost bond) exceeds the immediate gain from cheating.

In order to demonstrate nonseparability between potential bankruptcy and liquidation, we note that there may be future states of nature where the value of firm assets is altered such that the short-run gain from depreciating quality exceeds the value of nonsalvageable investment, inducing the firm to "cheat" consumers by attempting to depreciate quality. Such an action will drive the value of nonsalvageable assets (firm reputation) to zero and is appropriately construed as resulting in liquidation since all that remains is the liquidation value of salvageable assets.[3]

In the case of "imminent financial distress" due to a shift in asset value, consumers will anticipate quality depreciation and will reduce the price offered for the firm's product. This price decline prevents the firm from capturing the full gain from cheating and results in the loss of the nonsalvageable bonding investment.[4] We show that rational investors will anticipate the loss of firm value due to imminent bankruptcy and that the response to this is a cost of financial leverage. To complete the analysis, we demonstrate that a levered firm has the incentive to cheat in more states of nature than an identical unlevered firm. The resulting higher "costs of leverage" are impounded in current market values so that the value of a levered firm is less than that of an identical unlevered firm.[5]

Thus, our analysis identifies a clear and economically significant indirect cost of financial leverage (e.g. Altman, 1982) for which there has been no rigorous theoretical analysis. It also provides an explanation for the frequently observed phenomenon of firm market share declines which result from (rather than in) financial distress.[6]

In the second section, we review the theory that when product quality is costly to determine prior to purchase, nonsalvageable investments by the firm can provide quality assurance. We then proceed to develop the relationship between investment in nonsalvageable assets and firm value. The conditions under which an unlevered firm with a given investment in nonsalvageable assets will depreciate quality are examined in the subsequent section. The next section presents the main analysis of the paper. In this section, we introduce the capital structure decision and examine how this decision affects the value of nonsalvageable assets. The incurrence of costs of financial leverage is analyzed first for the case where bankruptcy is imminent and then for cases where it is not. The effect of the timing of public information on the financial condition of the firm is considered. We also examine the possibility of capital structure reorganization in this section to show that such reorganization cannot prevent the incurrence of leverage costs. The final section offers a brief summary of the analysis and implications of the paper.[7]

PRODUCT QUALITY, NONSALVAGEABLE ASSETS, AND FIRM VALUE

The value of any product or service depends on a vector of product characteristics such as performance, timely delivery, use related by-products or side effects, replacement policy, durability, and repair cost. In aggregate, the values of these characteristics may be thought of as describing the "quality" of the product. Since information about true product quality cannot be acquired by consumers without cost, there arises an informational asymmetry between the firm and its customers. Akerlof (1970) has demonstrated that in markets where consumers perceive products as undifferentiated (because the cost of differentiating is prohibitive), individual sellers can increase profitability by depreciating product quality and free-riding on the general reputation for quality in the industry. The net result of competition in such industries is to depress the overall level of quality.

The Problem of Quality Depreciation
and Nonsalvageable Investment

If product quality could be costlessly ascertained prior to purchase, the quality decision in one period would have no strategic implication for the future. In each period, the firm would choose product quality to maximize firm value without deception. In this context, a firm desiring to increase product quality could do so unilaterally.

The problem of quality depreciation arises because quality determination is not costless. To illustrate, assume that consumers are unable to determine quality prior to purchase and that one firm in an industry is able to costlessly misrepresent quality. Then starting from an initial (hypothetical) "noncheating" industry equilibrium, the value of this firm will be maximized by depreciating quality to save the cost of producing higher quality. With no strategic overlap of quality decisions (no firm reputation), the individual firm optimum would involve "cheating" in every period.

Assuming costless, undetectable quality depreciation to be feasible over some range to all firms, the industry would quickly converge to a Nash equilibrium where further unilateral quality depreciation would become unprofitable, either because it becomes less costly to detect or because depreciation itself becomes costly. This is the so-called "lemons problem" market failure, first formally discussed by Akerlof. Individual producers are unable to profitably supply anything but the lowest quality products.

For a single firm to profitably offer a higher level of quality than the industry average, consumers must first be able to distinguish that firm's product from others available in the market, and second, must be provided with an enforceable guarantee of quality. For consumers, identifiability is provided by a "brandname." But provision of the guarantee is more difficult, since settlement of claims for quality defects may involve large transaction costs and since claims cannot be easily enforced against bankrupt or liquidated firms. If enforceability were not feasible, then profit maximizing strategies would still involve quality depreciation. Thus, a mechanism to ensure against quality depreciation is needed.

The Role of Nonsalvageable Assets

Klein *et al.* (1978) describe the value of historical information about past levels of product quality as an appropriable quasi-rent accruing to the specialized assets of the firm. The consumer's original trial of a product is an investment in specialized information that can be appropriated by quality depreciation in a subsequent period. The consumer is induced to make the initial investment by evidence of the durability of resulting information in the form of a costlessly enforceable guarantee. Klein and Leffler (1981) suggest that existence of nonsalvageable investment signals that product quality will not be depreciated and provides the requisite enforceability.

The nature of the nonsalvageable investment is such that the firm expects to earn a normal return on the investment through repeat business with its customers provided it does not depreciate product quality, but less than a normal return otherwise. Customers perceive evidence of nonsalvageable investment as an implicit guarantee of product quality, and are willing to pay for it with a price premium sufficient to yield a normal return on the investment. The existence of nonsalvageable asset expenditures may thus be regarded as giving rise to firm reputations or "brandnames." Given such investments, consumers will not need to incur search costs by investing in information on quality through actual trial of the product. They simply observe whether the necessary nonsalvageable investments have been made. Nonsalvageable asset investments may take many forms. They will typically include advertising that does not provide specific product or price information, nonmarketable (or imperfectly marketable) information resulting from research and development, and firm-specific aspects of fixed asset investments and organizational capital development.

NONSALVAGEABLE INVESTMENT AND FIRM VALUE

In this section, we develop theoretical definitions of salvageable and nonsalvageable firm value. The purpose of the section is to demonstrate the relationship between potential gains from opportunistic quality depreciation, nonsalvageable investment and firm value in equilibrium. In subsequent analysis, we show that the value of nonsalvageable asset investment is diminished by financial leverage.

To facilitate the analysis, we assume throughout that the firm produces a single quality differentiated product. This differentiation results in the firm having its own demand curve given the decisions of other producers. The time horizon of the firm is assumed to be infinite. All investments are made at time zero with production and sale beginning at time one. For convenience, we define the period length to correspond to the time span required for customers to learn of quality depreciation by the firm. That is, the firm begins depreciating quality at time t, and this is known to all actual and potential customers at $t+1$. We assume no lag in information transfer among outsiders. Once one customer learns that quality has been depreciated, that information becomes immediately known to the market.[8] Thus, initially the market is assumed to be efficient with respect to information but imperfect with respect to product quality observability.[9]

Nonsalvageable investments are demanded by customers because of the firm's incentive to depreciate quality for opportunistic gain. Nonsalvageability (or product-specificity) of an asset is defined in the present study such that when the firm discontinues producing its current product (with all its quality attributes), the value of the nonsalvageable investment vanishes.[10] Subsequent to discovery of quality depreciation by the market, the firm is only able to sell products with quality that can be determined prior to purchase, unless it makes new investments in nonsalvageable assets.

All investments of the firm are assumed to be "fixed" and nondepreciating. Given this, production cost in each period depends on product quality and output quantity. There are no periodic fixed asset investments. Cost and demand conditions are expected to be static. With these assumptions, we can consider the amount of nonsalvageable investment that will be required by customers and the resulting firm value. In order to "guarantee" quality, the firm must make a nonsalvageable asset investment equal in present value to the one-time gain from cheating. This gain is given by

$$W = \int_{Q^m}^{Q^e} \frac{C_{(Q,\bar{X},A)}}{\partial Q} dQ \tag{9.1}$$

where Q is the product quality, Q^e is the quality level expected by customers, Q^m is the minimum quality level that can be supplied without detection by customers, $\bar{X}$ is the one-period equilibrium output when nonsalvageable expenditures are made and Q^e is expected, A is a measure of productive assets, and C is total cost as a function of Q, $\bar{X}$, and A. The right-hand side of equation (9.1) is simply cost savings from supplying Q^m rather than Q^e, say, at time 1. Quantity of time 1 sales is unchanged since depreciation is not detected by customers until time 2.[11] Customers are presumed to have some notion of the value of W; for convenience, they are assumed to know it with certainty.

The productive (variable cost reducing) asset investment of a firm may be partly product specific and nonsalvageable. If the nonsalvageable portion of productive assets is insufficient to guarantee product quality, then additional investment in nonsalvageable assets, E, will be necessary. We define the salvage value, V^s, of productive assets, A, owned by the firm as their highest alternative use value. Assuming that production of Q^m is the highest valued alternative use, then salvage value of A will be

$$V^s = \sum_t \frac{PX - C(Q^m, X, A)}{(1 + \Phi)^t} \tag{9.2}$$

where P is the (*ex-post*) equilibrium product price given Q^m, X is quantity sales given Q^m, and Φ is the discount rate. If productive assets are highly specialized to production of Q^e, then V^s will be small, as will the required investment in E (other things equal).

To determine the contribution of productive assets to the total nonsalvageable investment, we define their value in continued current use, V^c, as

$$V^c = \sum_t \frac{P^*X^* - C(Q^e, X^*, A)}{(1 + \Phi)^t} \tag{9.3}$$

This is a hypothetical firm value under the assumption that consumers can costlessly determine that Q^e is being produced. The variables P^* and X^* are equilibrium price and output values under this assumption. Thus, the contribution of productive assets to total nonsalvageable investment is $V^c - V^s$. It follows that the required level of nonsalvageable nonproductive[12] expenditures, E, is obtained as

$$E = W - V^c + V^s \tag{9.4}$$

It is clear from (9.4) that a firm which is able to substitute highly specialized productive assets for nonspecialized assets will require a smaller investment in E and will thus achieve profitable production at a lower price. The interesting cases of (9.4) are those for which the value of E is nonnegative ($E \geqslant 0$) or ($W \geqslant V^c - V^s$). Otherwise, the firm will not gain from quality depreciation because salvage value plus the one-time gain from depreciation ($V^s + W$) is already less than continued use value (V^c).

The market value of firm assets (both productive and nonproductive) in current use, V, is the value given that quality determination is costly. This value is obtained by substituting P and X, the resulting equilibrium product price and output, for P^* and X^*, in (9.3). By reorganizing the condition for a noncheating equilibrium given in equation (9.4), we can express firm value for the marginal firm in the industry as

$$V = V^c + E = V^s + W \tag{9.5}$$

The above discussion leads to the result that the current use value of nonsalvageable assets, V^n, is implicitly defined as the difference between the going-concern value of the firm and the salvage value of productive assets

$$V^n = V - V^s \tag{9.6}$$

Rationality on the part of firm owners would imply $V \geqslant V^s$ and thus $V^n \geqslant 0$. This inequality will hold in efficient markets for corporate assets. Consistent with this, we assume, henceforth, that whenever $V < V^s$, the firm immediately changes its line of business (i.e. liquidates) to increase the value of the firm to V^s. The notion of liquidation is theoretically appropriate and will be used throughout the chapter.

THE LIQUIDATION DECISION
AND QUALITY DEPRECIATION

The purpose of this section is to examine conditions under which quality depreciation and liquidation will occur. From (9.5) and (9.6), we note that in equilibrium the value of nonsalvageable assets, V^n, must equal the gain from cheating, W. As long as the future states result in $V^n > W$, the firm will continue to produce Q^e. But if $V^n < W$ holds, for example, due to unexpected changes in demand or cost conditions, the firm will have the incentive to depreciate quality to Q^m in order to collect W, and then liquidate. Thus, $V^n < W$ (or equivalently, $V < V^s + W$) is the disequilibrium condition which would induce the firm to optimally depreciate quality.

The firm's ability to capture W depends on when customers learn that $V^n < W$ holds. If customers receive the information at the same time as the firm, they will anticipate depreciation and will simply switch to products of other firms. In this case, the firm is unable to capture W but still experiences the decline in value to V^s as the value of nonsalvageable investment goes to zero. The inability of the firm to costlessly communicate its "honest intention not to cheat" is what causes the loss of V^n.

If customers receive the information with a lag relative to the firm, then a portion of W will be realized by the firm. With a full period lag, the entire W is captured. The case of information lag is considered further below.

The following section introduces the question of capital structure and examines how the condition for depreciation, $V^n < W$, is changed when a firm is financially levered. As we have argued above, customer reaction to the recognized incentive to cheat can bring about the loss of nonsalvageable asset value. It will be shown below that equityholders of a levered firm have the incentive to depreciate quality in a greater number of states than owners of an unlevered firm, and thus the expected value of the loss of V^n will increase with leverage.

CAPITAL STRUCTURE AND THE VALUE OF
NONSALVAGEABLE ASSETS

In this section, we consider how V and V^n change under alternative capital structures and profitability expectations of the firm. The discussion leads to a definition of what may be called "leverage costs" as the indirect costs that may cause (rather than result from) liquidation. Our analysis implies that sufficiently high levels of financial leverage may bring about the loss of V^n, at which point bankruptcy and liquidation (as we define it) result.

The relevancy of capital structure arises because equityholders, as agents of the debtholders in a levered firm, have the incentive to depreciate quality even in cases where $V^n > W$. Since this incentive may be anticipated by rational customers, the levered firm may simply experience the loss of V^n without realizing any gain from quality depreciation. Since the potential loss arises due to leverage, it is appropriately termed leverage cost rather than bankruptcy cost.

We retain the assumptions made in preceding sections. Also, it is convenient to focus initially on the case where $V^c \leqslant V^s$ so that the only nonsalvageable asset is the nonproductive investment in reputation, E. We assume for expositional simplicity that once a new state of nature obtains after the equilibrium as described above is established, this state is expected to hold indefinitely. Initially, all parties are assumed to learn of the new state at the same time, say time 1, prior to production and sale of the product. To focus on the cost of leverage, we (continue to) assume no corporate tax subsidy on interest payment, and no direct costs of bankruptcy.

We first consider the case of imminent bankruptcy (i.e. firm value less than contractual debt obligations) to show that the firm will lose the value of nonsalvageable assets. We then consider the cases where leverage costs are realized even when bankruptcy is not imminent. We then relax the assumption that all nonsalvageable assets are due to nonproductive investment in reputation. This enables us to derive the conditions under which informal reorganization, as described by Haugen and Senbet, will occur. As will be seen, even in this case, the firm will be unable to avoid incurring leverage costs.

In the following, subscripts L and U are used to denote the levered and unlevered firms, respectively. Also, the market values of equity and debt of the levered firm will be denoted as S and B, respectively, so that

$$V_L = V_L^n + V_L^s = S + B \tag{9.7}$$

Leverage Costs With Bankruptcy Imminent

Bulow and Shoven (1978) have derived the conditions for financial crisis or imminent bankruptcy with risk neutrality. Assuming that there is only one type of debt that will mature in the next period, the first of these conditions is stated as

$$V_L < rD + \frac{(1+r)D}{1+i} \tag{9.8}$$

where r is the coupon rate on bonds, i is the riskless discount rate, and D is the bond principal due in the next period. This condition merely states that the going concern value of the firm is less than the contractual value of liabilities. The second and third conditions given by Bulow and Shoven are that the value of the firm is insufficient to retire the debt immediately and that cash is insufficient to meet current debt claims.[13] Consider two firms that are identical except for their degrees of financial leverage and, in particular, have the same amount of E. Under the previously stated assumptions with respect to taxes and direct bankruptcy costs, it follows that $V_L = V_U$ and $V_L^n = V_U^n$.

When the first two bankruptcy conditions are in effect, equityholders are *expected* to receive nothing, regardless of whether bankruptcy occurs immediately or next period. Given these conditions, the firm cannot avoid bankruptcy by raising more cash either by borrowing or issuing equity shares and the third condition will force the firm into bankruptcy.[14] In the present study, bankruptcy is said to be imminent from the viewpoint of equityholders, debtholders or customers if the three conditions are known to be satisfied. Imminency is initially assumed to be learned by all parties at the same time. We will later consider the case of information lag on the part of customers.

Even though bankruptcy is imminent for the levered firm, the value of equity, S, should remain positive until bankruptcy. Once bankruptcy occurs, however, the share value of equity is guaranteed to be zero as implied by the second condition. It follows that the most profitable strategy for owners is to cash in on the reputation of the firm by not delivering anticipated quality.[15] This strategy would enable the firm to realize the one-time gain W as defined in (9.1).

The gain arising from quality depreciation is current earnings in accounting terminology. As such, it may be used to meet current debt obligations so that actual bankruptcy is delayed or avoided.[16] Alternatively, the gain may be distributed to equityholders as dividends prior to actual bankruptcy.[17] Once nonsalvageable capital has been depreciated by equityholders, firm value will decline to V_L^s.

The ability of debtholders to prevent quality depreciation, and the resulting loss of nonsalvageable asset value, will depend on the costs of recontracting and policing. These costs would appear to be significant for several reasons. First, the asset impairment rule in debt contracts cannot practically govern such intangible assets as firm reputation. Second, if quality depreciation were not difficult to detect, then equityholders would stand to gain very little from the strategy. Third, the imminence of bankruptcy may result rather quickly from an unanticipated event and, for reasons we address next, the size of gain from quality depreciation may depend on speed of implementation of the strategy. This immediacy adds to the cost of recontracting.

As alluded to above, the attempt by equityholders to collect W through quality depreciation will not be successful under the given assumption on the timing of information to customers. When customers perceive the imminent bankruptcy, they will anticipate the "last period" behavior of shareholders and thus terminate the implicit contract between the firm and themselves by basing demand on the presumption that quality level Q^m is being offered rather than Q^e. This expectation of quality depreciation alone is sufficient to occasion the loss of value of nonsalvageable brandname capital. Hence, the firm may not realize W and may only experience the loss of V_L^n. The resulting loss represents the indirect costs of bankruptcy crudely discussed in the literature. It is not a cost of liquidation, because the prospect of bankruptcy (and its perception by customers) has caused the cost. "Liquidation" (transfer of the productive assets to the production of other products) is only the result.

Cost of Capital and the Risk of Imminent Bankruptcy

The above conclusion on the indirect costs of bankruptcy can be easily demonstrated to imply a cost of capital disadvantage for financially levered firms. Suppose that $V_U^n > W$ is certain to hold in all future states so that an unlevered firm would never depreciate quality. In contrast, a levered firm facing imminent bankruptcy would be expected to depreciate quality, and would therefore lose V_U^n upon receipt of this information by customers. Thus, during imminent bankruptcy V_L falls below V_U due to the loss of nonsalvageable capital. If the probability of imminent bankruptcy in some future state is positive, the present value of the expected loss of V^n will be reflected in V_L when the leverage decision is announced. Thus, V_L will be less than V_U even when bankruptcy is not imminent. It follows that the cost of capital for the levered firm will be higher than that of the unlevered firm in the absence of offsetting benefits, such as a tax subsidy on the use of debt. An implication of the above is that the optimal debt to equity ratio will be an increasing function of the ratio of salvageable to nonsalvageable asset value. Thus, we conclude that the financial leverage decision of the firm cannot be separated from incurrence of the cost associated with loss of value of the investment in firm reputation due to bankruptcy.

It may be argued that the opportunity for "informal reorganization" of the firm's capital structure, as suggested by Haugen and Senbet (1978), will prevent such costs. However, such reorganization would have to be completed before customers received information of imminent bankruptcy. This is because termination of the implicit contract by customers occurs as soon as they receive the information, and this occasions the dissipation of brandname capital (reputation). Even though the firm starts reorganizing its capital structure upon receiving information of imminent bankruptcy, reorganization cannot be completed instantly. Any subsequent reorganization would require a new investment in E. A reorganization of capital structure *before* the occurrence of a state in which bankruptcy is known to be imminent, and before equityholders are expected to switch to the last period strategy, is equivalent to maintenance of a capital structure entailing a small probability of bankruptcy.

The Cost of Financial Leverage when Customers Learn of Imminent Bankruptcy with a Lag

So far, we have assumed that customers receive information on imminent bankruptcy at the same time as owners of the firm. By revising their quality expectation from Q^e to Q^m upon receiving the information, customers do not allow time for the firm (equityholders) to capture W. The firm simply loses V_L^n, the value of investment in reputation.

In reality, it is possible that customer information lags (or even leads) the firm. Since equityholders will not gain W unless they act prior to public arrival of bankruptcy information, they can be expected to disguise the firm's true condition for as long as possible. On the other hand, there are ongoing efforts in the market to forecast the firm's financial conditions (e.g. by the bond rating organizations, security analysts, etc.). It may be that these forecasts or even speculations may come even before (managers of) the firm fully realize its financial conditions in the immediate future).

If customers who are wary of quality depreciation terminate the relationship with the firm even before the firm realizes that bankruptcy is imminent, then again the indirect cost equals the full loss of V_L^n. However, if customers lag in information, then equityholders will realize at least part of W by successfully cheating customers. By the time customers receive information on the imminence of bankruptcy, the value of brandname capital will be lost. But since the firm will have realized some gain, not all of this loss in V_L^n represents the indirect cost of leverage. Only the difference between V_L^n and the gain from quality depreciation is such a cost. Note that the gain might be greater than the loss of V_L^n if $W > V_L^n$ ($= V_U^n$). But if this were the case, then nonlevered firms could do the same. Thus, in this regard, the levered firm has no advantage.

In summary, the levered firm will lose the entire value of non-salvageable, nonproductive investment if customers do not lag in information about financial distress. And even if customers lag in information, the firm may incur some loss in value. In no case does it have an advantage over the nonlevered firm. Assuming that each case has some nonzero probability, the expected value of leverage costs is positive. Thus, we conclude that the capital structure decision will reflect this expected cost.

Quality Depreciation and Leverage Costs when Bankruptcy is not Imminent

Starting with the assumption that the firm is already in financial crisis, we have argued that the firm's nonsalvageable investment is impaired due to customer recognition of the firm's inclination to depreciate anticipated quality. We now consider more general cases in which leverage costs are realized even when the risk of bankruptcy is not imminent. We continue to assume that customers receive information on the new state of nature at the same time as firm owners. Relaxation of this assumption can again be shown not to alter the conclusion.

Assume initially that $V_L = V_U$ and suppose that the bankruptcy conditions are not in effect so that

$$V_L^n + V_L^s > rD + \frac{(1+r)D}{1+i} \qquad (9.9)$$

Here we focus on the case of $V_U^n > W$, which implies that the unlevered firm has no incentive to supply deceptively low quality products. We want to derive the condition under which the levered firm can be expected to depreciate quality (while the unlevered firm would not) and accordingly will experience the loss of value of nonsalvageable assets. We consider two separate cases with respect to the level of contractual debt service:

$$V_L^s \geqslant rD + \frac{(1+r)D}{1+i} \qquad (9.10)$$

and

$$V_L^s < rD + \frac{(1+r)D}{1+i} \qquad (9.11)$$

Under (9.10) with salvage value sufficient to meet contractual debt service, the levered firm will not depreciate quality regardless of V_L^n. This result follows from the assumption that the current state of nature will prevail indefinitely. Thus, in this case, it holds that $B = rD = (1+r)D/(1+i)$ and therefore:

$$V_L^s \geqslant B \qquad (9.12)$$

which implies

$$V_L^n \leqslant S \qquad (9.13)$$

Under these conditions, it can be shown that the performance/nonperformance decision is independent of capital structure. Note that this is because the entire gain of W and loss of V_L^n due to cheating on quality will accrue to equityholders. Thus, a sufficient condition for nondepreciation by the levered firm is

$$S \geqslant W + V_L^s - B \quad \text{or} \quad S + B \geqslant W + V_L^s \tag{9.14}$$

Because of equation (9.7), the second inequality in (9.14) gives $V_L^n > W$. But this is exactly the noncheating condition for the unlevered firm. (Note that we started with the assumption that the two firm values are identical.) Therefore, as long as (9.12) is known to be satisfied, the value of nonsalvageable investment is not affected by leverage and thus the equality $V_L = V_U$ will be maintained. There is no leverage cost in this case where bankruptcy is not possible and the relevant Modigliani–Miller proposition holds.

Next, we assume that (9.11) instead of (9.10) is satisfied. Since we are assuming no direct costs of bankruptcy, it should be true that

$$V_L^s \leqslant B \tag{9.15}$$

This follows because bondholders will receive at least the salvage value of the firm. Expression (9.15) implies

$$V_L^n \geqslant S \tag{9.16}$$

Note that when (9.16) holds as a strict inequality, part of the loss of V_L^n in case of quality depreciation will be imposed on debtholders. It follows that there may be cases where shareholders are motivated to cheat. In particular, if equityholders can garner the full gain from quality depreciation then cheating by the levered firm will occur whenever the one-time gain is greater than the market value of equity without cheating. That is,

$$V_L^n > W > S \tag{9.17}$$

This condition cannot exist for an unlevered firm since V^n cannot exceed S except through the use of leverage.

As soon as equation (9.17) holds and is perceived by customers as being plausible, they will switch to competitors' products. The value of the firm will be decreased to V_L^s and liquidation (i.e. the production of a different product) will follow. The probabilities for the states of nature in which (9.17) holds will be reflected in the valuation of the firm when the firm is levered. This implies that the cost of capital for the firm is increased.

The significance of the cheating condition (9.17) is that, even when the firm is not facing bankruptcy as an immediate possibility, the incentive for the equityholders to behave opportunistically exists and this gives rise to leverage costs.[18] As has been noted above, the argument made by Haugen and Senbet (1978) that an informal reorganization of capital structure can solve the problem does not apply here. Such a reorganization would have to be done before the firm is thrown into the state where (9.17) holds, and this simply means that the firm should carry only a small amount of debt from the beginning. Hence, we conclude that as long as there are also advantages of using debt, firms will recognize the existence of an optimal capital structure.

Liquidation and Reorganization Decisions[19]

So far in this section, we have assumed that productive assets provide no contribution to the required nonsalvageable investment. With this assumption, upon the loss of the value of the nonsalvageable investment in E as caused by condition (9.17), firm value and the value of its debt will decrease to V_L^s and liquidation will result.

This result can be different if we change the assumption such that the value of the firm under the hypothetical, costless quality determination equilibrium, V^c, is greater than its salvage value. In this case, the productive assets are partly nonsalvageable. Customer anticipation of quality depreciation under (9.17) would still cause the value of the firm to decrease to V^s. However, if existing stocks and bonds can be retired at their market values, then equityholders, bondholders or outsiders in the capital market will want to reorganize the firm's capital structure and simultaneously make the nonsalvageable investment in E until the following equilibrium is obtained:

$$S > W$$

and

$$V_L = E + V_L^c = W + V_L^s$$

The second equality holds because of equation (9.4). The net change in V_L due to restoration of the value of the nonsalvageable portion of productive assets equals its equilibrium value minus its original (salvage) value and minus the new expenditure E, or

$$V_L - V_L^s - E = (E + V_L^c) - V_L^s - E = V^c - V^s$$

Therefore, as long as $V^c > V^s$, the reorganization of capital structure, as described by Haugen and Senbet (1978), will occur *and* the necessary investment in E will be made.[20] If debts cannot be retired at current market values, then it is in the interest of the bondholders to take over the firm and make the investment in E.

It is important to recognize that such reorganization does not imply the cost of leverage can be avoided. The cost in this case still equals E, the necessary expenditure on nonsalvageable assets to restore customer confidence.

CONCLUDING REMARKS

The chapter has shown that if firms use investments in nonsalvageable assets to signal product quality, the credibility of the signal is affected by the degree of financial leverage as the incentive to deliver expected quality is different between equityholders of a levered and an unlevered firm.

Public information on financial distress, coupled with the inability of the firm to restructure claims costlessly under such conditions, cause the loss of brandname (or reputation) capital acquired through investment in nonsalvageable assets. Consequently, liquidation may result because consumers cannot directly transact with the firm to prevent depreciation of product quality. The loss of value of the nonsalvageable assets is a cost of financial leverage and may represent an economically important "indirect cost of bankruptcy." The expected value of the loss will be reflected in the value of the levered firm and will, therefore, tend to militate against the use of debt.

The analysis presented here is rich in empirical and theoretical implications. With respect to corporate finance, it implies that firms or industries required to invest in nonsalvageable assets more than others will tend to use less debt.[21] More generally, it implies that firm behavior will reveal risk aversion. Diversification at the firm level may not be redundant even if investors could diversify costlessly in the capital market. Since the probability of occurrence of states in which bankruptcy will result can be decreased through diversification, the value of nonsalvageable asset investments may be better protected.[22] Thus, the analysis suggests that models of the firm which assume risk neutrality will not be appropriate for analyzing certain activities of firms.

Finally, we note that our analysis is similar to that of Myers (1977) in several respects. Both studies consider aspects of shareholder (agent) behavior which cause the value of a levered firm to decrease. Myers shows that shareholders of levered firms will have the incentive to pass up some growth opportunities with positive net present values. He concludes that firms with a large portion of value accounted for by growth opportunities will employ smaller amounts of debt. Our study shows that shareholders of levered firms have increased incentives to depreciate product quality in some states, thereby causing the value of nonsalvageable assets to vanish. This implies that financial leverage will be lower as the share of assets which are nonsalvageable increases. Financial leverage decisions of firms and their cross-sectional variation will be better explained once these indirect but potentially important costs of bankruptcy are included in the analysis.

NOTES

1 In more recent work, Miller (1977) has argued that the incentive of firms to fully exploit the tax advantage of financial leverage is mitigated by the investor's ability to achieve essentially the same benefit using homemade leverage. Despite this point, the wide variation in financial leverage decisions does not appear to be randomly distributed about the aggregate mean (or optimum), as would be implied by Miller's analysis. These deviations from the mean are still deserving of investigation. In a subsequent work, Modigliani (1982) points out that some implications of Miller are counterfactual and are due to the disregard of investors' risk aversion and diversification in Miller's framework.

2 The relationship of indirect bankruptcy costs to capital structure has been suggested in several studies, including those of Baxter (1967), Warner (1977) and also Jensen and Meckling (1976). An analysis of indirect bankruptcy costs associated with liquidation is provided by Scott (1976). However, in his analysis the distinction between liquidation and bankruptcy costs is blurred. He derives capital structure implications from the assumptions that bankruptcy always results in liquidation and that the secondary markets for firm assets are imperfect.

3 Implicit in our argument is the notion that the excess of going-concern value over liquidation value represents simply the value of nonsalvageable capital.

4 We do not mean to imply that the customers fully understand the connection between financial condition and quality depreciation (though some may), nor that they engage in sophisticated financial analysis of the firm prior to purchase. We require only that they (some of them) correctly perceive the empirical correlation between arrival of information that bankruptcy is imminent such as might appear in the *Wall Street Journal* and the increased probability of quality depreciation.

5 This assumes that creditors are unable to achieve an informal restructuring of claims prior to loss of the performance bond (i.e. the nonsalvageable investment). This inability may arise either from actual costs and delays of restructuring or from information lags. For a discussion relevant to this point, see White (1982).

6 An example is the case of International Harvester. See "Harvester's Financial Problems Test Loyalty of Customers and Dealers," *Wall Street Journal*, October 11, 1982, p. 23.

7 In a paper similar to the present study in some respects, Titman (1982) argues that firms will choose capital structures taking into account the costs of liquidation to be imposed on durable goods customers, employees, and others with firm-specific investments. Terms of trade (e.g. selling price) with these

parties are supposed to be improved because the capital structure ensures that the firm will liquidate only when liquidation is valuable after the costs to these parties are taken into account. Thus, in Titman's model, capital structure itself is used to guarantee (to some extent) an attribute of quality (service on durable goods). In contrast, our model assumes that quality guarantee is provided by nonsalvageable investment and it is this investment that gives rise to the cost of financial leverage. This cost affects the capital structure decision.

8   This assumption is made for convenience. The more realistic assumption of gradual dissemination of information or quality depreciation, though it is intuitively more clear, would unnecessarily complicate the analysis.

9   In reference to the semi-strong and strong forms of the efficient market hypothesis, we assume that the former is true but not the latter. The quality depreciation decision by the firm is inside information at the beginning of the period in which the firm cheats and becomes public only at the end of the period.

10 Nonsalvageability is therefore a concept which is stronger than the usual notion of firm specificity, which may not imply product specificity that is assigned to the nonsalvageable assets in this discussion.

11 The required investment in nonsalvageable investment at time 0 is W rather than the discounted (time 0) value of the R.H.S. of (9.1). This is because the product price premium absent depreciation will provide the firm a normal return on W and because (given the infinite life of the firm) the time 1 value of future premia still equals W.

12 These expenditures are nonproductive in the sense that they do not reduce the average variable cost of production, although they do serve as signals of quality to customers and thus command a product price premium.

13 These conditions can be stated algebraically as $V_L < rD + D$ and $C < rD$, where C is cash. Bulow and Shoven (1978) do not distinguish bankruptcy and liquidation, which is not appropriate for the present purpose. Thus, their second condition is modified; we use V_L rather than V_L^s, since it is assumed that $V_L \geqslant V_L^s$ always holds.

14 We assume that the firm is prohibited by indenture convenants from selling off or pledging its tangible assets to meet current debt obligations.

15 As previously noted, quality depreciation may take many forms: outright depreciation, lower level of service, etc. This behavior of the firm under the expectation of bankruptcy goes beyond the risk-taking behavior of equityholders to shift wealth from bondholders as discussed in the agency cost and option pricing literature (see, for example, Barnea *et al.*, 1981).

16 Avoiding bankruptcy by depreciation of nonsalvageable capital when it is otherwise imminent should be share value maximizing because, as demonstrated in the option pricing literature, the value of an expiring option (the common stock) is increased by extension of the expiration date. Upon expiration (bankruptcy) the option becomes valueless, but without immediate bankruptcy, owners may expect favorable random events affecting firm profitability.

17 As long as quality depreciation and default are not simultaneous, there are opportunities to garner the profit from quality depreciation. Me-first rules are not perfectly enforceable (Ang and Chua, 1980).

18 The objection may be raised that equityholders will be unable to engage in

deliberate quality depreciation because to do so would be contrary to the interest of firm managers and employees. The model can be easily extended to provide for this possibility.

First, employees of the firm will be indifferent to quality depreciation as long as their human capital is not product specific. Upon liquidation, the labor input will be converted (together with other physical assets) to production of one or more other products, including the reduced quality version of the current product.

Second, quality depreciation will not necessarily be known to employees early enough. Policies regarding replacement, research, delivery and input quality may be unobservable to employees or may be subject to so much cyclical or random variation that deliberate quality depreciation shifts will not be discernible. Frequently, quality depreciation is instantaneous, such as an abrupt termination of business in the face of prepaid but uncompleted contracts.

However, if employee skills are firm or product specific and if quality depreciation is detectable by employees, then it may be necessary to modify the condition under which quality depreciation will occur. We must consider two cases. In the first, if employee product-specific investments are not impaired in the process of expected quality depreciation (with or without imminent bankruptcy) and reorganization, then employees should again be indifferent to quality depreciation.

In the second, the value of employee product-specific investment may vanish in the process of quality depreciation. Then it may be necessary for owners to compensate employees. This implies that the conditions for quality depreciation must be modified. Imminent bankruptcy does not automatically imply quality depreciation. The gain from depreciation, W, must be greater than the required compensation to employees. Condition (9.17) derived under no imminent bankruptcy has to be modified as follows:

$$V_L^n > W > S + S'$$

where S' is the present value of employee compensation for their product-specific investments.

19 It should be recalled that liquidation here simply means discontinuation of the production of the current product with all its quality attributes. If the firm chooses to produce the product with Q^m, i.e. with a level of quality lower than before, this qualifies as liquidation in the present context. Similarly, reorganization here implies the firm's return to the production of the old product with its original high quality, in addition to its usual implication for the ownership and capital structure changes.

20 Thus, for example, the "new" Chrysler Corporation had to step up its advertising at the same time as it underwent capital structure reorganization. This was in addition to a massive capital expenditure program which would already contribute to its nonsalvageable investment requirement.

21 The more important of these nonsalvageable assets will include noninformative advertising, nonmarketable information derived from R&D, firm-specific human and organization capital, and certain physical assets specialized to a particular product.

22 Diversification through the combination of firms can in some cases increase

rather than decrease the risk of bankruptcy (see, for example, Higgins and Schall, 1975). It is, of course, also true that well-matched combinations can reduce this risk.

BIBLIOGRAPHY

Akerlof, G. A. 1970: The market for 'lemons': quality uncertainty and the market mechanism. *Quarterly Journal of Economics*, 84, August, 488–500.

Altman, E. I. 1982: A further empirical investigation of the bankruptcy cost question. Working Paper No. 277, Graduate School of Business, New York University, November.

Ang, J. S. and Chua, J. H. 1980: Coalitions, the me-first rule and the liquidity decision. *Bell Journal of Economics*, 11, Spring, 355–9.

Barnea, A., Haugen, R. A. and Senbet, L. W. 1981: Market imperfections, agency problems, and capital structure: a review. *Financial Management*, 10, Summer, 7–22.

Baxter, N. 1967: Leverage risk of ruin and the cost of capital. *Journal of Finance*, September, 395–404.

Black, F. and Scholes, M. 1983: The pricing of options and corporate liabilities. *Journal of Political Economy*, 81, 637–54.

Bulow, J. and Shoven, J. B. 1978: The bankruptcy decision. *Bell Journal of Economics*, 9, Autumn, 437–56.

Haugen, R. and Senbet, L. W. 1978: The insignificance of bankruptcy costs to the theory of optimal capital structure. *Journal of Finance*, May, 383–93.

Higgins, R. C. and Schall, L. D. 1975: Corporate bankruptcy and conglomerate merger. *Journal of Finance*, 30, March, 93–113.

Jensen, M. C. and Meckling, W. H. 1976: Theory of the firm: managerial behavior, agency costs and ownership structure. *Journal of Financial Economics*, 3, October, 305–60.

Klein, B. and Leffler, K. B. 1981: The role of market forces in assuring contractual performance. *Journal of Political Economy*, 89, August, 615–41.

Klein, B., Crawford, R. G. and Alchian, A. A. 1978: Vertical integration, appropriable rents and the competitive contracting process. *Journal of Law and Economics*, 21, October, 297–326.

Miller, M. H. 1977: Debt and taxes. *Journal of Finance*, 32, May, 261–76.

Modigliani, F. 1958: The cost of capital, corporation finance and the theory of investment. *American Economic Review*, 48, June, 261–97.

Modigliani, F. 1982: Debt, dividend policy, taxes, inflation and market valuation. *Journal of Finance*, 37, May, 255–93.

Modigliani, F. and Miller, M. H. 1963: Corporate income taxes and the cost of capital: a correction. *American Economic Review*, 53, June, 433–43.

Myers, S. C. 1977: Determinants of corporate borrowing. *Journal of Financial Economics*, 5, 147–75.

Scott, J. H. 1976: A theory of optimal capital structure. *The Bell Journal of Economics*, Spring, 33–54.

Stiglitz, J. E. 1969: A re-examination of the Modigliani–Miller theorem. *American Economic Review*, 59, December, 784–93.

Titman, S. 1982: The effect of capital structure on a firm's liquidation decision. U.C.L.A. Working Paper, October.

Warner, J. B. 1977: Bankruptcy costs: some evidence. *Journal of Finance*, 32, May, 337–48.

White, M. J. 1982: Economics of bankruptcy: liquidation and reorganization. New York University Working Paper.

10
Anatomy and Portfolio Strategies of the High Yield Debt Market

EDWARD I. ALTMAN
and SCOTT A. NAMMACHER

PREFACE
by EDWARD I. ALTMAN

Like many others who are contributing to this book, I consider Fred Weston to be my "academic father." My esteem and gratitude for his tutelage, guidance and role-model are immense. The initial contact with Professor Weston was via a letter that I wrote in 1963, while still an undergraduate in New York City, inquiring about the possibility of a research assistantship. After all, I had a few courses in finance under my belt and felt qualified for the position. I had heard about him from my brother who was then a graduate student in economics at U.C.L.A. His response was positive although he added that I probably did not really know much finance at that stage but to "come along anyway." So, off to L.A. I went – never suspecting that my training as a finance academic was about to begin. My horizon at that point was to get an M.B.A. – nothing more.

One of my most vivid memories of my four years working as Fred's R.A. at U.C.L.A. was his tireless work ethic and true scientific approach in everything he did. When an important, new sophisticated technique or concept was introduced, Fred was always amongst the first to immerse himself in the subject and emerge – sometimes a week or two later – as competent to evaluate its usefulness. Oftentimes, this meant that one of his assistants would enter his cloistered world for that short period and

The research for this paper was conducted while the authors were consultants to Morgan Stanley & Co., Incorporated. The opinions and conclusions are the sole responsibility of the authors. An earlier version of this paper was presented at the Institute for Quantitative Research in Finance ("Q" Group) conference in Scottsdale, Arizona, October 14, 1985.

all other efforts ceased. It was an awesome experience. Those were the *"hot days"* of capital structure controversy between Modigliani and Miller and the theories of some of the other more thoughtful and talented finance researchers. True to form, Fred's energies shifted to the capital structure and valuation debate.

Fred's work and influence, already evident in the scholarly academic literature for several decades, also showed up in his classic textbook Managerial Finance, on which I had the privilege of working for the second and third editions. It was exciting to participate in the evolution of corporate finance through those revisions.

Finally, it became time to strike out on my own and find a dissertation topic. Many of Fred's students, including myself, and those of the other superb faculty at U.C.L.A. in the mid-1960s, had already been bitten by the article writing bug but now it was time to find *"the topic."* One day I returned to my cubicle to find a hastily scribbled note from Fred – *"Why don't you look into the topic of corporate bankruptcy, Ed?"* Three months later after having pored through the records of several chapter X cases, I emerged somewhat confused. Each case appeared to be unique and a formal theory of bankruptcy seemed elusive. My energies shifted to the predictability of the bankruptcy event. It wasn't until over ten years later that I returned to the bankruptcy cost issue – one that I continue to believe is critical in the optimum capital structure controversy.

Interestingly, Fred was not convinced that accurate and reliable prediction of business distress through a combination of traditional financial techniques and statistical classification procedures was likely to be a fruitful area to investigate. Happily, he did not present any obstacles to my continuing in this direction – and I respect that as much as his enthusiasm for many of my other endeavors. In the ensuing two decades, we have been in consistent contact and I value that as well.

Before I finish, I must not forget to mention another reason that I am so very happy to have been given the chance to work for Fred. My wife of 19 years, Elaine, was also an assistant to Fred in 1965 and our first date came about because of a wager we made on an empirical test. And, we both won!

In reality anyone who had the privilege and rare opportunity to work closely with Fred Weston can consider him or herself a winner. I am very pleased to participate in this compendium in his honor.

INTRODUCTION

Rising interest rates and rapid expansion of the high yield corporate debt market since the late 1970s have led a wide variety of financial institutions to explore the relative attractions of lower-rated securities. In addition to the promised superior yields and realized impressive returns, the high yield bond (or "junk") sector now offers considerable liquidity and diversification potential. It has been estimated that total outstanding debt in this area was close to $90 billion by late 1985. The segment analyzed in this study, all low rated, public, non-convertible (straight) debt, grew from under $8 billion in 1978 to almost $42 billion in 1984 and was over $80 billion by late 1985. Estimates from individuals dealing in these markets indicate that an additional 10–15 percent of the $80 billion rated, straight debt can be found in nonrated, high yield securities. By 1984, the low-rated segment represented at least 11.2 percent of the total corporate, straight debt market, versus just 3.8 percent in 1978. In 1984 alone, nearly $15 billion in new straight, high-yield financing was issued and in the first nine months of 1985, an additional $12 billion came to market (including exchange offers). Given the market's size, growth rate, yield, and capital raising potential, it has become an increasingly important area for investors and the investment banking community.

The objectives of this study are first to explore the anatomy of the high-yield bond market, particularly over the most recent high-growth years. We will document the size, growth, and returns of high-yield bond securities and explore the characteristics of new issuers in this market. We will also review the default experience and other credit quality aspects of this market. The other major section of this paper will explore different portfolio strategies comparing risk and return performance of passive and active investment strategies over the period 1978–1984. We will construct various high-yield bond portfolios using different criteria for credit risk assessment and compare their historical performance with investment grade and default risk-free debt portfolios. This paper is a first step in exploring portfolio characteristics of junk bonds and does not attempt either to define or construct optimal and efficient portfolios.

MARKET ANATOMY

Size, Growth and Returns

The 1978 to 1984 period was an exceptionally volatile period for interest rates and corporate profitability. Interest rates on three-month T-bills and on ten-year government bonds rose from 7.4 percent and 8.4 percent yield levels respectively in early 1978, to record heights, peaking in mid-1981 at 17.2 percent and 15.3 percent respectively. By the fourth quarter of 1982, T-bills had dropped to 8 percent while ten-year governments were near the 10.5 percent level.

This volatility caused large variations in bond returns and yields over the period. Investment managers holding a portfolio equivalent to the Shearson Lehman Long-Term Government Bond Index would have experienced losses or marginally positive returns for all but two (1982 and

1984) years of the seven-year period from 1978 through 1984. With high quality bond returns fluctuating at or below zero returns from 1978 through 1981, portfolio managers began looking for new opportunities to boost their returns. High-yield bonds from 1978 to 1981 returned an average of 4.4 percent[1] on investment while long-term government bonds returned an average of − 1.1 percent. The high-yield bond marketplace became an increasingly attractive fixed income security option.

Based on data from the Morgan Stanley database, we found that portfolio managers investing in high yield bonds from December 31, 1977 to December 31, 1983 would have realized a compounded return of 11.45 percent versus 5.62 percent for long-term government bonds, a 583 basis point difference annually![2] That differential narrowed to 330 basis points by the end of 1984. The arithmetic average annual return spread was 3.70 percent or 370 basis points at the end of 1984 versus 5.37 percent or 537 basis points at the end of 1983. Calendar year returns and yields are

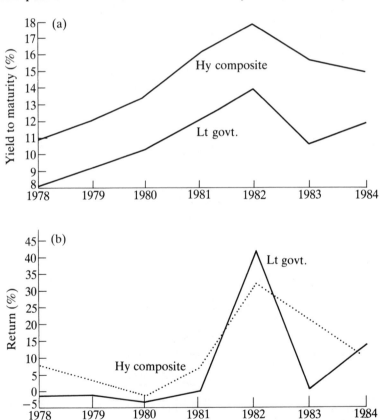

Figure 10.1   (a) Calendar year yields at the beginning of each year; (b) calendar year returns 1978 through 1984

displayed in figure 10.1. Thus the average yield spread (*ex-ante*) and average return spread (*ex-post*) from 1978–1984 were actually quite similar (3.57 percent versus 3.70 percent) but there is very little similarity in each specific year.

Figure 10.2 indicates the average fixed income mutual bond fund performance of a number of strategies over the period 1975–1984, for 1984 alone, and for the first six months of 1985. These statistics represent the average reinvested return performance of a number of funds investing in each category. Note that the return performance for the ten-year period is consistent with perceived risk attributes. The highest yielding funds were those of the high current yield category followed by general bonds, triple-B, single-A, and U.S. governments categories. Our own database calculations

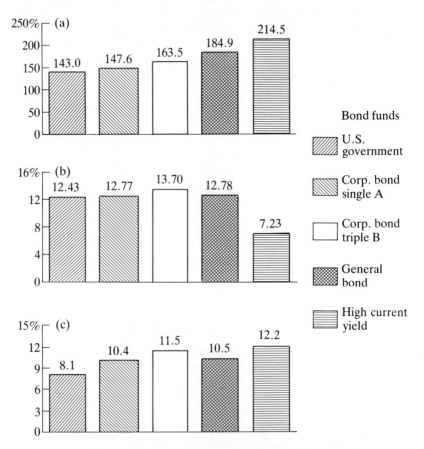

Figure 10.2   Selected groups of long-term taxable bond funds; total reinvested return for selected time periods: (a) ten years (1975–1984); (b) one year (1984); (c) six months (January–June 1985)
Source: Lipper Analytical Services, Inc.

for the period April 1978–April 1984 show the same relative rankings as the Lipper mutual fund rankings. This relative performance record also holds true approximately for the first six months of 1985, but not for 1984. In 1984, high-yield bonds recorded only a 7.23 percent return compared to over 12 percent for all other fixed income categories.

New Issues

The new issue public, straight debt marketplace (see table 10.1) has grown phenomenally, moving from the $1.5 billion level in 1978 to just under $15 billion in 1984 (with a 100 percent increase between 1983 and 1984).[3] The high-yield marketplace represented 15 percent of 1984's new, straight corporate debt issues. New issue business in 1984 alone accounted for over 48 percent of the total business in the high-yield marketplace since 1978 with a record number of issues with $200 million (par value) or more. The number of deals $100 million or larger rose from 2 in 1978, to 23 in 1983 and to 58 in 1984 (representing over 46 percent of the issues done in 1984, up from 27 percent in 1983). The average issue size has changed over the years, from $28 million in 1978 to over $120 million in 1984. The median issue in 1984 was $77 million.

The average "years to maturity" of new issues dropped as interest rates increased. In 1978, the average life was 19 years (ignoring sinking funds). By 1984 it had fallen to 12 years. The average "duration" of bonds in our high-yield universe was 6.45 years in 1983, down from 7.87 years in

Table 10.1   New non-convertible domestic debt issues: 1978–1984 ($MM)

| | Total new issues – public straight debt | | Total new high-yield debt issues[a] | | High-yield debt | | Variable rate debt | |
| | | | | | % new issue dollars | Issued with warrants or stock | | |
Year	Amount ($)	No.	Amount ($)	No.			Amount ($)	No.
1984	99,416	721	14,952	124	15.0	18	3,927	27
1983	46,903	511	7,417	86	15.8	35	—	—
1982	47,798	513	2,798	48	5.9	10	40	1
1981	41,651	357	1,648	32	4.0	6	104	2
1980	37,272	398	1,442	43	3.9	8	137	4
1979	25,678	277	1,307	45	5.0	14	—	—
1978	22,416	287	1,493	52	6.7	15	—	—
Total	321,134	3,064	31,057	430			4,208	34

[a] Not including exchange offers, tax exempts, convertibles, or government agencies.
Source: Morgan Stanley & Co. Incorporated.

1978, and has averaged 6.64 years over the six year period. The S.&P. rating distribution of new issues in recent years has been skewed toward single-B.

Default Experience on High-Yield Debt[4]

High-yield bond investors in the past have experienced significant return premiums over investment grade securities, but they have also experienced substantial defaults. Without a reliable measure of past losses from defaults, investors cannot intelligently estimate the net returns over time on high-yield bonds.

Default rates can be measured using several different base levels or denominators (i.e. total public debt, total straight debt, low-rated debt, etc.). The default rates discussed here were derived by dividing the par

Table 10.2 Historical default rates – low-rated, straight debt only[a] ($MM)

Year	Par value outstanding with utilities[b] ($)	Par value defaulted ($)	default rate (%)	Par value public outstanding less utilities[b] ($)	Default rate (%)
1984	41,700	344.16	0.825	32,120	1.071
1983	28,233	301.08	1.066	22,167	1.358
1982	18,536	752.34	4.059[c]	16,111	4.670
1981	17,362	27.00	0.155	15,010	0.180
1980	15,126	224.11	1.482	12,807	1.750
1979	10,675	20.00	0.187	10,031	0.199
1978	9,401	118.90	1.265	8,995	1.322
1977	8,479	380.57	4.488	7,548	5.042
1976	8,015	29.51	0.368	7,024	0.420
1975	7,720	204.10	2.644	6,971	2.928
1974	11,101[d]	122.82	1.106	7,445	1.650
1973	8,082	49.07	0.607	7,195	0.682
1972	7,106	193.25	2.719	6,245	3.094
1971	6,643	82.00	1.234	5,935	1.382
1970	6,996	796.71	11.388	6,448	12.356
Average default rate – 1970 to 1984			2.240		2.540
Average default rate – 1974 to 1984			1.604[c]		1.872
Average default rate – 1978 to 1984			1.291		1.507

[a] Issues rated below Baa3 by Moody's or BBB- by Standard & Poor's. Includes non-rated debt of issuers with other equivalently rated issues.
[b] *Source: Standard & Poor's Bond Guide* and *Moody's Bond Record*, July issues of each year.
[c] Excluding Johns Manville, the default rate for 1982 was 3.115 percent and it was 1.518 percent for the 1974–1984 period.
[d] Includes almost $2.7 billion of Consolidated Edison Co. debt.

value of defaulting debt by the total low-rated, straight debt outstanding. We found that the default rate on high yield bonds from 1974 to 1984 averaged 1.60 percent (or 160 basis points annually). Table 10.2 illustrates the annual default rates from 1970–1984. The default rate was 1.52 percent if Johns Manville's debt, the only issues rated investment grade just prior to default, is excluded. Year-to-year variations in this rate were substantial. This default level is significantly higher than rates generated using total straight debt outstanding as the base, i.e. 0.08 of 1 percent for the same period. We feel the higher rate is much more relevant to investors with portfolios in the high-yield area since virtually all defaults occur in the low-rated segment of the corporate debt market.

The actual losses from default, however, are considerably lower than these rates would imply. Defaulted bonds, far from becoming valueless, traded, on average, at 41 percent of par shortly after default. After accounting for the bonds' retained value and the loss of interest, the average reduction in returns to the investor would have been approximately 100 basis points annually, assuming purchase at par.

CREDIT QUALITY OF HIGH-YIELD DEBT

Measuring a Firm's Operating and Financial Risk

In our prior discussion, we documented the impressive increase in the number and size of new issues from 1978–1984. A lurking question related to this increase concerns the credit quality of these new issues and the impact that increased competition amongst underwriters has had on the profile of new, high-yield issuers. This section examines the overall trends of issuer credit quality in the market and looks at techniques to be used to identify and avoid credit deterioration. While the most "sensational" questions revolve around leveraged buyouts, hostile takeovers and defensive strategies used by firms issuing debt securities, our study does not address these new phenomena directly. Nor do we comment on the hearings being held in Congress on restricting federally insured financial institutions from investing in high-yield bonds.

We have chosen the Zeta credit evaluation scores to assess credit quality in our high-yield firm universe. Zeta was developed by Altman *et al.* (1977) to identify the bankruptcy risk of industrial corporations. Building upon earlier bankruptcy classification works, Zeta combines traditional financial measures with a multivariate technique known as discriminant analysis so as to lead to an overall "credit-score" for each of the firms being examined. This model is of the form

$$\text{Zeta} = a_0 + a_1 X_1 + a_2 X_2 + a_3 X_3 \ldots a_n X_n$$

where Zeta is the overall credit score, X_1-X_n are explanatory variables (ratios and market measures), and a_1-a_n are weightings or coefficients.

The explanatory variables include measures of a firm's profitability, stability of earnings, debt service capability, cumulative profitability, liquidity, capitalization and size. The lower the firm's Zeta score, the more "in-distress" the model reports for the firm. Negative Zetas do not indicate default or bankruptcy with certainty but the lower the score, the greater the similarity between that particular firm and those which have gone bankrupt in the past. The average Zeta score for past bankrupts was about -4.0 in the original sample and -5.0 for those filing bankruptcy petitions subsequent to the model's construction.

New Issuer Credit Quality

Based on average and median Zeta scores, newly issued, high yield securities appear to have experienced an upward (better quality) trend over the last eight years (with the exception of 1983 and also 1985). In 1978, the central tendency of new issuer scores was roughly equivalent or slightly above the average S.&P. single-B rated debt. Note that the high-yield new issuer's score increased from a -0.99 median in 1978 to -0.65 in 1980. But we observe that the trend was also favorable for all single-B rated debt and the BB/B average in that three-year period. Indeed, the median or average high-yield new issuer score was just about the same (-0.65) as all S.&P. single-B rated debt (-0.52) in 1980, but was still below the BB/B

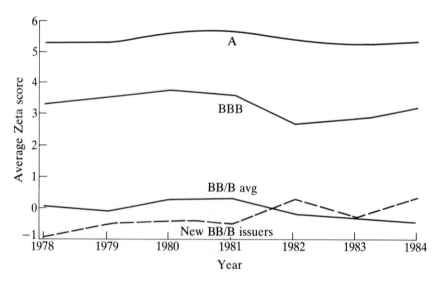

Figure 10.3   Zeta scores: new vs. existing issuers by S.&P. rating (from Zeta Services, Inc.)

average. There may be some bias in these results since Zeta scores were available on only 65 percent of the new issues.

The divergence between the trend in new issuer, high-yield debt and the entire debt market started to take place in 1981 and continued through 1984. Based on incomplete data for 1985, the median Zeta score for 37 new issues dropped to − 0.40, indicating a slight deterioration in credit quality. Figure 10.3 clearly illustrates these differences. The Zeta trend in new issuer debt rated BB/B continued to improve in the 1981–1984 period (except 1983), especially the median score, while the overall BB/B market deteriorated in the face of the recession. This deterioration has continued in the most recent expansionary years. No doubt a number of deteriorating higher grade securities, the so-called "fallen angels," helped to contribute to this decline. The trend in investment grade debt rated BBB and A was only slightly negative over this most recent period and was essentially unchanged from 1978–1984.

While the overall credit profile of new issuer, high-yield debt is still in the risky zone, around a Zeta of zero, we have observed an overall improvement in this group both in absolute and relative terms. This does not mean that the credit analyst can feel comfortable on all new issues since the distribution of scores is quite wide with several new issues fairly deep in the negative Zeta zone (7 of 46 (15 percent) had Zetas − 3.0 or below in 1983 and 7 of 53 (13 percent) in 1984).

PORTFOLIO STRATEGIES

We observe that high-yield bonds have provided substantial return premiums to their holders in recent years. Having examined the anatomy, default and credit aspects of this area, we now turn to its overall performance characteristics. In this section we attempt to quantify return premiums for different portfolio strategies and also measure additional risk dimensions. In doing so, we hope to answer several key questions:

1   What have been the expected yields and actual returns as well as the variation in these returns, for a diversified, passive investor in the high-yield market in recent years?
2   Are there ways to improve upon the risk–return relationship in this marketplace using specific, active portfolio selection strategies?
3   Do different high-yield portfolio strategies demonstrate statistically significant returns compared with strategies involving corporate investment grade or government bonds?

Data Base Properties

To answer these questions, an analytic database of 440 bonds was constructed to allow the tracking of period-by-period results from 1978 to 1984. It was designed to measure key aspects of any chosen portfolio, including average coupon, average bond rating, weighted and unweighted returns, yields, maturity date, and duration. In addition, our data base has a history of Zeta credit scores for each company going back to 1975 as well as the issues' bond ratings over time. For details of this data base and calculation procedures, see Appendix A.

Portfolio Construction

A number of index and strategy based high-yield debt portfolios are constructed for comparison. These include:

1   An index of low-rated (double-B or lower) bonds, called the High-Yield Composite (H.Y. Comp.).
2   An index for S.&P. rated bonds by rating (BB,B and CCC).
3   Portfolios based on Zeta scores:
    (a)   Zetas greater than or equal to 1 (Z ⩾ 1).
    (b)   Zetas greater than or equal to 1 with an uptick (positive change) over the prior year (Z ⩾ 1 +).
    (c)   Zetas greater than or equal to 1 with a downtick (negative change) from the prior year's score (Z ⩾ 1 −).
    (d)   Zetas greater than or equal to 2.5 (Z ⩾ 2.5).
    (e)   Zeta quartiles (Z Q − 1, Z Q − 2, Z Q − 3, Z Q − 4).

Benchmark Portfolios

In addition to the portfolio strategies containing high-yield bond issues, we also calculate yearly returns on the Shearson Lehman Long Term Government Index, the Salomon Brothers A-rated Bond Index, the Standard & Poor's BBB Index and the Common Stock S.&P. 500 Index. Since these benchmark portfolios do not exactly match our High-Yield Composite portfolio with respect to the average duration, we also construct and compare synthetic government bond portfolios with equivalent durations. We use these portfolios as benchmarks for comparison with the custom-built portfolios. Finally, we statistically test for differences in returns over the six annual periods and 72 monthly periods incorporating tests to account for covariance effects between strategies.

Portfolio Returns Over the Study Period

Since the Zeta scores are available in March, our study period is March 31, 1978 to March 31, 1984. We chose 1978 as the starting year due to a combination of factors including Zeta score availability and the start of the growth in the high-yield bond market.

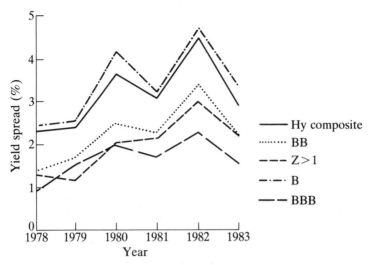

Figure 10.4   Yield spreads for major strategies off long-term government bonds –
March 1978 to March 1984

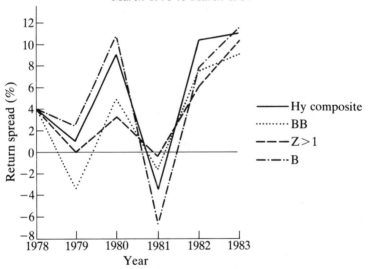

Figure 10.5   Return spreads for major strategies off long-term governments

Figures 10.4 and 10.5 illustrate yield and return spreads off long-term governments from March 31, 1978 to March 31, 1984. Yields are as of the start of the period, e.g. for 1978 it is as of March 31, 1978, and returns are for the period covering March 31, 1978 to March 31, 1979. Note that we have included the spreads for various high-yield portfolios including

Table 10.3 Investment strategies return comparison[a]

Strategy index	1978	1979	1980	1981	1982	1983	Averaged returns	Six-year averages Total compounded returns	Compounded annual returns	Zeta score	Standard deviation[b]
High-yield composite	5.85	−15.07	19.01	3.43	48.17	9.68	11.85	79.8	10.3	0.42	21.00
# of bonds	153	203	243	280	286	339					
Shearson Lehman Long-Term Government Index	1.52	−16.06	10.10	7.09	37.82	−1.17	6.55	36.9	5.4	NA	17.81
Salomon Brothers A-Rated Bond Index	1.41	−19.08	14.05	3.85	43.94	4.26	8.07	45.9	6.5	NA	20.50
Portfolio by S.&P. Rating											
BB-rated	3.14	−19.41	15.11	5.41	45.48	7.80	9.58	58.2	7.9	1.74	21.08
# bonds	34	51	61	49	55	70					
B-rated	5.78	−13.63	20.78	0.25	45.81	10.28	11.54	77.9	10.1	−0.35	20.28
# bonds	60	93	114	137	142	150					
CCC-rated	10.73	−10.62	27.75	5.25	76.15	13.82	20.51	166.8	17.8	−2.04	29.99
# bonds	17	14	16	23	21	35					
Zeta scores ⩾1 only	5.60	−16.03	13.34	6.75	43.71	9.03	10.40	68.1	9.0	3.25	19.26
# of bonds	56	64	75	87	97	123					
Zeta scores ⩾1 and an increase over prior years	6.10	−17.11	13.79	8.55	43.76	7.69	10.46	68.2	9.0	3.40	19.55
# of bonds	33	43	44	57	71	70					
Zeta scores ⩾1 and a decrease from prior year	4.84	−12.77	12.47	3.29	43.58	10.48	10.32	68.5	9.1	3.00	18.57
# of bonds	22	20	31	30	26	53					
Zeta scores ⩾2.5 only	6.81	−16.62	12.25	8.16	42.95	8.57	10.35	67.8	9.0	4.56	19.05
# of bonds	25	36	41	42	55	49					
Zeta scores by quartile											
First quartile (highest)	6.12	−15.67	12.05	7.39	43.88	8.26	10.34	67.7	9.0	3.59	19.16
Second quartile	4.38	−19.44	19.12	0.84	43.88	10.54	9.89	60.5	8.2	0.78	21.04
Third quartile	4.94	−12.86	22.66	4.31	54.97	7.68	13.62	95.2	11.8	−0.79	23.19
Lowest quartile	8.34	−11.81	24.20	0.86	50.63	13.33	14.26	104.4	12.6	−2.59	21.52
Approx. # of bonds/quartile	37	50	60	70	71	84					
S.&P. 500	19.99	6.16	40.07	−13.06	44.70	8.71	17.76	144.0	16.0	NA	21.88

[a] Returns are weighted by dollar amounts outstanding and are for twelve-month periods beginning March 31 of each year.
[b] Standard deviation of returns over six years (based on annual returns).

those with single-B and double-B ratings, Zeta greater than 1, as well as the High-Yield Composite.

Tables 10.3 and 10.4 list annual portfolio returns, arithmetic and compounded average returns, yields and durations over the six-year sample period. The returns are weighted by dollar amounts outstanding on each issue and were calculated by reconstituting the portfolios at the beginning of each annual period and then observing the return for that period's portfolio. In essence, the portfolio is liquidated at the end of the period and the proceeds reinvested in a new set of securities with the same characteristics. The number of securities in the various strategies over the sample period are also noted in table 10.3 and range from 153 in 1978 to 339 in 1983 for our High-Yield Composite, 56 to 123 for Zetas $\geqslant 1.0$, to between 17 and 35 issues for the CCC portfolio. The latter, while the highest return performer portfolio, is reported mainly for comparison purposes, realizing that the small number of issues probably makes that group of securities an impractical strategy.

The geometric or *compound* annual return over the six-year period ranged from 5.4 percent for the L.T. Govts. to 17.8 percent for CCC. Most of the relevant portfolios returned 8–9 percent with a few of the more credit risky (lower Zeta scores) returning around 12 percent. *Average* annual returns were somewhat higher for the entire period.

The return results for portfolios based on Zetas $\geqslant 1.0$ strategies were virtually identical, regardless of whether the score was accompanied by an uptick or a downtick. We observe that the quartile separation of Zeta resulted in higher returns for the lowest quartiles, no doubt reflecting their lower quality and higher promised yield situation. It appears that investors in high-yield debt reaped higher returns by taking more perceived risks.

The yield spreads are pretty much as one would expect with respect to the various bond rating categories. The highest yield spreads (of the rated portfolios) occurred in the CCC portfolio, followed by B and BB. The Morgan Stanley High Yield Composite can be found somewhere in the middle, on average. Interestingly, the High-Yield Composite's yield spread for the six-year period (3.15 percent) was slightly less than the B-rated group (3.44 percent) while the Composite's return spread (5.29 percent) was above that of the B's (4.99 percent). The average return was 11.85 percent on the Composite compared with 11.54 percent for Bs and 9.58 percent for BBs. All were considerably below the astounding 20.51 percent for our sample (admittedly small) of CCC-rated firms.

The major Zeta strategies (Z $\geqslant$ 1 and Z top quartile) produced yield spread levels lower than the BB rated portfolio, but return spreads considerably higher. The third and fourth quartile Zeta strategies produced yield spreads between the B- and CCC-rated portfolio spreads and had returns moderately higher than the B portfolio.

Table 10.4   *Investment strategies yield and duration comparison*[a]

Strategy		1978	1979	1980	1981	1982	1983	Average
High-yield composite								
	Yield	10.71	11.52	16.16	15.90	18.62	13.77	14.45
	Duration	7.87	7.52	6.25	6.12	5.63	6.45	6.64
Shearson Lehman Long-Term Govt. Bond Index								
	Yield	8.38	9.13	12.48	12.77	13.70	10.85	11.22
	Duration	9.90	9.55	8.04	7.84	7.44	8.44	8.53
Portfolio by S.&P. Rating								
BB-rated portfolio								
	Yield	9.80	10.85	14.99	15.12	17.21	13.07	13.51
	Duration	8.70	7.77	6.57	6.62	5.87	6.39	6.99
B-rated portfolio								
	Yield	10.83	11.79	16.73	15.96	18.50	14.20	14.67
	Duration	7.84	7.67	6.23	6.17	5.57	6.27	6.63
CCC-rated portfolio								
	Yield	12.86	13.38	17.89	17.91	22.70	15.60	16.72
	Duration	7.16	6.87	5.83	5.63	4.80	5.82	6.02
Zeta score $\geqslant 1$ only								
	Yield	9.70	10.32	14.56	14.96	16.78	13.10	13.24
	Duration	8.50	8.08	6.72	6.56	6.03	6.73	7.10
Zeta score $\geqslant 1$ plus uptick								
	Yield	9.52	10.18	14.66	14.80	16.83	13.04	13.17
	Duration	8.55	8.34	6.82	6.48	6.07	6.75	7.17
Zeta score $\geqslant 1$ plus downtick								
	Yield	9.92	10.78	14.37	15.25	16.65	13.15	13.35
	Duration	8.61	7.19	6.54	6.73	5.95	6.71	6.95
Zeta score $\geqslant 2.5$								
	Yield	9.56	10.01	14.36	14.77	16.56	12.99	13.04
	Duration	8.71	8.20	6.90	6.44	5.97	6.63	7.14
Zeta scores by quartile								
First quartile								
	Yield	9.58	10.79	14.37	15.11	16.68	12.99	13.25
	Duration	8.47	7.74	6.80	6.40	6.04	6.67	7.02
Second quartile								
	Yield	10.17	11.38	16.35	15.35	17.47	13.64	14.06
	Duration	8.37	7.71	6.13	6.53	5.65	6.50	6.81
Third quartile								
	Yield	11.43	12.06	17.23	16.19	19.27	13.48	14.94
	Duration	7.68	7.20	6.05	6.10	5.44	6.50	6.50
Lowest quartile								
	Yield	12.10	12.82	17.17	17.01	19.86	15.33	15.71
	Duration	7.10	7.07	5.84	5.67	5.36	5.98	6.17

[a] Yields and duration are from March 31 of each year and are weighted by the amounts outstanding.

Annual Return Performance

Three years, 1979, 1980, and 1982 are especially noteworthy with respect to returns. The jump in interest rates during the 1979 holding period caused substantial price deterioration in the fixed income market, leading to large annual negative returns (− 16 percent for L.T. Govts. and − 15 percent for the Morgan Stanley High Yield Composite). The superior coupon payment on high-yield debt softened the principal loss, especially for the CCC category. Note that returns in 1979 varied from − 19.4 percent for BB bonds to − 10.6 percent for CCCs. The following year, 1980, saw a reversal for all categories with CCCs again outperforming all other fixed income categories. The High-Yield Composite enjoyed a 19.0 percent return compared to just over 10 percent for L.T. Govts.

The most astonishing performance year was 1982 when prices rebounded as interest rates fell dramatically from their 1981 highs. Price appreciation accounted for most of 1982's returns of 38 percent on L.T. Govts., 44 percent on A-rated debt, 48 percent on the High-Yield Composite and an incredible 76 percent on CCC rated debt. One might be even more impressed since this remarkable performance was achieved despite 1982's relatively high default rate. However, as the largest of the defaults occurred in the beginning of the 1982 period, most of the price deterioration actually

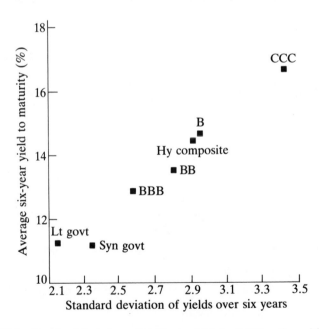

Figure 10.6   Standard deviation of yields vs. yields by S.&P. rating – March 1978 to March 1984

took place in 1981, or earlier. Hence, investors in these issues did not suffer substantial price depreciation in 1982.

Issues in Risk–Return Measurement

To understand the period-to-period risk of the portfolio in terms of yield and return variations, we can look at the variance of these factors over time. Figure 10.6 shows the standard deviations in yield to maturity by S.&P. ratings, calculated annually over the six-year sample period. As expected, the lower the rating the more volatile the yield. The High-Yield (H.Y.) Composite falls approximately where its average rating (B +) would have predicted it would.

The annual return deviations, however, show something quite different. While the averages show increased returns as ratings decrease (except for single-B rated bonds), there is a steep increase in return, with little difference in risk, over the A to B rating range (figure 10.7). Indeed, the standard deviation of returns over six years is virtually the same for the different ratings. The only exception is the CCC-rated category, with a standard deviation of about 50 percent higher than B, BB and most of the Zeta portfolios.

These return-generated results could be caused by the limited number of data points (6) used in calculating standard deviations. However, the

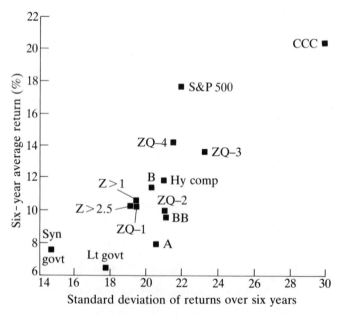

Figure 10.7   Risk vs. return for major strategies, annual data – March 1978 to March 1984

tendency of four of the portfolios (A, BB, B and H.Y. composite) to have little difference in risk agrees somewhat with the findings of a high-yield debt study done by Blume and Keim (1984). They actually found that higher rated debt had greater return volatility than did lower rated debt. In order to investigate this anomaly, we utilized our monthly return index so as to increase the number of data points and to allow for direct comparison with the Drexel Burnham Lambert and the Blume and Keim monthly indices.

Upon rerunning the major portfolio strategies using monthly data, the anomaly corrected itself for the portfolios from the Morgan Stanley high-yield data base, i.e. the ones selected by bond ratings and Zeta, but Salomon's A-rated index and Shearson's Long Term Government Bond index showed increased volatility and shifted to the right of even our B-rated portfolio (see figure 10.8). The number of data points does not appear to be the complete answer to the anomaly. The long-term government index has a longer average years to maturity and duration than the other indices, however, and this might explain the greater volatility in monthly returns. Indeed, when we plot Shearson Lehman's Short-Term Government/Corporate index for monthly returns, the standard deviation of returns is lower than the others. We will return to this issue in our section on duration matching.

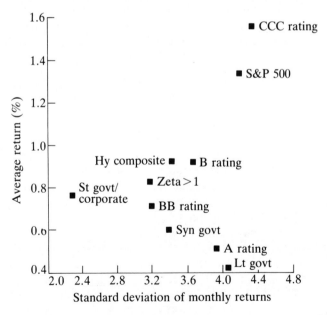

Figure 10.8   Average returns vs. standard deviation of return, monthly data – March 1978 to March 1984

One explanation for a risk–return anomaly could be that high yield bonds tend to trade with an equity component that offsets interest rate fluctuations more than anticipated. Investors in high quality bonds tend to key in on interest rates, with little regard to credit quality. Investors in low-rated bonds, however, are very credit conscious, and look more at the firm's operating fundamentals. While a company's stock is generally more volatile than its bonds, stock movements are usually not highly correlated to minor interest rate fluctuations. An equity component in low-rated debt may, as a result, help to counter some of the interest-rate-driven price fluctuations.

Annual Risk–Return Results

Using the less controversial (with respect to realized variance of returns) average annual return data, figure 10.7 combines all of the strategies tested in the risk–return environment. The bunching of the Zeta $\geqslant 1.0$ strategy and the Zeta top quartile (Q – 1) strategy in the lower risk range does seem to indicate that Zeta can be used to create more stable and, in some cases, higher returns distributions. Compound returns on these portfolios were an average of 110 basis points higher (annually) than the BB rated portfolio. The Zeta $\geqslant 1.0$ strategy also outperformed the A and Z Q – 2 portfolios by substantial margins, even though these latter portfolios registered higher risk levels. The B, CCC, HY Composite and low quality Zeta strategy (Z Q – 3 and Z Q – 4) portfolios had higher returns, but they were also accompanied by higher risk levels.

Significance Testing

There are a number of ways of analyzing the empirical results on the risk–return performance of our high yield portfolios. From an absolute return standpoint, the average annual results for the six-year period March 31, 1978 to March 31, 1984 are decent but not overwhelming. Most of the relevant portfolios had annual returns in the 10–12 percent range which was, on the one hand, quite good compared to investment grade fixed-income portfolios, but inferior to the return on common equities for the same period. Indeed, the S.&P. 500 returned an average of 17.8 percent annually. Also, since returns on various quality bond portfolios are highly correlated due to interest rate effects, simply looking at the average returns does not reveal the true significance of differential return performance. Finally, the variance of returns over time must be factored indirectly in determining whether differences in mean returns between portfolios are significant or not.

Difference in Means Tests

The objective of this section is to test rigorously for differential performance of the various portfolios listed and summarized earlier in table 10.3. Specifically, we will assess whether the high-yield portfolios demonstrated significantly different returns from our two investment grade series (i.e. L.T. Govts. and the A-rated index). We will also assess differential performance between high-yield portfolios.

The annual returns on various bond portfolios are *not* independent over time; thus, we must account for the covariance effect in our differential performance tests. Although there is some legitimate question of the efficiency of mean-variance tests in the high-yield segment,[5] we will utilize this framework in our tests. An appropriate test for analyzing return performance across portfolios is the *t*-test on annual mean difference measures, of the form

$$t = \frac{\bar{d}}{S_D/\sqrt{n}}$$

$$\bar{d} = \frac{\sum\limits_{i=1}^{n} d_i}{n}$$

$$S_D = \sqrt{\frac{\left(\sum\limits_{i=1}^{n} (d_i - \bar{d})^2\right)}{(n-1)}}$$

where d_i is the difference in annual return in period i for two portfolios being considered, $\bar{d}$ is the average difference between the two portfolios over the sample period, S_D is the standard deviation of the annual differences, and n is the number of periods.

For example, if we want to test the null hypothesis that the average annual return on the Morgan Stanley High Yield Composite compared with the L.T. Govt. index over the six-year sample period is not significantly different from zero, a one- and/or a two-tailed *t*-test of the annual differences would provide the answer. The differences in mean returns for these two series are given in table 10.5.

If we believe that the H.Y. Composite can be either above or below the L.T. Govt. index, a two-tailed test of significance shows that $t = 2.23$ with 5 degrees of freedom $(n-1)$ is significant at the 0.07 level, i.e. we are 93 percent confident that the rejection of the null hypothesis did not happen by chance. A one-tailed test, testing just for superior performance of the H.Y. Composite, is significant at the 0.035 level (96.5 percent confident). Hence, after adjusting for both the covariance effect and risk (variance

Table 10.5   Differences in mean returns

	H.Y. Composite	L.T. Govt.	=	Difference (d_i)
1978	5.85	1.52		4.33
1979	− 15.07	− 16.06		0.99
1980	19.01	10.10		8.91
1981	3.43	7.09		− 3.66
1982	48.17	37.82		10.35
1983	9.68	− 1.17		10.85
Average	11.85	6.55		5.30($\bar{d}$)

$S_D = 5.82$

$$t = \frac{\bar{d}}{S_D/\sqrt{n}} = \frac{5.30}{5.82/2.45} = 2.23$$

of return), the results show the H.Y. Composite significantly out-performing the L.T. Govt. index over the six-year period.

We have tested for the differences in the following strategies:

1   H.Y. Composite vs. L.T. Govt. index
2   Zeta first quartile vs. L.T. Govt. index
3   Zeta > 1.0 vs. L.T. Govt. index
4   Zeta > 2.5 vs. L.T. Govt. index
5   CCC vs. L.T. Govt. index
6   A-rated vs. L.T. Govt. index
7   H.Y. Composite vs. A-rated index
8   H.Y. Composite vs. Zeta > 1.0
9   H.Y. Composite vs. Zeta first quartile
10   Zeta > 1.0 vs. A-rated index
11   Zeta > 1.0 vs. Zeta first quartile
12   Zeta > 2.5 vs. A-rated index
13   CCC vs. H.Y. Composite
14   CCC vs. Zeta > 1.0
15   Zeta fourth quartile vs. H.Y. Composite
16   S.&P. 500 vs. H.Y. Composite

The resulting *t*-test statistics and significance levels are given in table 10.6.

Table 10.6

	Test	*t*-statistic	Two-tailed significance level (%)
1	H.Y. Composite vs. L.T. Govt. index	2.23	0.070
2	Zeta first quartile vs. L.T. Govt. index	2.58	0.050
3	Zeta > 1.0 vs. L.T. Govt. index	2.40	0.061
4	Zeta > 2.5 vs. L.T. Govt. index	2.50	0.055
5	CCC vs. L.T. Govt. index	2.48	0.056
6	A-rated vs. L.T. Govt. index	0.89	0.420
7	H.Y. Composite vs. A-rated index	4.37	0.007
8	H.Y. Composite vs. Zeta > 1.0	1.10	0.320
9	H.Y. Composite vs. Zeta first quartile	0.98	0.370
10	Zeta > 1.0 vs. A-rated index	2.50	0.055
11	Zeta > 1.0 vs. Zeta first quartile	0.25	0.750
12	Zeta > 2.5 vs. A-rated index	2.60	0.048
13	CCC vs. H.Y. Composite	2.18	0.080
14	CCC vs. Zeta > 1.0	2.05	0.095
15	Zeta fourth quartile vs. H.Y. Composite	2.18	0.080
16	S.&P. 500 vs. H.Y. Composite	0.82	0.470

An Additional Mean-Difference Test

Another test for the statistical significance of the differences in a matched paired sample (i.e. annual mean differences in rates of return) comparison is the "Wilcoxon matched-pairs signed-ranks" test (Wilcoxon and Wilcox, 1964; Siegel, 1956). This test considers the magnitude of the annual differences in the rates of return as well as the sign of the differences, but concentrates on ranks of the differences, instead of the absolute differences. For example, if we rank the annual differences in returns (ignoring the sign) between the H.Y. Composite and L.T. Govt. portfolios we observe the results given in table 10.7.

Table 10.7

Year	Differences (H.Y.–L.T.)	Rank	Sign of rank
1978	4.33	3	+
1979	0.99	1	+
1980	8.91	4	+
1981	− 3.66	2	−
1982	10.35	5	+
1983	10.85	6	+

$N = 6$, $T = 2$, Significance = 0.035 level

The relevant statistic is $T=2$, which is the sum of the ranks of the *smaller* like-signed ranks. The significance level of $T=2$ is at the 0.035 level, concluding that the annual mean differences in return between the H.Y. Composite and our L.T. Govt. benchmark are quite significant. This result is consistent with the difference in mean returns test, discussed earlier.

Discussion of Results

The overwhelming result of these tests is that every high-yield strategy performed significantly better than either the L.T. Govt. or the A-rated index. Our t-test confirms these differentials as significant after adjusting for covariance and variance effects. Also, with the exception of the CCC category and Zeta fourth quartile, none of the high-yield strategies performed significantly differently from any of the others. Finally, the A-rated vs. L.T. Govt. returns were insignificantly different from each other, but the H.Y. Composite was most significantly higher vs. the A-rated portfolio; even more so than the risk-free government index.

Despite the high average annual differential between the S.&P. 500 index and the H.Y. Composite index (5.91 percent per year), the differential is not statistically significant due to the high standard deviation of the annual differences. Hence, we cannot be confident that a passive investor buying the equity index could expect to continue receiving such sizeable premiums over the passive high-yield bond investment strategy.

PORTFOLIO RESULTS ADJUSTED FOR DURATION

Duration Comparisons

Up to this point, we have compared portfolio risks and returns for various long-term bond portfolios but we have not matched these portfolios exactly in terms of their maturities or duration. Duration, the average life of a security weighted by the timing of cash flow payments, has interesting patterns in our analysis. The concept of duration, first postulated by Macauley (1938), and revived in recent years, has become an increasingly popular tool of fixed income managers for matching of portfolios and as a means to estimate the volatility or sensitivity of the portfolio's market value to changes in interest rates. It is a particularly useful matching concept for high-yield bond comparisons vis-à-vis government bonds and other investment grade portfolios since coupon levels, i.e. cash flows, are quite different. Matching by maturities only considers the final cash flow.

We have seen earlier that the average duration of our portfolios increases as the credit risk is reduced (table 10.4). For example, the highest six-year average duration was for the Shearson Lehman L.T. Government Bond index (8.53 years) followed by the Zeta $\geqslant 1.0$ plus uptick and Zeta $\geqslant 2.5$

(7.17 and 7.14 years). Note also that the quartile Zeta duration rankings are highest for the top quartile (7.02 years) and consistently lower as the quartiles also move lower. The same phenomenon is observed as we go from the BB category (6.99 years) to the CCC (6.02 years). It is quite clear that the coupon rate and promised yield are greater as the credit quality of our portfolios diminish. Since coupon payments affect duration, we are not surprised by these results.

Constructing Synthetic Duration Government Portfolios

We have shown that all of the high yield portfolios have outperformed the L.T. Govt. and other investment grade portfolios. We have also found that the return volatility of the Long Term Government portfolio was actually greater than the high-yield portfolios when we used monthly return observations. This was consistent with Blume and Keim's (1984) findings, also using monthly data. Could these results be caused by the differences in duration patterns? Will our results still show that the high yield portfolios outperform the risk-free government indexes when we match portfolios by duration?

To answer these questions, we constructed synthetic government portfolios exactly matching them for duration, for each year, to our High-Yield Composite index. We combined the Shearson Lehman Long Term Government index with their Government Short Term index so that the weighted average return was based on a duration of 7.88 years in 1978, 7.52 years in 1979, etc. The six-year average duration was therefore equal to 6.64 years for our synthetic government portfolio – exactly the same as our High-Yield Composite. In each year, the weightings were approximately two-thirds long term and one-third short term, with 1978 and 1979 showing a 70–30 percent split and 1982 showing a 62–38 percent split.

Table 10.8   Annual rates of return for the synthetic government bond portfolio (matched to H.Y. Composite by duration)

Year	Duration (years)	H.Y. Comp. return (%)	Syn. Govt. return (%)	L.T. Govt. return (%)
1978	7.88	5.85	2.41	1.52
1979	7.52	– 15.07	– 11.55	– 16.06
1980	6.24	19.01	11.32	10.01
1981	6.11	3.43	8.83	7.09
1982	5.63	48.17	32.79	37.82
1983	6.45	9.68	1.66	– 1.17
Average	6.64	11.85	7.58	6.55
Std. deviation		21.00	14.69	17.82

Table 10.8 indicates the realized annual rates of return and standard deviation of return on our High-Yield Composite portfolio and the Synthetic Government Bond index as well as the L.T. Govt. grouping, with the yearly duration noted. The average annual return for the High-Yield Composite was 4.27 percent greater than the synthetic portfolio's return. Recall that the differential was even greater at 5.30 percent with the L.T. Government index.

The new synthetic government portfolio's (Syn. Govt.) yield to maturity vs. standard deviation of the yields is indicated in figure 10.6. The annual return and standard deviation of return results are noted in table 10.8 and figure 10.7 and the monthly returns can be found in figure 10.8. We observe that both the monthly and annual risk–return results are more in line with expectations, especially the annual results where the synthetic government returns are lower and less volatile than the high yield portfolios. The *monthly* standard deviation of return for the synthetic government (3.34 percent) is considerably lower than the long-term index but very similar to our high-yield portfolios. It appears that some of the monthly risk–return anomaly, first observed by Blume and Keim (1984), can be explained by the duration effect.

We next tested the statistical significance of the average annual and average monthly return differences between our High-Yield Composite and the Synthetic Government index. We find that the average *annual* H.Y. Composite return (11.85 percent) vs. the average annual Syn. Govt. return (7.58 percent) is still significant but less so than the L.T. Govt. index comparison. The t-test statistic is lower at $t = 1.47$, indicating a significance at the 0.10 level; the comparable statistic was significant at the 0.035 level for our earlier test on the L.T. Govt. index vs. the H.Y. Composite index.

The average monthly return for the H.Y. Composite was 0.92 percent (3.42 standard deviation) compared to the Syn. Govt.'s 0.60 percent return (3.34 standard deviation). The monthly differences result in $t = 1.30$, which is also significant at the 0.10 level (with 71 degrees of freedom). The results using the other significance test, the Wilcoxon matched-pairs signed-ranked test, on the annual differences calculated $T = 7$ for this test which is significant only at the 0.23 level indicating that the annual differences between the H.Y. Composite and the Syn. Govt. returns are less conclusive than we had determined based on the difference in means test.

The monthly Wilcoxon test, however, indicates greater confidence with $Z = 1.73$, significant at the 0.08 level for the two-tailed test. We therefore continue to find that the H.Y. Composite outperforms the risk-free Government bond portfolios, but somewhat less so when the various portfolios are matched for duration.[6]

High-Yield – High-Default Risk Portfolios

As indicated above, two of the high-yield portfolios performed significantly better than the others. These are the CCC-rated groups and Zeta fourth quartile. Both had the greatest default rate but a combination of offsetting higher returns and the one-year holding periods mitigated the impact of defaults. It is important to point out these differences to investors with a broad range of options and match these options with investor utility functions.[7]

We also have not explored analytic techniques for achieving efficient portfolios in the traditional mean-variance framework. Preliminary work by Bookstaber and Jacob (1985), indicates that randomly selected portfolios can achieve minimum variance of returns with a small number of debt securities and that adding a large number of issues may actually increase return variability. In addition, a potentially important dimension relating to "systematic crisis risk" for a large number of securities has not been explored. For example, the question can be asked as to what impact a $5 per barrel change in oil prices will have on the default risk of a diversified portfolio, or, the impact of domestic changes in inflation and real interest rates. Finally, such other micro-portfolio factors as principal repayment schedules could be relevant.

High-Yield – High-Quality portfolios – A Concluding Note

We have demonstrated that high-yield portfolios with minimal default risk qualities (high quality approach) can be achieved with some type of credit evaluation methodology. Returns significantly above investment grade debt securities were observed for portfolios based on the computerized credit screen Zeta technique. If such an approach were adopted, we recommend that traditional, subjective credit evaluation techniques, inherent in a sophisticated credit research environment, complement the computerized approach for at least three reasons:

1 To provide more timely modifications to the portfolio as conditions change *between* the reporting period of the model;
2 To monitor results, especially when a large financial statement data base, such as *Compustat*, reports possible abnormal results, e.g., large annual changes in a credit's profile;
3 To add securities to the "acceptable list" for a fund when the computerized model would not have selected the security. For example, to include securities where data is insufficient to provide a Zeta score, or the firm is not covered by the data base, or the credit deterioration risk is deemed acceptable based on qualitative assessments, etc.

As in most risk–return frameworks, we believe that the greater the risk reduction qualities of an approach, the greater will be the sacrifice in promised yields and also, it appears based on our findings, the lower the realized *ex-post* returns.

APPENDIX A
DATA BASE CHARACTERISTICS AND CALCULATIONS

The following is a description of our data base and a discussion of comparisons with other, similar composites.

Analytic Methods – Return Calculations

For the purposes of portfolio comparisons, the individual period lengths analyzed are restricted to twelve months. The data base can, however, accommodate varying period lengths based on six-month intervals of time. The time period for calculating returns covered by the study is March 31, 1978 through March 31, 1984. In addition, monthly wealth indices are analyzed.

Our High-Yield Composite index is based on a weighted average return calculation of individual bonds (coupon and reinvestment income + change in price)/beginning investment, weighted by dollar amounts outstanding and then summed over the entire portfolio.

Bonds pay coupons on different dates over the calendar year. Within portfolios, coupon income payments arrive throughout the year. This study assumed all coupons, on average, would be paid six months into each holding period. The coupon income was immediately reinvested in the same bond until the end of the calculation period. At period's end, the portfolio was sold and reconstructed for the next period. Symbolically, the rate of return on an individual bond can be represented as

$$R_{i,t} = \{[(1 + \frac{1/2\,C}{(P_6)})(1 + \frac{1/2\,C}{(P_{12})})P_{12}]/P_0\} - 1$$

where $R_{i,t}$ is the return on bond i in month t, C is the coupon amount, P_0 is the price at start of month, P_6 is the price at end of six months, and P_{12} is the price at end of twelve months.

Defaulting bonds were included in the portfolio up until the end of period in which they defaulted. When a default occurred, one half of coupon income due for the six-month period (in which the default occurred) was assumed to be received on all issues outstanding for the defaulting company. No additional coupon income was received. At the end of the period, the bond was sold. Bonds in default at the beginning of a new period were not included in the new portfolio. This is an arbitrary assumption and in many cases defaulted bonds can be bought or sold on a post-default basis.

Monthly Return Index

A monthly return index was also calculated for each of the major portfolio strategies tested. These returns were derived using the following simplified approach:

$$R_{i,t} = \frac{1/12\,C + P_1 - P_0}{P_0}$$

where $R_{i,t}$ is the return on bond i in month t, C is the coupon amount, P_1 is the price at end of month, and P_0 is the price at beginning of month.

This methodology, while not perfectly accurate for calculating total compounded returns over longer periods of time (due to our use of a proxy for accrued interest), does provide a good indication of the month-to-month variations in returns. To verify the reliability of our results, we compared our monthly High-Yield (H.Y.) Composite to those of Blume and Keim (1984) and also the monthly returns published by Drexel Burnham Lambert (D.B.L.). As noted below, we found the three series to be very highly correlated for the period January 1982 to March 1984.

	Correlation coefficient (R)
Morgan Stanley H.Y. Composite vs. Blume and Keim index	0.95
Morgan Stanley H.Y. Composite vs. D.B.L. index	0.93
Blume and Keim index vs. D.B.L. index	0.95

We calculated also the correlation between these three indexes and Shearson Lehman's Long-Term Government Bond index, and found significant but lower correlations.

Sample Description

The sample consisted of 440 fixed rate bonds representing 244 issuers from the high yield universe as it existed between 1978 and 1984. Bonds qualified for the sample only if their issuer had a Zeta score for five or more years. The model is not appropriate for utilities and financial firms so these were removed. Also, in a handful of cases when companies merged and the debt was assumed, the Zeta score of the parent firm was extended to the merged (issuing) firm from the point of merger onward. Our sample represented, on average, 62 percent of the total debt outstanding in the low-rated universe with utilities comprising the bulk of the bonds not included.

The study sample consisted of 16 industry categories, the largest of which were: manufacturing/heavy industry (61 issues), conglomerates/ (non-bank) holding companies (36 issuers), oil and gas (36 issuers), and high-tech/communications (33 issuers).

Data Base Information Sources

Totally reliable pricing in the high-yield bond area is probably impossible to find. In the past, because of a lack of interest in the area, very few of the bonds were directly priced, except when a transaction occurred. Because the majority of the study's bonds are traded on the New York and American Exchanges, it was felt that exchange-based prices would give a less biased view of actual market fluctuations than either pure matrix prices or "broker's quotes."

Matrix models use specific "bellwether" bonds and also the yield curve to drive the prices of all other bonds (based on their relative coupons, ratings, level of subordination, maturity dates, etc.). Using pure matrix prices would have meant that prices are determined more by mathematical models than by the characteristics of the high-yield market itself. Broker quotes have their own individual bias. "Quotes" can also incorporate a large degree of matrix pricing and may not be continuous due to lack of trading activity.

Our bond price data was derived from the data tapes of the Interactive Data Corp. which essentially provides exchange-listed prices with a small amount of matrix prices. Month-end closing prices or the price closest to the month-end were used. In the majority of cases we had only "ask" prices which could have presented some bias but it turns out the correlation of these prices was very high with Blume and Keim's (1984) broker quote prices.

We also considered using data based on a combination of broker quotes and matrix prices and ran some tests to determine differences in the two data bases. Monthly prices on 12 bonds were compared over the period 1975–1984 with 46 percent of the prices matching exactly and 37 percent having prices within $20 of each other. Given the close correlation of the two types of pricing available, the decision to use the exchange price data base was a pragmatic one since more complete data histories were available.

Outstanding dollar amounts of each issue came from the May issues of Standard & Poor's Bond Guide and the bond ratings were taken from the July issues of S.&P. and Moody's (consistent with our earlier default rate study (Altman and Nammacher, 1985)). The May issue was used because of specific investment timing assumptions, since the year-end Zeta is not available until April, at the earliest, and investment decisions would have to wait at least until this date.

APPENDIX B

Table 10.9 Contribution of total return from coupon (C) and price changes (P)I[a] March 1978 to March 1984

Portfolio	1978 C (%)	1978 P (%)	1979 C (%)	1979 P (%)	1980 C (%)	1980 P (%)	1981 C (%)	1981 P (%)	1982 C (%)	1982 P (%)	1983 C (%)	1983 P (%)
High-yield composite	181.39	−81.39	−66.27	166.27	80.90	19.10	454.69	−354.69	39.17	60.83	134.94	−34.94
BB rated	299.03	−199.03	−50.41	150.41	92.30	7.70	283.73	−183.73	38.60	61.40	164.69	−64.69
B rated	188.57	−88.57	−76.56	176.56	79.59	20.41	3,041.73	−2,941.73	41.70	58.30	127.75	−27.75
CCC rated	102.70	−2.70	−95.87	195.87	53.43	46.57	295.10	−195.10	31.88	68.20	105.52	−5.52
Zeta ≥ 1	172.64	−72.64	54.90	−154.90	98.87	1.13	226.79	−126.79	39.44	60.56	140.32	−40.32

[a] The numbers in the table indicate the percentage of the total return attributable to coupon income and price changes, and were calculated as follows:

$$\frac{\text{Total coupon return (\%)}}{\text{Total return (\%)}} = C$$

$$\frac{\text{Total return (\%) from price change}}{\text{Total return (\%)}} = P$$

Example: Total return = 9%
        Coupon return = 12%
        Price return = −3%

$$\frac{12\%}{9\%} = 133.33\% \ (C) \qquad \frac{-3\%}{9\%} = -33.33\% \ (P)$$

NOTES

1   The high-yield portfolio results come from the Morgan Stanley database described in detail in Appendix A.
2   Returns are very sensitive to the time period examined. For example, the return spread for the period 31 March, 1978 to 31 March, 1984 was 490 basis points. A three-month shift caused a 93 basis point change in returns.
3   Not including exchange offers, best effort offerings or convertibles.
4   This brief section summarizes an earlier study by the authors, "The Default Rate Experience on High Yield Corporate Debt" (Altman and Nammacher, 1985a) reprinted in *The Financial Analysts Journal*, July–August 1985.
5   See Bookstaber and Clark (1985) for a discussion of this issue, which revolves around the problems of a mean-variance framework for securities with implicit options.
6   The test comparing the Zeta ≥ 1.0 portfolio returns with a matched duration government bond index indicated very similar results to what we find using the H.Y. Composite. The Z statistic rather than the T is used for large samples.
7   For example, if hedging strategies are introduced (see Bookstaber and Jacob, 1985) into a high-yield investment strategy, even the greatest default risk potential portfolio might become acceptable.

BIBLIOGRAPHY

Altman, E. I. and Nammacher, S. 1985a: *The Default Rate Experience on High Yield Debt*, New York: Morgan Stanley. Reprinted in *Financial Analysts Journal*, July–August 1985.
Altman, E. I. and Nammacher, S. 1985b: *The Anatomy of the High Yield Debt Market*, New York: Morgan Stanley.
Altman, E. I. and Nammacher, S. 1985c: *Portfolio Analysis in the High Yield Debt Market*, New York: Morgan Stanley.
Altman, E. I., Haldeman, R. and Narayanan, P. 1977: Zeta™ Analysis, a new model to identify bankruptcy risk of corporations. *Journal of Banking & Finance*, June.
Atkinson, T. R. 1967: Trends in corporate bond quality. Cambridge Mass.: National Bureau of Economic Research.
Blume, M. E. and Keim, D. B. 1984: Risk and return characteristics of lower-grade bonds. Working Paper, Rodney White Center for Financial Research, The Wharton School, Philadelphia, PA 19104.
Bookstaber, R. and Clark, R. 1985: Problems in evaluating the performance of portfolios with options. *Financial Analysts Journal*, January–February.
Bookstaber, R. and Jacob, D. 1985: *The Composite Hedge. Controlling the Credit Risk of High Yield Bonds*, New York: Morgan Stanley, *Financial Analysts Journal*, forthcoming.
Drexel Burnham Lambert, *High Yield Newsletter*, Los Angeles, CA, monthly 1982–5.
Drexel Burnham Lambert, 1985: *The Case for High Yield Bonds*, Los Angeles, CA.

Hickman, W. B. 1958: *Corporate Bond Quality And Investor Experience.* Princeton University Press and the National Bureau of Economic Research.

Macauley, F. 1938: *Some Theoretical Problems Suggested by the Movements of Interest Rates, Bond Yields and Stock Prices in the U.S. Since 1856,* National Bureau of Economic Research.

Siegel, S. 1956: *Non-Parametric Statistics,* New York: McGraw-Hill.

Wilcoxon, F. and Wilcox, F. 1964: *Some Rapid Approximate Statistical Procedures,* Pearl River, N.Y.; Lederle Laboratories, American Cyanamid, revised.

11
Comparative Efficiency of Market Indices: An Empirical Study

CHI-CHENG HSIA

PREFACE

Since I received my degree and left U.C.L.A., Dr. J. Fred Weston has continued to educate me by sending me the working papers which he valued highly. About three years ago, I received a copy of Kandel's working paper: "The Likelihood Ratio Test Statistic of Mean-Variance Efficiency without a Riskless Asset," which Kandel presented at the U.C.L.A. finance workshop. Then, about one-half year later, I received from Dr. Weston a copy of Roll's working paper: "A Note on the Geometry of Shanken's C.S.R. T^2 Test for Mean-Variance Efficiency," and from Dr. Roll copies of Shanken's paper: "Multivariate Tests of the Zero-Beta C.A.P.M.," and Ross' paper: "A Test of the Efficiency of a Given Portfolio." Having read these and the related papers, I realized that they can be integrated into one model which can be used to rank portfolios in terms of comparative efficiency without having to know the true *market portfolio. I transformed the Shanken and Kandel statistics into efficiency measures which I call the S and K measures.*

Tests of the model are interesting. In spite of the fact that the efficient frontiers fluctuate widely over the 11 sample periods, the rankings of eight different market indices are remarkably consistent period by period. The C.R.S.P. equally-weighted, C.R.S.P. value-weighted, and S.&P. 500 consistently emerge as the three most efficient indices under all market

The author wishes to thank Stephen Brown, Richard Roll, Fred Weston, Russell Fuller, Halbert Kerr, Wenchi Wong, and an anonymous referee for their helpful comments, and also Johnnie Chen for computational assistance. This paper first appeared in *Journal of Financial Research* 9(2), 123–35 and is reprinted with permission.

conditions. Between the two measures, the S *measure appears to be preferred, because the efficiency scores measured by* K *are close together such that they are susceptible to rounding errors. However, the* S *and* K *measure give almost identical rankings.*

Upon completion of the draft, I presented the paper to Dr. Weston for comment. He carefully read the paper, made editorial changes, and offered me valuable comments for further improvements. If this paper makes any contribution to the finance literature, I'd like to attribute it to the continuing education, encouragement, and inspiration provided by Dr. Weston, my life-time teacher.

INTRODUCTION

A number of market indices describing the general movements of capital markets are widely used in the financial community. Qualitative evaluations of these indices have been documented in the investment literature. However, for the purpose of financial analysis and empirical studies, a systematic ranking of these indices is clearly needed. Stambough (1982) constructed four market indices with returns on bonds, real estate, and consumer durables in addition to common stocks. Using the Lagrangian multiplier (L.M.) test, Stambough found that the mean-variance efficiency hypothesis could not be rejected for the four indices he constructed. However, no systematic ranking of the four indices was given by the L.M. test of Stambough. The objective of this study is to provide measures for systematically ranking market indices in terms of comparative mean-variance efficiency.

The ranking measures used in this study are derived from the most recent developments in financial econometrics. Roll (1980) shows that the mean-variance efficiency of a given portfolio can be measured by the magnitude of deviations of the portfolio from the efficient frontier. Assuming the existence of a riskless asset and multivariate normality of asset returns, Ross (1980) introduces a likelihood ratio test of the mean-variance efficiency of a given portfolio. Kandel (1984) extends the Ross model to obtain a likelihood ratio test statistic of mean-variance efficiency for a given portfolio without the existence of a riskless asset.

Independent of Kandel, Shanken (1985) derives a generalized least squares cross-sectional regression (C.S.R.) Hotelling T^2 test for the mean-variance efficiency of a given portfolio. Roll (1985) further develops Shanken's test to obtain a geometric representation of the Shanken statistic. This study uses two efficiency scores developed from the statistics of Kandel, Shanken, and Roll, as the criteria for ranking the comparative efficiency of market indices.

The paper is organized as follows: the second section provides two efficiency scores, S and K, derived from the Roll geometric representation of the Shanken statistic and the likelihood ratio test statistic of Kandel, respectively. The third section describes the data and reports the estimated values of parameters. The next section presents the results of the tests and discusses the implications. The final section is a summary of the findings and concludes the paper.

EFFICIENCY SCORES

This section consists of three subsections. In the first two subsections, the efficiency scores S and K are derived respectively. The third subsection discusses the similarities and differences between S and K.

Efficiency Score S

The Shanken test statistic Q_s is a sum of residual squares obtained from a generalized least squares (G.L.S.) cross-sectional regression:

$$Q_s = T\mathbf{u}' \, V^{-1}\mathbf{u} \tag{11.1}$$

where T is the time series sample size, $\mathbf{u} = (n \times 1)$ vector of residuals from a generalized least squares cross-sectional regression on betas for n assets, and $V = (n \times n)$ sample covariance matrix.

Roll (1985) extends equation (11.1) to obtain a geometric representation and shows that Q_s can be written as

$$Q_s = T\Omega \, \frac{\sigma_m^2 - \sigma_{m*}^2}{\sigma_m^2 - \sigma_o^2} \tag{11.2}$$

where σ_m^2 is the sample variance of a given index m which has a sample mean return r_m, σ_{m*}^2 is the sample variance of a portfolio which is sample mean-variance efficient and has the same sample mean as r_m, σ_o^2 is the sample variance of the global minimum variance portfolio, and $\Omega = D/L$.

The quantities L, M, N, and D are the four elements of the information matrix of the sample efficient frontier. They are defined as: $L = \mathbf{e}' V^{-1}\mathbf{e}$, $M = \mathbf{e}' V^{-1}\mathbf{R}$, $N = \mathbf{R}' V^{-1}\mathbf{R}$, and $D = NL - M^2$, where $\mathbf{e}$ is an $(n \times 1)$ vector of 1s and $\mathbf{R}$ is an $(n \times 1)$ vector of sample mean returns. The quantity Ω is determined by the curvature of the sample efficient frontier, which is unrelated to the particular index being tested (cf. Roll, 1985, p. 352).

Note that equation (11.2) can be written as $Q_s = T\Omega(1 - S)$, where S is a ratio of tangents of two angles x and y (see figure 11.1a)

$$S = \frac{\tan x}{\tan y} \tag{11.3}$$

where

$$\tan x = \frac{r_m - r_o}{\sigma_m^2 - \sigma_o^2} = \frac{r_o - \gamma_o}{\sigma_o^2}$$

$$\tan y = \frac{r_m - r_o}{\sigma_{m*}^2 - \sigma_o^2} = \frac{r_o - \gamma_2}{\sigma_o^2}$$

$$\gamma_o = \frac{r_o \sigma_m^2 - r_m \sigma_o^2}{\sigma_m^2 - \sigma_o^2}$$

and

$$\gamma_2 = \frac{N - M r_m}{M - L r_m}$$

The r_o is the sample mean return of the global minimum variance portfolio; γ_o is the intercept of a line passing through the positions of O (the global minimum variance portfolio) and m (the index being tested); and γ_2 is the intercept of a line passing through the positions of O and $m*$ (the efficient portfolio that has the same sample mean as m).

Equation (11.3) has two advantages. First, since S is a ratio of tangents, the trigonometric relationship can be used conveniently. This advantage will greatly facilitate the comparison between the properties of S and K, because K is also a ratio of tangents of two angles. Second, the value of S can be used to rank unambiguously competing indices in terms of mean-variance efficiency. This is because $S \leqslant 1$, where the equity holds if and only if the index m being tested is *ex-post* mean-variance efficient, in which case m converges to $m*$. For all other cases, $0 < S < 1$. The closer is the similarity of the two triangles (i.e. $\Delta r_o O \gamma_o$ and $\Delta r_o O \gamma_2$, see figures 11.1(a) and (b)), the higher is the value of S, and the higher is the comparative efficiency of the index being tested; and conversely.

In figure 11.1(a), there are two efficient frontiers: the sample efficient frontier and the constrained efficient frontier. The sample efficient frontier (the outer parabola) is generated by the function (cf. Merton, 1972; Roll, 1977) $\sigma_p^2 = (1/D)(L r_p^2 - 2 M r_p + N)$. The constrained efficient frontier (the inner parabola) is generated by the same sample with additional constraints that the index m being tested is *ex-ante* mean-variance efficient and is orthogonal to γ_2. There exists a simple and direct relationship between these two efficient frontiers. Let L_c, M_c, N_c, and D_c be the elements of the information matrix of the constrained efficient frontier corresponding to the elements L, M, N, and D of the sample efficient frontier. Appendix A shows that the constrained efficient frontier is generated by

$$\sigma_p^2 = \frac{1}{D_c}(L_c r_p^2 - 2 M_c r_p + N_c) \tag{11.4}$$

where
$$L_c = L - G$$
$$M_c = M - r_m G$$
$$N_c = N - r_m^2 G$$
$$D_c = D(1 - \sigma_m^2 * G)$$

and

$$G = \frac{1}{\sigma_{m*}^2} - \frac{1}{\sigma_m^2} \geqslant 0$$

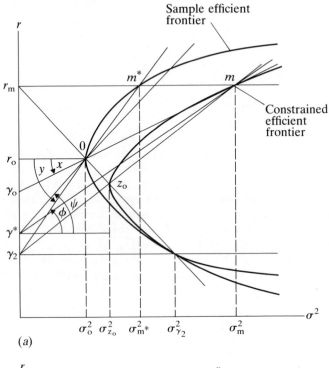

(a)

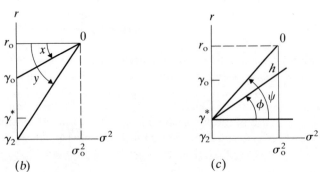

(b)   (c)

Figure 11.1   (a) Efficiency scores S and K, S = (tan x)/(tan y), K = (tan φ)/(tan ψ); (b) score S (c) score K

Equation (11.4) specifies the direct relationship between the two efficient frontiers. The degree of mean-variance inefficiency of the index m is related to the quantity G, which measures the difference between the reciprocals of σ_{m*}^2 *and* σ_m^2. If $G=0$, the two efficient frontiers coincide. The larger is the value of G, the further apart are the two efficient frontiers, and the worse off is the mean-variance efficiency of the index m being tested.

Efficiency Score K

The Kandel (1984) likelihood ratio test (L.R.T.) statistic is (see figure 11.1(c))

$$Q_k = T \log \frac{\tan \psi}{\tan \phi} \tag{11.5}$$

where

$$\tan \psi = \frac{r_0 - \gamma^*}{\sigma_0^2}$$

$$\tan \phi = \frac{r_m - \gamma^*}{\sigma_m^2} = \frac{h - \gamma^*}{\sigma_0^2}$$

The unique point of the Kandel statistic is γ^*. It is the smaller (larger) of the two roots of a quadratic function $H(r)$, if $r_m > r_0$ (if $r_m < r_0$). The quadratic function $H(r)$ is

$$H(r) = Ar^2 + Br + C \tag{11.6}$$

where

$$A = -1$$

$$B = -\frac{L(\sigma_m^2 + r_m^2) - (1 + N)}{M - Lr_m}$$

$$C = \frac{M(\sigma_m^2 + r_m^2) - r_m(1 + N)}{M - Lr_m}$$

Note that equation (11.5) can be written as $Q_k = T \log(1/K)$ where

$$K = \frac{\tan \phi}{\tan \psi} \leqslant 1 \tag{11.7}$$

The efficiency score K, similarly to the efficiency score S, can also unambiguously rank competing indices in terms of comparative mean-variance efficiency. This is because $K = 1$ if and only if the index m being tested is *ex-post* mean-variance efficient. For all other cases, $0 < K < 1$. The larger is the value of K, the higher is the mean-variance efficiency of the index, and conversely.

A Comparison between S and K

Since the empirical test that follows will be performed by using both scores S and K, their similarities and differences are summarized below.

1   Similarities
    (a) Both measures can be generated by the same elements of the information matrix (L, M, N, and D).
    (b) Both measures assume the non-existence of a riskless asset.
    (c) Both measures evaluate similarities of two triangles.
    (d) Both measures can unambiguously rank competing indices in terms of mean-variance efficiency.
2   Differences
    (a) The triangles measured by S are predicated on γ_0 and γ_2, while the triangles measured by K are predicated on γ^*. Kandel shows that $\gamma_0 > \gamma^* > \gamma_2$ if $r_m > r_o$; and the converse.
    (b) It can be shown that $K > S$, because $\tan \phi > \tan x$ and $\tan \psi < \tan y$.

DATA AND ESTIMATION

Data and Sample Periods

The data used in this study consists of eight widely used market indices. They are: S.&P. 500, N.Y.E. (New York Stock Exchange Composite Index), A.M.X. (American Stock Exchange Index), O.T.C., (Over-the-counter N.A.S.D.A.Q. Composite Index), D.J.I. (Dow-Jones Industrial Average), D.J.C. (Dow-Jones Composite Index), V.W. (C.R.S.P., value-weighted with dividends), and E.W. (C.R.S.P., equally-weighted with dividends).

Ten years of monthly data covering the period from January 1973 to December 1982 were collected from the following sources: V.W. and E.W., Center for Research in Security Prices of the University of Chicago; S.&P. 500, *Stocks, Bonds, and Inflation: The Past and The Future* (Ibbotson and Sinquefield, 1984); N.Y.E., A.M.X., O.T.C., D.J.I., and D.J.C., from *Wall Street Journal*. The return series are computed by using the formula $(I_t - I_{t-1})/(I_{t-1})$, where I is the month-end value of the index reported in *Wall Street Journal*.

The tests are repeated with varying time spans from six to ten years with different starting and ending periods. There are, in total, 11 overlapping test samples. Figure 11.2 explains the sample size and sample period covered by each of the 11 test samples.

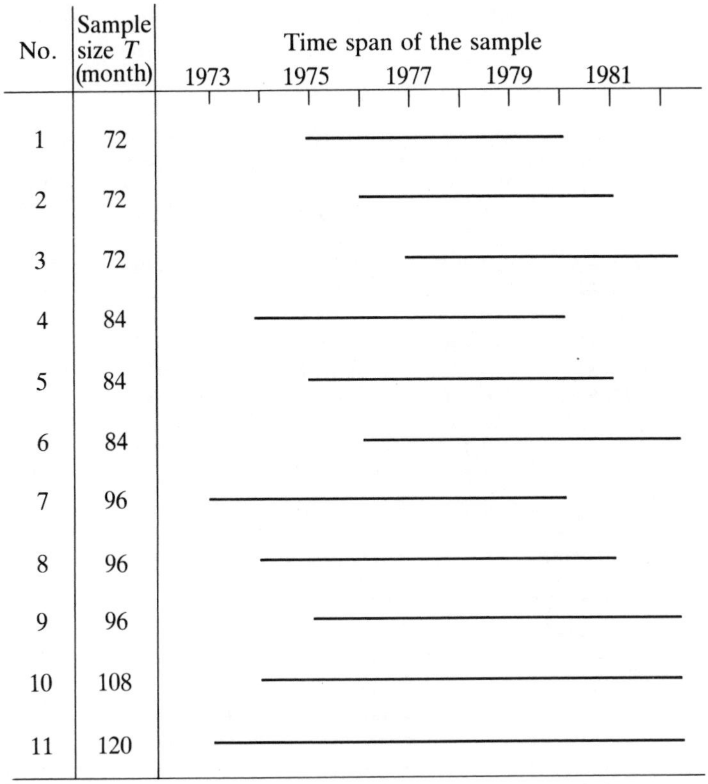

No.	Sample size T (month)	Time span of the sample

Figure 11.2   Sample size and sample periods of the tests

Estimation

Table 11.1 summarizes the estimated values of the 11 sample efficient frontiers. Table 11.1A reports the estimated values of the four elements of the information matrix (L, M, N, D) for each of the 11 test samples. Table 11.1B presents the estimated coefficients of the sample efficient frontiers. An examination of table 11.1 reveals that the sample efficient frontiers fluctuate widely over time. For example, the value of L/D, which is the coefficient of r_p^2, varies from 4.053 in the period of 1975–1982 to 13.86 in the period of 1973–1982.

Using equation (11.4) and the estimated values of L, M, N, and D of table 11.1, we have generated 88 constrained efficient frontiers, one for each of the eight indices in each of the 11 test sample periods. Further, using equation (11.6) and the same set of information (L, M, N, D), we have also generated 88 $H(r)$ functions for determining the values of

Table 11.1   Information matrix and sample efficient frontiers

A   Information matrix

T	Period	L $(\mathbf{e}'V^{-1}\mathbf{e})$	M $(\mathbf{R}'V^{-1}\mathbf{e})$	N $(\mathbf{R}'V^{-1}\mathbf{R})$	D $(LN-M^2)$
72	1975–80	754.696	3.27582	0.208294	146.468
	1976–81	783.232	0.26121	0.203919	159.647
	1977–82	758.309	1.01640	0.194584	146.522
84	1974–80	527.394	1.31574	0.104994	53.694
	1975–81	751.219	1.62477	0.187237	138.016
	1976–82	740.233	2.12002	0.172665	123.318
96	1973–80	527.490	2.03626	0.227280	115.741
	1974–81	554.789	0.55582	0.100740	55.582
	1975–82	716.220	1.62939	0.250320	176.727
108	1974–82	550.796	1.07429	0.107105	57.839
120	1973–82	547.728	0.80803	0.073339	39.517

B   Coefficients of the sample efficient frontiers $\sigma_p^2 = (L/D)r_p^2 - (2M/D)r_p + (N/D)$

T	Period	L/D	$2M/D$	N/D
72	1975–80	5.153	0.0447	0.0014
	1976–81	4.906	0.0033	0.0013
	1977–82	5.175	0.0139	0.0013
84	1974–80	9.831	0.0490	0.0020
	1975–81	5.443	0.0235	0.0014
	1976–82	6.003	0.0344	0.0014
96	1973–80	4.558	0.0352	0.0020
	1974–81	9.981	0.0200	0.0018
	1975–82	4.053	0.0184	0.0014
108	1974–82	9.523	0.0371	0.0019
120	1973–82	13.860	0.0409	0.0019

Table 11.2

Period	G value
1975–80	46.04
1976–81	23.72
1977–82	52.05
1974–80	44.09
1975–81	27.01
1976–82	17.73
1973–80	237.17
1974–81	27.27
1975–82	65.33
1974–82	25.54
1973–82	45.31

γ^* estimates. The detailed values of these estimates are not reported due to space limitations, but they are all available upon request.

One interesting point worth noting is the behavior of G estimates (see equation (11.4)). As a typical example, the estimated values of G associated with the C.R.S.P. equally-weighted index for the 11 sample periods are summarized in table 11.2.

Note that the G estimate for the period of 1973–1980 ($G = 237.17$) is particularly large, which implies that the index E.W. is far off the sample efficient frontiers. This information provides evidence of mean-variance inefficiency of the index E.W. in that period (see discussions following equation (11.4).

TEST RESULTS

S *Scores and Rankings of Indices*

Table 11.3 reports the S scores and rankings of the eight indices being tested. The scores are ranked from high to low in each of the 11 sample periods. The last two columns provide the weighted average scores and the corresponding rankings, where the weights are the sample size of the respective sample period.

Note the remarkable consistency in rankings over the 11 sample periods, even though, as noted earlier, the sample efficient frontiers fluctuate widely over time. The evidence indicates that the eight indices can be classified into three distinct groups. The first group consists of three indices: E.W. (the equally-weighted C.R.S.P.), V.W. (the value-weighted C.R.S.P.), and S.&P. 500. These three indices almost always rank in the top three over the 11 sample periods. On average (see the last two columns), E.W. ranks first, V.W. second, and S.&P. third. Their average scores are all above 60 percent with $S(\text{E.W.}) = 73$ percent, $S(\text{V.W.}) = 68$ percent, and $S(\text{S.\&P.}) = 64$ percent. One possible reason that the average efficiency score of E.W. is higher than that of V.W. might be due to the small firm effect, which is not tested in this paper because it is beyond the scope of this study.

In contrast, the N.Y.E. and D.J.I. indices consistently emerge at the bottom of the list with average scores below 20 percent (S (N.Y.E.) = 16 percent and S (D.J.I.) = 15.6 percent). The remaining three indices (A.M.X., O.T.C., and D.J.C.) consistently rank in the middle with average scores below 50 percent and above 20 percent (S (A.M.X.) = 46 percent, S (O.T.C.) = 39 percent, and S (D.J.C.) = 24 percent). One possible reason that the N.Y.E. index is being dominated in the mean-variance space might be due to the "dividend effect," because both N.Y.E. and V.W. are value-weighted indices with a similar population, but N.Y.E. includes no dividend while V.W. is dividend adjusted.

Table 11.3 S scores and rankings

T = 72 and T = 84

| | T = 72 | | | | | | T = 84 | | | | | |
| | 1975–80 | | 1976–81 | | 1977–82 | | 1974–80 | | 1975–81 | | 1976–82 | |
Index	Score	Rank	Score	Rank	Score	Rank	Score	Rank	Score	Rank	Score	Rank
S.&P.	0.80701	2	0.79803	3	0.39821	4	0.68222	3	0.88383	2	0.55140	3
N.Y.E.	0.20269	7	0.47617	6	0.21045	6	0.06310	8	0.19956	8	0.27723	5
A.M.X.	0.66542	5	0.68142	4	0.40536	3	0.65432	4	0.55365	4	0.49815	4
O.T.C.	0.66900	4	0.48842	5	0.36837	5	0.43799	5	0.50289	5	0.42557	6
D.J.I.	0.19480	8	0.17214	8	0.13316	7	0.09896	7	0.22839	7	0.14180	8
D.J.C.	0.33173	6	0.37360	7	0.09506	8	0.23609	6	0.40526	6	0.18107	7
V.W.	0.87805	1	0.84060	2	0.49188	2	0.72642	1	0.92554	1	0.64671	2
E.W.	0.76754	3	0.88463	1	0.75958	1	0.71518	2	0.85759	3	0.90822	1

T = 96, T = 108, T = 120, W. average

| | T = 96 | | | | | | T = 108 | | T = 120 | | W. average | |
| | 1973–80 | | 1974–81 | | 1975–82 | | 1974–82 | | 1973–82 | | Whole sample | |
Index	Score	Rank	Score	Rank	Score	Rank	Score	Rank	Score	Rank	Score	Rank
S.&P.	0.07264	4	0.73828	3	0.67844	3	0.63481	2	0.67400	3	0.63633	3
N.Y.E.	0.00276	7	0.06157	8	0.17915	8	0.05625	8	0.03986	8	0.16080	7
A.M.X.	0.09083	2	0.53546	4	0.33240	6	0.37539	4	0.28456	4	0.46154	4
O.T.C.	0.02561	5	0.38875	5	0.38153	4	0.35705	5	0.25958	5	0.39134	5
D.J.I.	0.00884	6	0.11493	7	0.30730	7	0.20420	6	0.10724	7	0.15561	8
D.J.C.	0.00094	8	0.28766	6	0.34255	5	0.19784	7	0.16702	6	0.23907	6
V.W.	0.09061	3	0.76393	2	0.69064	1	0.69352	3	0.71233	2	0.67820	2
E.W.	0.11082	1	0.82102	1	0.68812	2	0.83053	1	0.71737	1	0.73278	1

V.W. and E.W. stand for the value-weighted and equally-weighted C.R.S.P. monthly returns.

Table 11.4 K scores and rankings

Index	T=72 1975–80 Score	Rank	1976–81 Score	Rank	1977–82 Score	Rank	T=84 1974–80 Score	Rank	1975–81 Score	Rank	1976–82 Score	Rank
S.&P.	0.97620	2	0.97623	3	0.92147	3	0.97639	2	0.98731	2	0.95128	3
N.Y.E.	0.88448	7	0.93287	5	0.88666	7	0.91543	8	0.88899	8	0.91291	6
A.M.X.	0.94877	5	0.94899	4	0.90272	4	0.96962	4	0.93405	4	0.93100	4
O.T.C.	0.95259	4	0.91871	7	0.90202	5	0.95136	5	0.92760	6	0.92208	5
D.J.I.	0.88343	8	0.89786	8	0.89999	6	0.92350	7	0.89715	7	0.90950	7
D.J.C.	0.91636	6	0.92897	6	0.86893	8	0.94666	6	0.93241	5	0.90327	8
V.W.	0.98428	1	0.97957	2	0.92936	2	0.97877	1	0.99098	1	0.95821	2
E.W.	0.96454	3	0.98252	1	0.96507	1	0.97507	3	0.97946	3	0.98819	1

Index	T=96 1973–80 Score	Rank	1974–81 Score	Rank	1975–82 Score	Rank	T=108 1974–82 Score	Rank	T=120 1973–82 Score	Rank	W. average Whole sample Score	Rank
S.&P.	0.85587	1	0.98109	3	0.95633	1	0.97251	3	0.98180	2	0.95613	3
N.Y.E	0.72734	8	0.91634	8	0.86274	8	0.91228	8	0.93602	8	0.89004	8
A.M.X.	0.83832	4	0.95930	4	0.87369	7	0.94236	5	0.95241	4	0.92545	4
O.T.C.	0.82627	5	0.94642	6	0.88639	6	0.94121	6	0.95107	5	0.91884	5
D.J.I.	0.78850	7	0.92730	7	0.90147	5	0.93871	7	0.94294	7	0.90078	7
D.J.C.	0.81856	6	0.95153	5	0.91039	4	0.94417	4	0.94801	6	0.91500	6
V.W.	0.85060	2	0.98204	2	0.95297	2	0.97533	2	0.98288	1	0.95833	2
E.W.	0.84304	3	0.98467	1	0.94367	3	0.98496	1	0.98170	3	0.96049	1

Recall from table 11.1 that the efficient frontiers fluctuate widely over the sample periods. This evidence indicates that, regardless of market conditions (i.e. upward or downward markets), the E.W., V.W., and S.&P. are the highest mean-variance efficient indices among the eight widely used indices during the period of 1973–1982.

K *Scores and Rankings of Indices*

The test results using the K score are summarized in table 11.4. The K score rankings are almost perfectly consistent with the S score rankings. The rank correlation coefficient between the K and S rankings over the 11 sample periods is above 91 percent. As shown in the last two columns of table 11.4, the K score rankings of the top three indices (E.W. first, V.W. second, and S.&P. third) are on average exactly the same as those ranked by the S scores.

Further, the middle class indices (A.M.X., O.T.C., and D.J.C.) remain in the middle as the fourth, fifth, and sixth respectively. The K score ranks D.J.I. seventh and N.Y.E. eighth, but the difference between the two is minimal.

CONCLUSIONS

Using the efficiency scores S and K, and ten years of monthly data during the period of 1973–1982, this study tests the comparative mean-variance efficiency of eight widely used market indices. The results indicate that the C.R.S.P. equally-weighted, C.R.S.P. value-weighted, and S.&P. 500 consistently emerge as the three most efficient indices under all market conditions for the 11 tested samples.

APPENDIX

This appendix provides a proof for equation (11.4) which shows the direct relationship between the constrained efficient frontier and the sample efficient frontier (see figure 11.1). Note that an efficient frontier is a parabolic function, which can be determined by the means and variances of any two efficient portfolios and the covariance between these two portfolios. Since the covariance between r_m and γ_2 is zero by constraint, the elements of the information matrix of the constrained efficient frontier can be determined by

$$L_c = \begin{bmatrix} 1 & 1 \end{bmatrix} \begin{bmatrix} \sigma_m^2 & 0 \\ 0 & \sigma_{\gamma_2}^2 \end{bmatrix}^{-1} \begin{bmatrix} 1 \\ 1 \end{bmatrix} = \frac{1}{\sigma_m^2} + \frac{1}{\sigma_{\gamma_2}^2} \qquad (11.A1)$$

and similarly,

$$M_c = \frac{r_m}{\sigma_m^2} + \frac{\gamma_2}{\sigma_{\gamma_2}^2} \tag{11.A2}$$

$$N_c = \frac{r_m^2}{\sigma_m^2} + \frac{\gamma_2^2}{\sigma_{\gamma_2}^2} \tag{11.A3}$$

Since $(r_o - \gamma_2)/\sigma_o^2 = (r_m - \gamma_2)/\sigma_{m^*}^2$, *(see figure 11.1(a))*

$$\gamma_2 = \frac{r_o \sigma_{m^*}^2 - r_m \sigma_o^2}{\sigma_{m^*}^2 - \sigma_o^2} \tag{11.A4}$$

Further, since $(r_m - r_o)/\sigma_o^2 = (r_m - \gamma_2)/\sigma_{\gamma_2}^2$,

$$\sigma_{\gamma_2}^2 = \frac{\sigma_o^2(r_m - \gamma_2)}{r_m - r_o} \tag{11.A5}$$

Substituting (11.A4) into (11.A5) and simplifying terms we obtain

$$\frac{1}{\sigma_{\gamma_2}^2} = \frac{1}{\sigma_o^2} - \frac{1}{\sigma_{m^*}^2} \tag{11.A6}$$

Substituting (11.A6) back to (11.A1), we have the first element,

$$L_c = L - G \tag{11.A7}$$

where

$$G = \frac{1}{\sigma_{m^*}^2} - \frac{1}{\sigma_m^2} \tag{11.A7a}$$

Next, using (11.A4) and (11.A6) in (11.A2), the second element is

$$M_c = M - r_m G \tag{11.A8}$$

Further, since γ_2 is orthogonal to m on the constrained efficient frontier, and is also orthogonal to m^* on the sample efficient frontier,

$$\gamma_2 = \frac{N_c - M_c r_m}{M_c - L_c r_m} = \frac{N - M r_m}{M - L r_m} \tag{11A.9}$$

Using (11.A7) and (11.A8), the denominators of (11.A9) are equal, i.e. $M_c - L_c r_m = M - Lr_m$. Thus, (11.A9) reduces to

$$N_c - M_c r_m = N - Mr_m$$

Therefore,

$$N_c = N - r_m(M - M_c) = N - r_m^2 G \qquad (11.A10)$$

Finally, using (11.A7), (11.A8), and (11.A10) in the relation $D_c = N_c L_c - M_c^2$,

$$D_c = D(1 - \sigma_{m*}^2 G) \qquad (11.A11)$$

Equations (11.A7), (11.A8), (11.A10), and (11.A11) constitute the four elements of the constrained efficient frontier, with (11.A7a) defining the parameter G, which is written as equation (11.4) of the text.

BIBLIOGRAPHY

Cootner, P. H. 1978: Stock market indices: fallacy and illusions. *Commercial and Financial Chronicle*, September, 1966, reprinted in *Modern Development in Investment Management*, 2nd edn, Dryden Press, Hinsdale Ill., 94–100.

Fisher, L. 1966: Some new stock market indexes. *Journal of Business*, January, 191–225.

Fisher, L. and Lorie, J. 1964: Rates of return on investments in common stock. *Journal of Business*, January, 1–21.

Ibbotson, R. G. and Sinquefield, R. A. 1984: *Stocks, Bonds, and Inflation: The Past and The Future*, The Financial Analysts Research Foundation, University of Virginia.

Kandel, S. 1984: The likelihood ratio test statistic of mean-variance efficiency without a riskless asset. *Journal of Financial Economics*, 13, December, 575–92.

Lorie, J. H. and Hamilton, M. T. 1978: Stock market indices, In *Modern Development in Investment Management*, 2nd edn, Dryden Press, Hinsdale Ill.

Merton, R. C. 1972: An analytic derivation and the efficient portfolio frontier. *Journal of Financial and Quantitative Analysis*, 7, 1851–72.

Roll, R. 1977: A critique of the asset pricing theory's tests. *Journal of Financial Economics*, 4, 129–76.

Roll, R. 1980: Orthogonal portfolios. *Journal of Financial and Quantitative Analysis*, 5, 1005–23.

Roll, R. 1985: A note on the geometry of Shanken's C.R.S. *T*2 Test for mean-variance efficiency. *Journal of Financial Economics*, 14, 349–57.

Ross, S. A. 1980: A test of the efficiency of a given portfolio. Working Paper, Yale University.

Shanken, J. 1985: Multivariate tests of the zero-beta C.A.P.M. *Journal of Financial Economics*, 14, 327–48.

Stambaugh, R. F. 1982: On the exclusion of assets from tests of the two-parameter model. *Journal of Financial Economics*, 10, 237–68.

12

Financial Disclosure, Asymmetric Information and Financial Risk Assessment

WILLIAM BERANEK

PREFACE

Of the many favorable impressions I have of Weston as a mentor there is one that stands alone: his emphasis on objectivity. This fact is not easily lost on an impressionable student. And in terms of this precept, Weston practiced what he preached. As a research assistant I was exposed to the many opportunities he had of yielding to the temptation of failing to report undesirable evidence, or of overlooking compelling contrary arguments.

Weston was a constant source of encouragement and enlightened guidance. Among all mentors he was the one who not only provided me with the most inspiration to pursue graduate work, but who also introduced me to the then relatively undeveloped area of financial economics. He opened my eyes to this fertile field of research and his persistence gave me the courage to attempt to employ the full range of analytical techniques to the study of financial economics, both positive and normative.

There were still other acts for which I will be eternally grateful. Graduate students are not noted for their affluence and many of us were increasingly seeking means to support our studies. Weston never failed either to find some remunerative task or, failing that, to extend a personal loan to tide one over the all too frequent financial barriers that dogged our lives.

In my opinion Weston's greatest single gift to the finance profession is his exceptional ability to interpret the passing scene of scholarly research. All members of the profession were touched at some time in their careers by his incisive commentaries, and all have been enriched by his imaginative insights.

Finally, Weston was one of the early vigorous exponents of the need to develop positive financial theories as the most fruitful path for research

*development. He held this heretical view at a time when the profession
was dominated by institutionalists. Today the profession is richer because
of his leadership and scholarly contributions, and a number of former
students who owe so much to him regret that they can only repay him
with so little.*

INTRODUCTION

The private corporation may be viewed as a legal fiction "which serves
as a nexus for contracting relationships" (Jensen and Meckling, 1976).
Knowledge of these relationships and their implications is available in a
perfect market, so that the public has all relevant information pertaining
to security values. Such a state implies the absence of asymmetry in the
distribution of information.

A certain kind of information asymmetry exists in the *form* in which
financial statements are disclosed. The overwhelming majority of
corporations report to stockholders only consolidated financial statements.
Some report both consolidated and parent statements. A few publish just
parent statements. While shareholders of firms that issue both statements
receive more information than shareholders of firms that publish just
consolidated statements, it can be shown that under certain conditions
this greater information leads to a more accurate assessment of firm
financial risk, and hence, of firm value.

These information differences have only begun to be explored. Beranek
and Dillon (1982a; 1982b) point out that if a wholly owned subsidiary has
any debt owned by outsiders, the debt to equity ratio from the consolidated
statement will *always exceed* the corresponding parent company ratio. They
suggest that this relationship will often hold for partially owned
subsidiaries. An exploratory sample of 10 K reports revealed that the ratio
of the consolidated debt to equity ratio to the parent ratio ranged from
1.08 to 17.57. Conditions were also set forth under which the consolidated
interest-coverage ratio was related to the parent's ratio. Similarly,
conditions which spell a relationship between the parent's working-capital
ratio and the corresponding consolidated ratio were established.

Beranek and Clayton (1985) provide a formal proof of the above debt
to equity theorem. They also produce some evidence supporting the
hypothesis that the betas of firms that report only consolidated statements
(O.C.S.) tend to exceed those of appropriately matched firms that report
both forms of statements indicating that investors, when given full
information, do not believe that the parent always views subsidiary debt
as an unconditional obligation of the parent, or of other affiliated
subsidiaries.

Parents may wish to support the debt of some or all of their subsidiaries.
Clayton and Beranek (1985) suggest that subsidiaries essential to the

parent's mission tend to find their debt being parent supported. This implies that vertically integrated systems should enjoy more support than horizontal or conglomerate systems. While this hypothesis cannot be tested directly, an indirect test conducted by Clayton and Beranek led to its confirmation.

The purpose of this effort is to summarize the literature in this area of information differences and perceived financial risk and to extend these lines of investigation. The first section reviews the debt to equity theorem, derives further implications, and discusses the findings of the earlier studies mentioned above. The second section reviews explanations for financial-statement informational asymmetry. The final section contains suggestions for further research.

CONSOLIDATED STATEMENTS AND FINANCIAL RISK

Legal Liability, Letters of Support, and the Color of Liability

Generally, a parent is not legally responsible *per se* for the contractual debts of its subsidiary. An additional step must be taken by the parent to extend such responsibility. An explicit written guarantee is one such step. Others the firm may take are much weaker, and very difficult to enforce against the parent but nevertheless may be adequate to win a judgement in a court of law. A court may give relief to a subsidiary creditor when it is convinced that the parent gave an overwhelming impression of subsidiary support. If such a color of assumption of responsibility would lead a reasonable person to conclude that the parent does guarantee the debt, the court may hold the parent secondarily liable.[1] This is indeed a murky, gray area but the possibility of relief here does exist.

A creditor of a subsidiary will normally attempt to secure a parent's explicit guarantee for a loan to its subsidiary. In the absence of a guarantee, many creditors will obtain so-called "letters of support" or "comfort letters" from either the parent or a strong affiliate. These letters usually say no more than that it is of interest to the signer that the borrower repay the debt. There is no guarantee. Indeed, many courts have ruled that these letters do no more than provide "comfort" to the lender.

The Entity Theory and Consolidated Statements

Where effective control is in the hands of a parent, the entity theory (Moonitz, 1951) of an affiliated group of firms provides that the group should be viewed "as if" it were an economic unit. This accounting theory then suggests that the corporate veil should be pierced, so to speak, so that financial results are presented for the whole economic entity. Such an entity is a legal fiction, of course, for it has no charter, no stockholders, no bondholders, and no legal standing as an "as if" unit.

Consolidated statements can and do convey some useful information. They can also be mischievous. If the parent has guaranteed all subsidiary obligations, then consolidated debt can be viewed as an obligation of the parent. Where this is not the case, however, and there is some doubt as to the degree that a parent will support subsidiary debt, consolidated debt may overstate the total of parent obligations. If the firm issues O.C.S., then consolidated debt will exceed the debt for which the parent is apparently liable.

This presents no problem when, either in footnotes or otherwise, subsidiary debt issues appearing on financial statements are clearly identified, permitting the reader to isolate direct parent debt. To what extent this practice is observed is an empirical question. Unless otherwise specified, when we refer to debt we mean risky debt.

Reporting O.C.S. may give the unwary the impression that consolidated debt is the parent company's responsibility. And in the absence of subsidiary identified debt on the consolidated balance sheet, even the wary investor has no easy alternative but to equate consolidated debt with parent debt.

In cases where a subsidiary's securities are registered with the S.E.C., subsidiary statements must be issued in compliance with S.E.C. regulations. This may help mitigate the dichotomy of information that exists in consolidated systems that report O.C.S.

Valuation Implications

Regardless of what form financial reporting assumes in this context, the parent is the only legal entity with outstanding shares – there is no legal entity labeled the consolidated unit and investors cannot purchase shares in such a fictitious entity. The value of parent shares depends in part on the extent to which it has assumed liability for subsidiary debt.[2] More precisely, value depends on investor perceptions of this liability. Investor perceptions in turn are a function of the firm's disclosure of relevant information and the impression the firm wishes to convey through various signals. Financial risk is the variation in stockholder returns due to the firm's financial structure, which is a set of contractual relationships between the firm, a legal entity, and other parties. There are other potential dimensions to this risk. Even in the absence of an explicit contract the firm may voluntarily assume obligations of third parties. This may be done, for example, to support the debt of an important subsidiary when it is in financial distress. While the firm may find itself subject to other court-imposed liabilities of its subsidiary, such as, for example, unfunded pension liabilities in connection with labor contracts, these are better classified as business risks. The same holds for both product and personnel liability claims, the amounts and timing of which may occur at random.

The axiom of investor rationality implies that investors will take account of perceived financial risk in their bid prices for shares of parent stock. A firm with perceived guaranteed consolidated debt (whether explicitly guaranteed or not) will, all other things given, be valued lower in the market than in the absence of this perception. In terms of the now classic asset pricing model, and if Hamada (1972) and Rubinstein (1973) (and others) are correct, the betas of perceived consolidated-debt-responsible firms should be higher than if they had forsaken the responsibility, and hence, *ceteris paribus*, the value of the firm's equity will be lower.

We assumed that all other things were given. However, one factor cannot be easily held constant in this context. If a firm gives the impression of subsidiary debt support, the reserve borrowing power of the subsidiary may be enhanced and this may have value to the parent. The value of the increased borrowing power will offset some of the decline in value due to increased perceived financial risk. To what degree this may take place is not at all clear for the theory of valuing borrowing power is not well developed and quite inconclusive (Myers and Majluf, 1984; Myers, 1974).

Debt to Equity Theorems

The preceding discussion pointed out that if (1) consolidated debt is equal to or greater than parent debt, and (2) subsidiary debt is not identified, then perceived financial risk of the parent may be upwardly biased. These intuitive arguments should be made more precise and their qualifications set forth.

Let E_p be the book equity of parent, E_{si} the book equity subsidiary i, D_p the debt of parent, D_{si} the external debt of subsidiary i, $L_p = D_p/E_p$ the debt ratio of parent, $L_s = \Sigma D_s/\Sigma E_{si}$ the weighted debt ratios of all subsidiaries, and α_i the fraction of minority interest in subsidiary i ($0 < \alpha_i < 0.5$).

The consolidated debt to equity ratio, L_c, can be defined in two ways. Either

$$L_c = \frac{D_p + \Sigma D_{si}}{E_p + \Sigma \alpha_i E_{si}} \tag{12.1}$$

where minority interest is included in consolidated equity, or

$$L_c^* = \frac{D_p + \Sigma D_{si}}{E_p} \tag{12.2}$$

where the minority interest is excluded. L_c^* also denotes the case of a wholly owned subsidiary since in this instance $\alpha_i = 0$ for all i.

Theorem 1. If all subsidiaries are wholly owned and one or more of the subsidiaries have amounts of external debt greater than or equal to zero, the consolidated debt to equity ratio (debt ratio) will equal or exceed the parent's ratio and conversely.

Corollary 1A. As a special case of Theorem 1, if one or more subsidiaries have any external debt, the consolidated debt ratio will exceed the parent's ratio and conversely.

The reader should be convinced of the validity of these assertions just by casual reflection. Nevertheless, a simple proof is offered in order to generate qualifications and other implications.

Proof. Theorem 1 follows from rewriting equation (12.2) as

$$L_c^* = \frac{D_p}{E_p} + \frac{\Sigma D_{si}}{E_p}$$

If $\Sigma D_{si} \geqslant 0$, then $L_c^* \geqslant L_p$. The converse follows by reversing the argument. Corollary 1A emerges by setting $\Sigma D_{si} > 0$ and hence $L_c^* > L_p$.

The following theorems apply when minority interest is included in consolidated equity.

Theorem 2. If the debt ratio of the parent is equal to L_s, the weighted average of all subsidiary debt ratios, the consolidated debt ratio inclusive of minority interest will exceed the parent's ratio and conversely.

Proof. This theorem is established by noting that if $L_p = L_s$, equation (12.1) implies

$$L_c = \frac{L_p(E_p + \Sigma E_{si})}{E_p + \Sigma \alpha_i E_{si}}$$

Since $\alpha < 0.5$ for all i, $\Sigma E_{si} > \Sigma \alpha_i E_{si}$ and hence $L_c > L_p$. The converse is proven by reversing the argument.

Theorem 3. If the consolidated debt ratio inclusive of minority interest exceeds the parent's ratio, then the ratio of all subsidiary debt to the book value of all minority interests must exceed the parent's debt ratio and conversely. Similarly, if the consolidated debt ratio is less than the parent's ratio, then the ratio of total subsidiary debt to total minority interest must be less than the parent's debt ratio. Analytically, if

$$L_p \lessgtr \frac{\Sigma D_{si}}{\Sigma \alpha_i E_{si}} \quad \text{then } L_c \gtrless L_p$$

Note that L_c can be less than L_p in this case because minority interest is included in the consolidated debt ratio.

Proof. The first part of this theorem is most easily proved by first assuming it is not true, i.e. if

$$L_p < \frac{\Sigma D_{si}}{\Sigma \alpha_i E_{si}} \quad \text{then } L_c \leqslant L_p \tag{12.3}$$

Equation (12.1) can be expressed as

$$L_c = \frac{L_p E_p + L_s \Sigma E_{si}}{E_p + \Sigma \alpha_i E_{si}}$$

Substituting this result for L_c in the implied proposition of (12.3) yields

$$L_p E_p + L_s \Sigma E_{si} \leqslant L_p (E_p + \Sigma \alpha_i E_{si})$$

and hence

$$L_s \Sigma E_{si} \leqslant L_p \Sigma \alpha_i E_{si}$$

which implies $L_p \geqslant \Sigma D_{si} / \Sigma \alpha_i E_{si}$, a contradiction since (12.3) assumed

$$L_p < \frac{\Sigma D_{si}}{\Sigma \alpha_i E_{si}}$$

To prove the converse we follow an analogous argument. The denial of the converse implies the theorem

$$\text{if } L_c > L_p, \text{ then } L_p \geqslant \frac{\Sigma D_{si}}{\Sigma \alpha_i E_{si}} \tag{12.4}$$

Manipulating (12.1) we obtain

$$\frac{\Sigma D_{si}}{\Sigma \alpha_i E_{si}} = \frac{L_c E_p - D_p}{\Sigma \alpha_i E_{si}} + L_c$$

and substituting for $\Sigma D_{si} / \Sigma \alpha_i E_{si}$ in the implication of (12.4) and simplifying yields

$$L_p \geqslant L_c$$

again a contradiction since (12.4) assumes $L_c > L_p$. The second part of Theorem 3 is proved by similar arguments.

Theorem 3 provides interesting insights. With L_p, ΣD_{si} and ΣE_{si} given, large values of α_i make the condition $L_p < \Sigma D_{si}/\Sigma \alpha_i E_{si}$ difficult to satisfy, which, in turn, leads to more difficulty in yielding the condition $L_c > L_p$. As α_i is reduced, however, the condition $L_p < \Sigma D_{si}/\Sigma \alpha_i E_{si}$ is easier to satisfy and hence, so is the result $L_c > L_p$. In the limiting case where $\alpha_i \to 0$ we approach the wholly owned firm, and if $\Sigma D_{si} > 0$ this result approaches Corollary 1A, as expected.

Interest-Coverage Ratio

The interest-coverage ratio, another frequently used measure of financial risk, provides difficulties as well. The consolidated ratio can either over- or under-estimate the parent's ratio. It is an easy exercise to show that the consolidated ratio exceeds the parent's ratio if, and only if, the subsidiary's ratio exceeds the ratio of the parent.[3]

Working-Capital Ratio

The working-capital ratio, often labelled the current ratio, is sometimes employed as a measure of liquidity and hence as an indirect measure of financial risk. The relationship between the consolidated working-capital ratio and the parent's ratio is identical to the above relationship between the parent's interest-coverage ratio and the corresponding consolidated ratio.[4] The interest-coverage theorem as well as the working-capital theorem do not depend on any minority interest.

Amplification of Parent Financial Risk

If the parent does not support subsidiary debt, combinations of certain conditions will amplify estimated parent financial risk while other combinations will attenuate the estimates. First, if subsidiary interest coverage is less than the parent's coverage, consolidated interest coverage will underestimate parent coverage and thus overestimate parent financial risk. Second, conditions set forth in the section on debt to equity theorems can also lead to an overestimate of parent risk. Finally, if the subsidiary working-capital ratio is less than the parent's ratio, the consolidated ratio will underestimate the parent's ratio and again lead to an overestimate of parent financial risk. Thus if the above three conditions exist jointly, estimated parent financial risk from consolidated statements is amplified. The denial of these conditions leads, of course, to an attenuation of overestimation and, in the extreme case, depending on the order of magnitude of these factors and how they are assessed by the analyst, even to a possible underestimation of parent financial risk.

Analysts are expected to make trade-offs among these three measures of financial risk. How on average this is actually done remains an unanswered question warranting further research. On a priori grounds we conjecture that the working-capital ratio would have less impact on financial risk than either the interest-coverage ratio or the debt ratio. Speculating beyond that would be hazardous but, we repeat, a fruitful area for valuable research.

SUMMARY OF EMPIRICAL WORK AND NEW HYPOTHESES

Accounting Data

Beranek and Dillon (B.&D.) developed an exploratory sample of 81 New York Stock Exchange firms for which 10 K reports were locally at hand. Seventeen of these firms (21 percent of their sample) filed parent company as well as consolidated statements. But further research is needed. A comprehensive sample should be drawn of all reporting firms to establish the proportion reporting O.C.S. as well as the trends in such disclosure.

As noted earlier, B.&D. found marked differences among the ratio of consolidated to parent debt ratios. Consolidated interest-coverage ratio overestimated the parent's ratio 15 out of 17 times. The consolidated current ratio as a percentage of the parent ratio ranged from a low of 5 percent to a high of 708 percent.

The proposed comprehensive sample alluded to above should yield more definitive estimates of these quantities, and hence a firm notion of the possible error involved in estimating parent parameters on the basis of consolidated data. Such information would be of particular importance to analysts and others who must estimate parent quantities and who only have consolidated data at hand.

Financial Hypotheses

Several propositions have been derived from the foregoing discussion and tested.

The Financial Risk Hypothesis. If some parents will not support the debt of their subsidiaries, the debt to equity theorems imply that the perceived financial risk of parents who report only consolidated statements will be over-estimated. If all three conditions for over-estimation hold then the upward bias is magnified. Of course, attenuation of the debt to equity effect through favorable interest-coverage and working-capital ratios is always possible. However, it is extremely unlikely that this would cause average financial risk to be underestimated. Beranek and Clayton (B.&C.) hypothesized that, all other things equal, the betas of firms that report both consolidated and parent statements should be less than those of firms that report only consolidated statements.

Firms that issue both statements (class A firms) were matched with those that reported O.C.S. (class B firms). Matching was made by four-digit industry code (to control for industry and operating risk) and by debt ratio. Debt ratios in each class were calculated on a consolidated basis. Hence, if perceived financial risk is really less for class A firms, this phenomenon would be detected by observing smaller betas for class A firms. Smaller betas would be observed (1) if there is some doubt about parent support, and (2) because of the debt to equity theorems.

For a sample of 25 pairs B.&C. found a mean difference between the betas of matched firms (class B beta less the class A beta) of 0.1673 with a t-statistic of 1.848 which is significant at the 5 percent level. This test was replicated over four additional periods with almost similar results. Thus, investors implicitly impute greater financial risk to class B firms than to class A firms.

B.&C. did not establish if the imputation was intentional (investors believe parent will support subsidiary debt) or unintentional (investors have no other information other than consolidated statements). Further research is needed to distinguish between these two motives.

In a more refined test of the risk-difference hypothesis, business risk may be controlled better by other means and thus lead to a possible substantial increase in the sample size. Consideration might be given to the use of the standard deviation of earnings before interest and taxes as a measure of business risk. Another alternative measure might be the standard deviation of the residual around a time-series regression of such earnings.

New Hypotheses. Additional tests are suggested by the above analysis. Given that business and financial risk is controlled, firms that satisfied the three strong conditions for risk amplification should have significantly larger betas than those that display conditions for high attenuation. This could be tested by comparing firms that report both types of statements with those from the attenuated class. An appropriate criterion for selecting firms for the attenuated class would have to be developed.

Firms may issue O.C.S. for a number of reasons. One motive may be to signal a higher debt capacity than would be inferred from parent balance sheets. As noted earlier, if this is to increase shareholder wealth the value of the apparent added debt capacity must exceed the negative effect of the enhanced perceived financial risk. To test for this effect some measure of the value of debt capacity change would be needed.

An indirect test of this hypothesis might be made by noting that markedly more firms switch from reporting O.C.S. to the practice of issuing both statements than do those changing from the latter to the former. An event study might be performed of the price changes in the stocks of firms that did switch from O.C.S. to both statements. If the evidence were to show abnormal positive returns after the switch, then this would be consistent with the notion that the valuation effect of the perceived reduction in financial risk swamps the value contribution of the apparent added debt capacity.

Parent Support of Subsidiary Debt Hypothesis. Even in the absence of an explicit guarantee some parents will support the debt of certain subsidiaries. While a number of reasons could be cited for such support, Clayton and Beranek (C.&B.) suggest that support would be forthcoming if the operation of the subsidiary were vital to the effective functioning of the parent or of one or more of its affiliated subsidiaries.

This implies that default rates among vertically integrated subsidiaries should be less than those among conglomerate or horizontal combinations. Obtaining information on defaults is difficult because they are so rare among medium to large firms. One reason for the lack of defaults is that when subsidiaries are in financial difficulty, parents often attempt to divest them before they are beset by extreme difficulties. These divestitures are rarely, if ever, spun off; they are either sold off or merged into other firms.

Divestiture rates are thus expected to be higher among conglomerate-horizontal systems than among vertical combinations. Another reason reinforces this hypothesis. There is the belief that in conglomerate-horizontal systems the principal reason for holding a subsidiary is to further a "pure" investment-portfolio motive, while in a vertical combination the primary motive is synergism. Portfolio rebalancing is much less likely in vertical groups because such subsidiaries are important to the operation of such systems.

C.&B. test this hypothesis by examining divestitures rates among those firms that were listed continuously among Fortune's 500 firms from 1970 to 1979. The mean number of disassociations among vertical firms over this period was 0.7333 while the mean for nonvertical firms was 2.1086. The mean difference of 1.3753 had a t-statistic of 3.4977, which is statistically very significant.

Because the above test does not control for the firm's portfolio rebalancing motive it is not clear whether the avoidance of debt default or mere rebalancing is the dominant motive in conglomerate disassociations. Since 1979, however, there have been a number of reported debt defaults among subsidiaries. Adequate default data might now be available to provide a direct test of the differential default rate hypothesis.

REASONS FOR O.C.S. REPORTING PRACTICES

Some reasons for the practice of disclosing only consolidated statements have already been given. If firms wish to signal subsidiary debt support and yet avoid the commitment of an express guarantee, they may issue consolidated statements only. This gives the impression that all resources are available to buttress total consolidated debt, and that there is but one economic entity. The entity theory of accounting also justifies the issuance of such statements. Moreover, signaling such support through the issuance of O.C.S. also may increase the debt capacity of individual subsidiaries, thus contributing to the enhancement of parent shareholder wealth. This assumes that the value of the incremental debt capacity is expected to exceed the negative effect of the greater imputed financial risk.

The most important single reason for an O.C.S. policy may be the desire among firms to avoid the disclosure of information to rivals and other potential competitors. The consolidated income statement in particular serves as a powerful device for masking information that may be useful to competitors. The line-of-business reporting requirement of the F.T.C. helps, but falls far short of ameliorating this asymmetry.

Finally, and reinforcing the previous motive, is the desire on the part of management for confidentiality, *per se*. There are firms that would issue O.C.S. even in the absence of competitors. This is true because they neither want to attract potential competitors to enter the industry nor do anything to ease their entry. Making vital information less accessible serves this objective.

ADDITIONAL COMMENTS

This article has served to introduce the reader to a variety of reporting and financial issues. It has suggested numerous areas for fruitful research. In addition, we need better explanations for reporting practices and trends in these practices. We need to establish conditions which discriminate between subsidiary debt support and the absence of such support. What means do firms use for signaling such support? What is the likely magnitude of errors involved when parent parameters are estimated on the basis of consolidated data? How do investors, on average, trade off the debt ratio against interest-coverage and current ratios in assessing financial risk? How should they make this choice? These are only some of the questions that present current research challenges.

NOTES

1   At least five legal theories have been invoked to establish parent liability. These include (1) the alter ego theory, (2) the agency theory, (3) the instrumentality rule, (4) the identity theory, and (5) the estoppel theory. These are not general rules, however, and their applicability depends on the special circumstances of the cases (see American Law Reports 1971).
2   An explicit guarantee may assume different forms. It may consist of a flat agreement to pay interest and principal on the subsidiary's debt. Frequently

it is expressed as an "income maintenance" agreement whereby the parent contributes a specified amount of funds to the subsidiary if its income falls below a given level.

3 Let Y_s and Y_p denote earnings before interest for all subsidiaries and the parent respectively, and I_s and I_p interest payments to outsiders for all subsidiaries and the parent respectively. If the consolidated coverage ratio exceeds the parent's ratio then

$$\frac{Y_s + Y_p}{I_s + I_p} > \frac{Y_p}{I_p}$$

$$Y_s + Y_p > \frac{Y_p}{I_p}(I_s + I_p)$$

and hence

$$\frac{Y_s}{I_s} > \frac{Y_p}{I_p}$$

i.e. the subsidiaries' ratio exceeds the parent's ratio. The converse is proved by reversing the argument.

4 Let CA_s and CA_p denote current asset of all subsidiaries and the parent, respectively, and CL_s and CL_p current liabilities of all subsidiaries and the parent, respectively. Let these quantities be defined after intercompany eliminations. Consolidated working-capital ratio exceeds the parent ratio if

$$\frac{CA_s + CA_p}{CL_s + CL_p} > \frac{CA_p}{CL_p}$$

hence

$$\frac{CA_s}{CL_s} > \frac{CA_p}{CL_p}$$

Again, the converse of this argument can be established by reversing the steps in the argument.

BIBLIOGRAPHY

American Law Reports: Cases and Annotations 1971: *Liability of Corporation For Contracts of Subsidiary*, vol. 38, Rochester, N.Y.: The Lawyers Cooperative Publishing Co., pp. 1102–93.

Beranek, W. and Clayton R. J. 1985: Risk differences and financial reporting. *Journal of Financial Research*, 8, Winter, 327–34.

Beranek, W. and Dillon, G. 1982a: Pitfalls in assessing financial risk from consolidated statements. *Journal of Financial Education*, 11, Fall, 32–9.

Beranek, W. and Dillon, G. J. 1982b: Consolidated financial statements: sufficient for loan decisions? *Journal of Commercial Bank Lending*, 63, October, 71–6.

Clayton, R. J. and Beranek, W. 1985: Dissociations and legal combinations. *Financial Management*, 14, Summer, 24–8.

Hamada, R. S. 1972: The effect of the firm's capital structure on the systematic risk of common stock. *Journal of Finance*, 27, May, 435–52.

Jensen, M. C. and Meckling, W. H. 1976: Theory of the firm: managerial behavior, agency costs, and ownership structure. *Journal of Financial Economics*, 3, October, 305–60.

Myers, S. C. 1974: Interactions of corporate financing and investment decisions – implications for capital budgeting. *Journal of Finance*, 29, March, 1–26.

Myers, S. C. and Majluf, N. S. 1984: Corporate financing and investment decisions when firms have information that investors do not have. *Journal of Financial Economics*, 13, 188–221.

Moonitz, M. 1951: *The entity theory of consolidated statements*, New York: Foundation Press.

Rubinstein, M. E. 1973: A mean-variance synthesis of corporate financial theory. *Journal of Finance*, 28, January, 167–81.

13
The Value of Information in Impersonal and Personal Markets

JEFFREY F. JAFFE AND MARK RUBINSTEIN

PREFACE
by MARK RUBINSTEIN

This paper was written in 1974–1975, shortly after I graduated from U.C.L.A. Even at that remove, it reflects the continuing influence of Fred Weston who provided unceasing encouragement and optimism (as well as financial assistance) about some of my earlier research which led up to this joint paper with Jeffrey Jaffe. The paper is one of the first attempts to deal with the problem of optimal trading strategies in a situation where an uninformed investor needs to trade for liquidity reasons but fears that he will be at the mercy of a better-informed investor who will take the other side of his trade.

INTRODUCTION

Until recently, theoretical research in finance has been exclusively focused on competitive securities markets in which those with whom any consumer trades are not identified to him. In this context, it has been argued, for example by Hirshleifer (1971), that information[1] about the future aggregate supply of resources in the economy is *privately* valuable to consumers since it permits informed consumers to profit at the expense of the uninformed. Moreover, if information cannot affect aggregate production decisions, then it is also *not socially* valuable since what one consumer gains another loses.[2] *Ex post*, in terms of realized consumption

We wish to thank Fischer Black, John Harsanyi, Roger Ibbotson, and David Ng for helpful discussion.

at the same date, since the social total of consumption is fixed by assumption, the last conclusion is trivially true. However, *ex ante*, in terms of expected utility of consumption, the conclusion requires a more subtle justification.

This paper first reexamines the impersonal and competitive economy of Hirshleifer. We concur with Hirshleifer that information has private value and that the *production* of new public information does not *ex ante* have social value;[3] however, the *dissemination* of existing private information may have social value; and for the same reason the production of new private information, even if costless, can be socially harmful. In particular, if existing information is already fully reflected in security prices, then its free dissemination is *ex-ante* Pareto efficient.[4] Moreover, even if this information is not fully reflected in security prices, there always exists a way of redistributing resources concomitant with disseminating the information so that this dissemination is Pareto efficient. As a corollary, if a prior market for the sale of information can be properly organized, informed consumers will always benefit more from selling their information than from withholding it and making speculative side bets in the securities market with uninformed consumers. The dissemination (for a price) of existing private information therefore has both private and social value.

While information about supply conditions has private value and may even have social value in an impersonal and competitive pure exchange economy, this value will be substantially reduced if consumers are assumed to have direct information about demand conditions; that is, knowledge of the economic characteristics (resources, tastes and beliefs) of other consumers.[5] Such personalization is common in insurance and loan markets where the buyer has more information than the seller and the seller knows it. One may think of a continuum beginning with an impersonal market where each consumer views others as completely unidentified. Markets become more personal as each consumer learns more about those with whom he is trading. Increased personalization may occur gradually over time among a relatively small group of traders, as for example, among coaches and managers in the professional sports market for the allocation of athletes among competing teams.

Here we show that even under arbitrary exchange arrangements (possibly not competitive), personalization of the market limits the private value of information about supply conditions. In particular, with sufficient personalization consumers can identify and may even be able to rank Pareto-efficient allocations independent of their information about supply conditions. Consequently, if the endowed allocation is itself Pareto efficient, then information (about supply conditions) will be valueless. However, if the endowed allocation is not Pareto efficient, then information may be valuable for comparing Pareto-inefficient with Pareto-efficient allocations. But, even in this case, if exchange arrangements are competitive and "average" beliefs exist, information will be valueless. This is true even though poorly informed consumers cannot infer the beliefs of better informed consumers from security prices.

IMPERSONAL MARKETS

Consider a two-date $(t = 0, 1)$, $E(e = 1,2, \ldots, E)$ state, $I(i = 1,2, \ldots, I)$ consumer perfect and competitive *pure exchange* economy, where each consumer i endowed with resources $\{\bar{W}_e^i\}$, selects state-contingent claims $\{W_e^i\}$ at present prices $\{P_e\}$ so as to maximize the expected utility $(\Sigma_e \pi_e U_i(W_e^i))$ of his future wealth subject to

$$\Sigma_e P_e W_e^i = W_0^i \equiv \Sigma_e P_e \bar{W}_e^i$$

with $\pi_e^i > 0$, $U_i' > 0$ and $U_i'' < 0$. The final allocation across all consumers must also satisfy the closure conditions

$$\Sigma_i W_e^i = W_e^M \equiv \Sigma_i \bar{W}_e^i$$

for all e. Each consumer is assumed to know only his resources, tastes and beliefs, and the opportunities – prices – the market makes available to him.

Let us say, of two consumers, one has *superior information* about supply conditions if by revealing his information he can convince the other to adopt his beliefs. Consumers with superior information can benefit from it by making speculative side bets with others via the securities market or by selling it to others in a prior market for information before the securities market convenes. To see that superior information is *privately* valuable, we compare the expected utility to the same consumer of the choices he would make with and without the superior information, where *expectations are assessed with respect to beliefs which reflect the superior information*.

The simplest illustration is furnished by an economy in which all consumers have logarithmic utility functions and are identical except for their beliefs. In this instance,[6] competitive equilibrium is characterized by

$$W_e^i = \left(\frac{\pi_e^i - \pi_e}{\pi_e} \right) W_e + W_e \quad \text{for all } i \text{ and } e$$

where $\pi_e \equiv \Sigma_i \pi_e^i / I$ and $W_e \equiv \Sigma_i W_e^i / I$. When all consumers have the same beliefs, all speculative side bets $[(\pi_e^i - \pi_e)/\pi_e] W_e = 0$ and each consumer's state-contingent future wealth is exactly the per capita amount. With differences in beliefs, consumers plan for more wealth in those states toward which they are optimistic $(\pi_e^i > \pi_e)$ and less in those states toward which they are pessimistic $(\pi_e^i < \pi_e)$.[7] Suppose that $\{\pi_e^*\}$ represents beliefs based on superior information. This information is privately valuable to consumer i if and only if

$$\Sigma_e \pi_e^* \ln W_e^* - \Sigma_e \pi_e^* \ln W_e^i > 0$$

where $W_e^* = (\pi_e^*/\pi_e) W_e$, the choices based on superior information, and $W_e^i = (\pi_e^i/\pi_e) W_e$, the choices based on inferior information $\{\pi_e^i \neq \pi_e^*\}$.[8] Consequently, superior information is privately valuable if and only if

$$\Sigma_e \pi_e^* \ln \pi_e^* - \Sigma_e \pi_e^* \ln \pi_e^i > 0$$

To see that this must be positive, solve the following programming problem by choosing $\{\pi_e'\}$ such that

$$\max_{\{\pi_e'\}} \Sigma_e \pi_e^* \ln \pi_e' - \lambda(\Sigma_e \pi_e' - 1)$$

Observe that at the maximum $\pi_e' = \pi_e^*$ for all e.

To see that the dissemination of information may also be *socially* valuable, suppose that, before dissemination, security prices fully reflect the superior information. In that case, revealing the information leaves prices, and hence "consensus beliefs,"[9] unchanged. In the logarithmic utility illustration, consensus beliefs $\pi_e \equiv \Sigma_i \pi_e^i / I$ for all e and the difference in expected utility with and without the dissemination of the information is again $\Sigma_e \pi_e \ln \pi_e - \Sigma_e \pi_e \ln \pi_e^i$ for consumer i. Clearly, this is positive for all uninformed consumers $\{\pi_e^i \neq \pi_e\}$ and zero for all informed consumers $\{\pi_e^i = \pi_e\}$. Note that Pareto efficiency has been assessed with respect to beliefs which reflect the superior information. This type of Pareto efficiency will be termed "full information efficiency"; it defines a situation which would be Pareto efficient after all private information has been released. Hereafter, the term "Pareto efficient" will refer unambiguously to this full information definition of the concept.

Observe that if the informed consumers were to sell their superior information at a positive (but not too high) price, then even informed (as well as uninformed) consumers would be better off as a result of the dissemination of the information. To derive the maximum price[10] an uninformed consumer would pay for the superior information (assuming it were disseminated to all consumers), find that proportion γ_i of initial wealth for which

$$\Sigma_e \pi_e \ln[(1-\gamma_i) W_e] - \Sigma_e \pi_e \ln \left(\frac{\pi_e^i}{\pi_e} W_e \right) = 0$$

It follows that

$$\gamma_i = 1 - \Pi_e \left(\frac{\pi_e^i}{\pi_e} \right)^{\pi_e}$$

a fraction between zero and one.

This analysis suggests that even if superior information is not fully reflected in security prices, there always exists a way of redistributing resources concomitant with disseminating the information so that this dissemination would be socially valuable. In particular, suppose a prior market for information, if it were utilized, did not use up aggregate resources. That is, for each state e, W_e^M would remain the same before and after the sale of private information. Moreover, suppose the sale of private information were to bring about agreement in beliefs. Without a prior market for information, uninformed consumers would make disadvantageous side bets. With a prior market for information, while no side bets would later be taken in the securities market, poorly informed consumers would instead deplete their wealth by purchasing superior information. They would then enter the securities market poorer but wiser.

Is it possible to organize a prior market for information so that its use is preferred by all consumers in the economy to the alternative of making side bets in an impersonal competitive market?

Theorem 1. Impersonal Markets. In an impersonal competitive market, given at least some disagreement, there always exists a way of redistributing resources through a prior market for information such that all consumers will be better off.

Proof. In an impersonal competitive market, each consumer i

$$\max_{\{W_e^i\}} \Sigma_e \pi_e^i U_i(W_e^i) - \lambda_i(\Sigma_e P_e W_e^i - W_0^i)$$

Since U_i is concave, $U_i'(W_e^i)/U_i'(W_s) = P_e \pi_e^i/(P_s \pi_s^i)$, for any two states e and s and all i, are the necessary and sufficient conditions for an equilibrium. Consequently, consumers have the same beliefs if and only if for any two states e and s, $U_i'(W_e^i)/U_i'(W_s^i)$ is the same for all i. Therefore, the equilibrium allocation under heterogeneous beliefs cannot be the same as the equilibrium allocation under homogeneous beliefs. Only the equilibrium under homogeneous beliefs can be Pareto efficient (with respect to the beliefs reflecting the superior information). If consumers were to trade without convening a prior market for information, they would not have the same beliefs and thus would not reach a Pareto-efficient allocation. Therefore, all consumers can be made better off by holding a prior market for information, and then all entering the securities market with the same beliefs.

In short, the benefits from buying and selling information in a properly organized prior market for information exceed the benefits from speculative side bets for all consumers in the economy.[11] This may *partially* explain the empirical evidence supporting the speed with which the securities market digests new information, since disclosure for a price is more profitable than taking a speculative position and waiting for nature to reveal the true state. Taking a speculative position and then disclosing the information for a price will also *not* be preferred to pure disclosure for a price, since the prior speculative position, even by its slight effect on prices in a large market, will diminish the benefits to poorly informed individuals from later disclosure, causing them to pay less for the information.

The theorem only asserts that it is *possible* to redistribute resources via a prior market for information so that all consumers are better off. However, due to the special characteristics of information as a "commodity," such a prior market will be difficult to design. For an informed consumer to benefit more from selling information than from speculating, its value (benefits its disclosure confers upon others) must be sufficient appropriable. However, because of the Pareto inefficiency of heterogeneous beliefs, this value need not be *completely* appropriable to its owner.

Since heterogeneous beliefs are full information inefficient and the production of private information tends to increase the heterogeneity of beliefs, then the production of private information, even if costless, is socially harmful. The society therefore has an incentive to implement full information efficiency by establishing regulatory bodies to prevent the production of private information. For example, insider trading laws, which strive to control profits earned by corporate officials on their information, may reduce the amount of private information produced. Similarly, the public dissemination of private information helps to create homogeneous beliefs and therefore full information efficiency. Hence authorities may create disclosure laws, even if the dissemination of information is costly. The key to full information efficiency is the homogeneity of beliefs, not the amount of information. It is important to stress that these public policy implications have not been justified in this paper by recourse to equity arguments. Rather, they have been justified by considerations of Pareto efficiency alone.

PERSONAL MARKETS

Assume the economy is described as before except that the securities market is completely personal with arbitrary exchange arrangements. The securities market is said to be *completely personal* if, in addition to his own resources, tastes, and beliefs, each consumer knows (1) the resources of all other consumers, (2) the tastes of all other consumers, (3) the "type" of information he and all others have. By knowledge of type of information, we mean all consumers agree on the ranking of informativeness of all consumers in the economy, although they do not know the content of this information. Although the exchange arrangements are arbitrary,[12] in a completely personal market it seems reasonable to impose the restriction that the final allocation be Pareto efficient (with respect to the beliefs reflecting superior information $\{\pi_e^*\}$). As we have seen in the preceding section, any Pareto-inefficient allocation could not be stable since an informed consumer can always sell his superior information at a positive price. More precisely, we require that the final allocation $\{W_e^i\}$ be feasible so that $\Sigma_i W_e^i = \Sigma_i \bar{W}_e^i$ for all e and there exists no other feasible allocation $\{\hat{W}_e^i\}$ for which

$$\Sigma_e \pi_e^* U_i(\hat{W}_e^i) - \Sigma_e \pi_e^* U_i(W_e^i)$$

be greater or equal to zero for all consumers i and greater than zero for some consumers i. In addition to Pareto efficiency, we require that each consumer perceive his final allocation as superior to his endowed allocation. That is, by whatever beliefs $\{\pi_e^i\}$ he chooses to use

$$\Sigma_e \pi_e^i U_i(W_e^i) - \Sigma_e \pi_e^i U_i(\bar{W}_e^i)$$

be greater than or equal to zero.

With this preamble, we are prepared for the following theorem.

Theorem 2. Personal Markets. In a completely personal market,[13] consumers can identify Pareto-efficient allocations independent of their beliefs.

Proof. It is well known that for concave utility, an allocation is Pareto efficient if and only if it maximizes a positively weighted sum of consumer utilities subject to closure conditions:

$$\max_{\{W_e^i\}} \Sigma_i k_i \Sigma_e \pi_e^i U_i(W_e^i) - \Sigma_e \lambda_e (\Sigma_i W_e^i - \Sigma_i \bar{W}_e^i)$$

where $k_i > 0$ for all i and $\{\lambda_e\}$ are Lagrangian multipliers. The necessary and sufficient conditions for efficiency are then $k_i \pi_e^i U_i'(W_e^i) = k_1 \pi_e^1 U_1'(W_e^1)$ for all i and e and the closure conditions. Assessing Pareto efficiency with respect to beliefs which reflect superior information amounts to setting $\pi_e^i = \pi_e^1 = \pi_e^*$ for all e so that $k_i U_i'(W_e^i) = k_1 U_1'(W_e^1)$ for all i and e. These equations and the closure conditions describe the exhaustive set of Pareto-efficient allocations (by varying $\{k_i\}$) and are independent of $\{\pi_e^*\}$. Moreover, since the market is completely personal, all consumers can calculate this set.

Information, in a completely personal market, therefore, does not acquire private value because it assists in identifying ending portfolio positions; irrespective of the beliefs an uninformed consumer attributes to an informed consumer, the set of full information efficient allocations is the same. The following corollary emphasizes this result.

Corollary. In a completely personal market, if the endowed allocation is Pareto efficient, then no consumer will trade and the private value of information is zero.

Proof. From the theorem, since each consumer knows the resources and tastes of all consumers, even though he does not know the beliefs of the best-informed consumer, he can calculate the set of Pareto-efficient allocations. Therefore, each consumer knows the endowed allocation is Pareto efficient. Since (1) no well-informed consumer will offer to trade with a poorly-informed consumer unless the well-informed consumer will benefit *ex ante*, (2) the poorly-informed consumer must lose *ex-ante* in this exchange (since the endowed allocation is already Pareto efficient), and (3) the poorly-informed consumer knows this and that he is poorly informed (since the market is personal), he will refuse to trade. Superior information about supply conditions, i.e. the probability distribution of $\{W_e^M\}$, clearly has no value in a personal market if the endowed allocation is Pareto efficient. Even if it is publicized, there will be no trade.

For example, in an economy in which all consumers have the same endowed resources and tastes, the endowed allocation is Pareto efficient and information has no private value.

Therefore, the private value (if it has any) of information in a personal market must arise from the necessity of *ranking* Pareto-efficient allocations or *comparing* Pareto-efficient with Pareto-inefficient allocations. As long as the endowed allocation is not itself Pareto efficient, in the process of trading consumers will move from a Pareto-inefficient to a Pareto-efficient allocation. In this process, consumers must choose among alternative Pareto-efficient allocations. However, in general a poorly-informed consumer does not know which direction of movement along the contract curve will be to his advantage and information will therefore have private value. None the less, there are special situations where Pareto-efficient allocations can be ranked, as well as identified, independent of beliefs.

Theorem 3. Personal Markets. In a completely personal market, consumers can rank Pareto-efficient allocations independent of their beliefs if either

1 there are only two consumers in the market, or
2 all consumers have H.A.R.A. (linear risk tolerance) utility functions with the same cautiousness.[14]

Proof. Consider first the case of two consumers. From the observation in the previous proof, Pareto efficiency with respect to homogeneous beliefs, requires that

$$\frac{U_1'(W_e^1)}{U_2'(W_e^2)} = \frac{U_1'(W_s^1)}{U_2'(W_s^2)} = \ldots \quad \text{for all states } e \text{ and } s$$

Consider any other Pareto-efficient allocation; it must likewise satisfy

$$\frac{U_1'(\hat{W}_e^1)}{U_2'(\hat{W}_e^2)} = \frac{U_1'(\hat{W}_s^1)}{U_2'(\hat{W}_s^2)} = \ldots \quad \text{for all states } e \text{ and } s$$

Together with $W_e^1 + W_e^2 = \hat{W}_e^1 + \hat{W}_e^2 \equiv W_e^M$ for all e, these conditions are necessary and sufficient for Pareto efficiency. Therefore, if $\hat{W}_e^1 > W_e^1$, then since U_i is concave $U_1'(\hat{W}_e^1) < U_1'(W_e^1)$; also by closure, $\hat{W}_e^2 < W_e^2$ so that similarly $U_2'(\hat{W}_e^2) > U_2'(W_e^2)$. In short, if $\hat{W}_e^1 > W_e^1$, then

$$\frac{U_1'(\hat{W}_e^1)}{U_2'(\hat{W}_e^2)} < \frac{U_1'(W_e^1)}{U_2'(W_e^2)}$$

For any other state s, this implies

$$\frac{U_1'(\hat{W}_s^1)}{U_2'(\hat{W}_s^2)} < \frac{U_1'(W_s^1)}{U_2'(W_s^2)}$$

Repeating the same reasoning backwards, this in turn implies $\hat{W}_s^1 > W_s^1$ and $\hat{W}_s^2 < W_s^2$. In brief, any two Pareto-efficient allocations must either be characterized by $\hat{W}_e^1 > W_e^1$ and $\hat{W}_e^2 < W_e^2$ for all states e or by $\hat{W}_e^1 < W_e^1$ and $\hat{W}_e^2 > W_e^2$ for all states e. Consequently, the nonsatiation property ($U_i' > 0$) of consumer tastes allows consumers to rank Pareto-efficient allocations independent of their beliefs.[15]

Consider now the case of H.A.R.A. utility functions. As developed in Rubinstein (1974a), a necessary and sufficient condition for a Pareto-efficient allocation is

$$W_e^i = \frac{A_M W_0^i - A_i W_0^M}{A_M \phi + B W_0^M} + \frac{A_i \phi + B W_0^i}{A_M \phi + B W_0^M} W_e^M \quad \text{for all } e \text{ and } i$$

where $\phi \equiv \Sigma_e P_e$, $W_0^M \equiv \Sigma_e P_e W_e^M$, and $A_M \equiv \Sigma_i A_i$. Although this condition was derived in the context of a competitive market (as in the preceding section), it applies even in the absence of a competitive market. This follows since all Pareto-efficient allocations can be spanned by an appropriate redistribution of resources (i.e. redistribution of $\{W_0^i\}$). Moreover, from his resource distribution irrelevancy theorem, Rubinstein (1974a) proved that the price system is independent of the distribution of resources; therefore, ϕ and W_0^M remain fixed through any redistribution of resources. This motivates rewriting the condition for Pareto efficiency as

$$W_e^i = \alpha_e A_i + \beta_e W_0^i \quad \text{for all } e \text{ and } i$$

where

$$\alpha_e \equiv \frac{\phi W_e^M - W_0^M}{A_M \phi + B W_0^M}$$

and

$$\beta_e \equiv \frac{A_M + B W_e^M}{A_M \phi + B W_0^M}$$

As the set of Pareto-efficient allocations is spanned by redistributing resources, α_e, A_i and β_e remain fixed. Since, as is easy to show, $\beta_e > 0$ for all e, for any given consumer i, Pareto-efficient allocations must either be characterized by $\hat{W}_e^i > W_e^i$ or $\hat{W}_e^i < W_e^i$ for all e. Again, the nonsatiation property ($U_i' > 0$) of consumer tastes allows consumers to rank Pareto-efficient allocations independent of their beliefs.

However, even if information is not needed to identify and rank Pareto-efficient allocations, it may still be useful in comparing Pareto-efficient with Pareto-inefficient allocations. In the process of moving from a Pareto-inefficient to a Pareto-efficient allocation, each consumer will insist that he be made at least as well off as his endowed allocation. That is, by whatever beliefs $\{\pi_e^i\}$ he chooses to use, he will require that

$$\Sigma_e \pi_e^i U_i(W_e^i) - \Sigma_e \pi_e^i U_i(\bar{W}_e^i)$$

be greater than or equal to zero. Unlike the ranking of Pareto-efficient allocations, information will generally affect the perceived sign of this expression. The consumer with information $\{\pi_e^*\}$ superior to all others in the economy will be in the enviable position of "knowing" under what allocations its sign is positive. An uninformed consumer, even though he knows he is uninformed, cannot in general evaluate the sign of this expression independent of the beliefs he attributes to informed consumers.

While information would appear to derive positive private value from its assistance in comparing Pareto-inefficient with Pareto-efficient allocations, the absolute size of its private value will depend on the bargaining arrangements among consumers (for example, see Harsanyi and Selton, 1972). Except for the special competitive case, we have little to add. However, we speculate if uninformed consumers tend to overestimate the private value of their endowed resources ($\Sigma_e \pi_e^i U_i(\bar{W}_e^i) > \Sigma_e \pi_e^* U_i(\bar{W}_e^i)$), informed consumers may find it in their interest to disclose their superior information to quash the unduly tough bargaining stance of uninformed consumers. Similarly, if $\Sigma_e \pi_e^i U_i(\bar{W}_e^i) < \Sigma_e \pi_e^* U_i(\bar{W}_e^i)$, then informed consumers should tend to keep their superior information to themselves. Unfortunately, the consequent ability of an uninformed consumer to infer the undue optimism or pessimism of his own beliefs from the decision of informed consumers to reveal or not reveal their information complicates this speculation.

Although private information appears generally to have some value in a personal market with arbitrary exchange arrangements, this value can fall to zero in a completely personal market with competitive exchange opportunities, even though the endowed allocation is not Pareto efficient. The simplest illustration is furnished by an economy in which all consumers have logarithmic utility functions but are otherwise different. In this instance, competitive equilibrium is characterized by

$$W_e^i = \left(\frac{\pi_e^i - \pi_e}{\pi_e}\right)\left(\frac{W_0^i - W_0}{W_0}\right)W_e + \left(\frac{\pi_e^i - \pi_e}{\pi_e}\right)W_e + \left(\frac{W_0^i - W_0}{W_0}\right)W_e + W_e$$

$$\text{(WB)} \qquad\qquad \text{(B)} \qquad\qquad \text{(W)}$$

where

$$\pi_e \equiv \Sigma_i \left(\frac{W_0^i}{W_0}\right)\pi_e^i$$

$$W_0 \equiv \frac{\Sigma_i W_0^i}{I}$$

and

$$W_e \equiv \frac{\Sigma_i W_e^i}{I}$$

When all consumers have the same wealth and beliefs, then each consumer's state-contingent future wealth is exactly the per capita amount (W_e). With differences in initial wealth, rich consumers ($W_0^i > W_0$) plan for more future wealth under all states (term W); with differences in beliefs, optimistic consumers ($\pi_e^i > \pi_e$) plan for more wealth in those states (term B). The additional joint demand created by both differences in wealth and beliefs is captured by the remaining term (WB). Clearly, informed consumers will be most anxious to take on side bets (terms B and WB) with uninformed consumers. However, the uninformed consumers have an easy way of preventing such unfavorable trades: they can act as if they have the same beliefs as the informed consumers without knowing what these beliefs are. This follows since in a personal competitive market they can calculate the above sharing rule and make their choices satisfy

$$W_e^i = \left(\frac{W_0^i - W_0}{W_0} \right) W_e + W_e$$

what they would have been had all consumers had the same information.[16]

Kihlstrom and Mirman (1975) have derived a similar result for personal competitive markets. They show that private superior information is valueless when a one-to-one correspondence exists between security prices and the beliefs based on superior information. Superior private information then leaks out through the price system. The above example suggests that in complete markets, a necessary and sufficient condition for this leakage is the existence of consensus beliefs $\{\pi_e\}$. As noted elsewhere (Rubinstein, 1975), their existence is a necessary condition for security prices to fully reflect all available information. That is, security market "efficiency" demands that there exist some set of beliefs which, if commonly held by all consumers, is capable of explaining actual security prices.

Perhaps unfortunately, consensus beliefs do not generally exist. The only examples of which the authors are aware are:

1 all consumers have logarithmic utility, or
2 all consumers have exponential utility, or
3 all consumers are identical except for their beliefs.

This last case we owe to David Ng. It, of course, is already covered by the corollary to Theorem 2.

NOTES

1 For the purposes of this paper, it is useful to categorize three types of information:

   1 *Personal information:* A consumer's knowledge of his own resources and tastes.
   2 *Information about supply:* A consumer's knowledge of the aggregate supply of future consumption.

3 *Information about demand:* A consumer's knowledge of the resources and tastes of other consumers, and his knowledge of other consumers' information about supply and demand.

2 This theme was first discussed by Samuelson (1957, p. 209) who wrote in reference to the commodities market:

> Suppose my reactions are not better than those of other speculators but rather just one second quicker . . . In a world of uncertainty, I note the consequences of each changing event one second faster than anyone else. I make my fortune – not once, but every day that important events happen. Would anyone be foolish enough to argue that in my absence the equilibrium pattern would fail to be reestablished? . . . There is no necessary correspondence between the income effects realized by any person's actions and the amount of meritorious substitutions that his actions can alone bring into being.

3 Although Hirshleifer (1971) couches his analysis of information production in an economy consisting of identical consumers, as Marshall (1974) and Ng (1975) have shown, his results are quite general carrying over to perfect and competitive economies with arbitrary heterogeneity among consumers (but with the same beliefs). In particular, Ng shows that good news tends to increase the risk-free interest rate making lenders better off and borrowers worse off.

4 See Rubinstein (1974) on the *ex-ante* issue. Ng (1974) has extended the Pareto efficiency of free dissemination even to certain cases where existing superior information is *not* fully reflected in security prices. Starr (1972) has further shown that full dissemination of information (i.e. homogeneous beliefs) is required for *ex-post* Pareto efficiency if consumption occurs at two dates. Without homogeneous beliefs, when uncertainty is resolved at the second date for at least one state, there will be at least two consumers who will regret their consumption decisions at the first date; thus, one would realize more utility with less initial consumption (and consequently more later consumption) and the other would realize more utility with more initial consumption (and consequently less later consumption). Consequently, if only they could have forecast the future with certainty, they would have made a mutually beneficial exchange at the first date.

5 Other recent papers modelling personal markets include those of Grossman (1977) and Rothchild and Stiglitz (1976).

6 To derive this sharing rule

$$\max_{\{W_e^i\}} \Sigma_e \pi_e \ln W_e^i - \lambda_i (\Sigma_e P_e W_e^i - W_0)$$

which has first order conditions $W_e^i = (\pi_e^i / P_e) W_0$ for all e and i. Summing this over all i and dividing by I, $W_e = (\pi_e / P_e) W_0$.

7 Note that

$$\Sigma_i \left(\frac{\pi_e^i - \pi_e}{\pi_e} \right) W_e = \Sigma_e P_e \left(\frac{\pi_e^i - \pi_e}{\pi_e} \right) W_e = 0$$

for all i and e.

8　This analysis is somewhat simplified in that it ignores the likely second-order effect of the conversion of the beliefs of a single consumer on $\{\pi_e\}$, the "average" beliefs. Were this second-order effect considered, our conclusion concerning the private value of information would be unaffected.

9　Consensus beliefs are those beliefs which, if held by all consumers in an otherwise similar economy, would generate the same equilibrium prices as in the actual economy (see Rubinstein, 1975).

10　For an extended analysis, considering choice of information structures, see Morris (1974).

11　Hirshleifer (1971) has argued that given the opportunity to purchase information in a prior market, consumers would actually pay *not* to have information released and therefore such a market would be inactive. Each consumer would view the release of information new to him as creating a fair gamble and risk averters are willing to pay to avoid fair gambles. However, the prior market for information envisioned here contains a special feature which militates against this behavior. Concomitant with the release of information is a *redistribution of resources*. The theorem implies it is possible, by redistributing resources, to guarantee that all consumers will be better off. As a result, all consumers want the information to be released. Either by itself, releasing the information or redistributing resources, would not be Pareto efficient.

12　In particular, we no longer require that there exist prices $\{P_e\}$ such that $\Sigma_e P_e W_e^i = \Sigma_e P_e \bar{W}_e^i$ for all i.

13　For this theorem to hold, we can weaken the information requirements of a completely personal market and require in place of (1) that each consumer knows only the aggregate resources $\{W_e^M\}$ available in each state and not their distribution among consumers. In addition, there are some special cases for which these information requirements can be further weakened. For example, with no aggregate uncertainty (i.e. W_e^M is the same for all e), in place of (2) consumers only need know that all other consumers are risk averse. In this case, irrespective of tastes, all Pareto-efficient allocations are characterized for each consumer i by W_e^i the same for all e.

14　The H.A.R.A. class of utility functions is described by the solution to the differential equation $-U_i'(W_e^i)/U_i''(W_e^i) = A_i + B_i W_e^i$ where A_i and B_i are constants. Requiring identical cautiousness implies $B_i = B$ (independent of i) for all consumers. The solution includes most popular utility functions including quadratic, exponential, logarithmic, and power utility. These utility functions possess a surprising constellation of properties some of which are developed in Rubinstein (1974, 1981). In particular, Brennan and Kraus (1975) have recently shown that in a perfect and competitive financial market with homogeneous beliefs, condition (2) is necessary and sufficient for all consumers to have parallel linear Engle curves.

15　We are indebted to David Ng for teaching us that this proof does not generalize to economies with more than two consumers.

16　Observe also that even though only a few consumers are sophisticated, their information is fully reflected in security prices.

BIBLIOGRAPHY

Brennan, M. and Kraus, A. 1978: Necessary conditions for aggregation in securities markets. *Journal of Financial and Quantitative Analysis*, September, 407–18.

Grossman, S. 1977: The existence of future markets, noisy rational expectations and informational externalities. *Review of Economic Studies*, May, 431–49.

Harsanyi, J. and Selten, R. 1972: A generalized Nash solution for two-person bargaining games with incomplete information. *Management Science*, XVIII, part 2, 80–106.

Hirshleifer, J. 1971: The private and social value of information and the reward to inventive activity. *American Economic Review*, LXI, 561–74.

Kihlstrom, R. and Mirman, L. 1975: Information and market equilibrium. *Bell Journal of Economics and Management Science*, 6(1), 357–76.

Marshall, J. 1974: Private incentives and public information. *American Economic Review*, LXIV, 373–90.

Morris, J. 1974: The logarithmic investor's decision to acquire costly information. *Management Science*, XXI, 383–91.

Ng, D. 1974: Social value of authentic information, Berkeley, unpublished manuscript.

Ng, D. 1975: Informational accuracy and social welfare under homogeneous beliefs. *Journal of Financial Economics*, March, 53–70.

Rothchild, M. and Stiglitz, J. 1976: Equilibrium in competitive insurance markets: the economics of imperfect information, *Quarterly Journal of Economics*, November, 629–49.

Rubinstein, M. 1974: An aggregation theorem for security markets. *Journal of Financial Economics*, 1(3), 225–44.

Rubinstein, M. 1975: Security market efficiency in an Arrow–Debreu economy. *American Economic Review*, December.

Rubinstein, M. 1981: A discrete-time synthesis of financial theory. *Research in Finance*, 3, 53–102, Jai Press Inc.

Samuelson, P. 1957: Intertemporal price equilibrium: a prologue to the theory of speculation. *Weltwirtschaftliches Archiv*, 179–217.

Starr, R. 1972: Optimal production and allocation under uncertainty. *Quarterly Journal of Economics*, March, 81–95.

Index

Index by Ann Hall